THE
BONES
OF A
KING

THE BONES OF A KING

RICHARD III
REDISCOVERED

The Greyfriars Research Team
with Maev Kennedy and Lin Foxhall

WILEY Blackwell

Library of Congress Cataloging-in-Publication data is available for this title.

ISBN: 9781118783146 (hardback)

A catalogue record for this book is available from the British Library.

Cover image: Boar badge of Richard III, discovered at Bosworth Field
© Leicestershire County Council Museums Service; Background image
© clearviewstock / iStockphoto.
Cover design by Simon Levy

Set in 10.5/13pt Galliard by SPi Publisher Services, Pondicherry, India
Printed and bound in Great Britain by TJ International Ltd. Padstow

1 2015

Contents

ILLUSTRATIONS

Figures

Maps

Plates

THE GREYFRIARS
RESEARCH TEAM

Dr Jo Appleby (JA)
Lecturer in Human Bioarchaeology, School of Archaeology and Ancient History, University of Leicester
Project osteoarchaeologist (human bones specialist)

Dr Richard Buckley (RB)
Co-Director, University of Leicester Archaeological Services (ULAS), School of Archaeology and Ancient History, University of Leicester
Lead archaeologist

Professor Jane Evans (JE)
Geoarchaeologist, British Geological Survey, Natural Environment Research Council
Isotopes expert

Professor Sarah Hainsworth (SH)
Graduate Dean and Professor of Materials and Forensic Engineering, University of Leicester
Weapons and tool-marks expert

Professor Russell Harris (RH)
Professor of Medical Engineering and Advanced Manufacturing, School of Mechanical and Manufacturing Engineering, Loughborough University
3D printing expert

Professor Norman Housley (NH)
Professor of History, School of History, University of Leicester
Expert in medieval history

Dr Turi King (TK)
Lecturer in Genetics and Archaeology, Department of Genetics and School of Archaeology and Ancient History, University of Leicester
Project geneticist

Dr Sarah Knight (SK)
Senior Lecturer in Renaissance Literature, School of English, University of Leicester
Expert in literature and historical sources

Dr Angela Lamb (AL)
Isotope geochemist, British Geological Survey, Natural Environment Research Council
Isotopes expert

Professor Mark Lansdale (ML)
Professor of Psychology, School of Psychology, University of Leicester
Expert in cognitive and applied psychology

Dr Mary Ann Lund (MAL)
Lecturer in Early Modern English Literature, School of English, University of Leicester
Expert in literature and historical sources

Mr Ather Mirza (AM)
Press Officer, External Relations, University of Leicester

Dr Piers Mitchell (PM)
Department of Archaeology and Anthropology, University of Cambridge and Consultant Children's Orthopaedic Surgeon, Peterborough City Hospital
Bioarchaeology and scoliosis expert

Professor Bruno Morgan (BM)
Professor of Cancer Imaging and Radiology, Department of Cancer Studies and Molecular Medicine, University of Leicester
Forensic radiologist

Mr Mathew Morris (MM)
ULAS, School of Archaeology and Ancient History, University of Leicester
Archaeologist (Roman, medieval, urban archaeology), Greyfriars site director

Ms Deirdre O'Sullivan (DOS)
Lecturer in Archaeology, School of Archaeology and Ancient History, University of Leicester
Academic advisor to the Greyfriars project and specialist in medieval archaeology and friaries

Professor Guy Rutty (GR)
Chief Forensic Pathologist, East Midlands Forensic Pathology Unit, University of Leicester

Professor Kevin Schürer (KS)
Pro-Vice Chancellor for Research, University of Leicester
Historian specialising in historical demography (population) of medieval and early modern Britain

Mr Richard Taylor (RT)
Former Marketing Director, University of Leicester (now Chief Operating Officer, Loughborough University)

Mr Carl Vivian (CV)
Video Producer, External Relations, University of Leicester

Mr Robert C. Woosnam-Savage (RWS)
The Royal Armouries, Leeds
Senior Curator of European Edged Weapons
Expert in medieval arms and armour and battlefield archaeology

ACKNOWLEDGEMENTS

Above all we would like to thank the team of contributors whose research made this book possible. Beyond the team we owe special thanks to Patricia Balaresque, Julian Boon, Alison Brough, Louise Carr, Graham Clark, Steffan Davies, Wendy Duldig, Richard Earp, Vicky Eves, Helen Foxhall Forbes, Steven Gunn, Frederick Hepburn, Carly Hilts, Pete Hobson, Michael Hofreiter, Nick Holder, John Holt, Michael Ibsen, Loveday Ingram, Philip Lindley, David Monteith, Claire Robinson, David Thompson, Thomas Veit, Darren Watts, Mike Webb, Vanessa Wilkie and the Huntington Library, The Royal Armouries in Leeds and the staff at Wiley Blackwell.

Investigating the Bones of a King

This book is about the discovery of the grave of one of England's most notorious and enigmatic monarchs, Richard III. For five centuries he lay buried under the dismantled remains of the church of the Greyfriars, the Franciscans' church in the centre of Leicester, in a location which by the twenty-first century had become a car park. The archaeological excavation which recovered his remains was made possible by a joint project between the Richard III Society, the University of Leicester and the city of Leicester. However, as the story unfolds it will become clear that many other people became involved in the subsequent research on the bones of the king led by the University of Leicester. A glance at the members of the team makes clear that only with the expertise of researchers from a wide range of academic disciplines from archaeology to art history, engineering, forensics, genetics, geology, history, medicine and beyond, could the bones have revealed so much about the life, death and burial of this man.

Even during his lifetime Richard attracted controversy, and from the time of his death up to the present day, the nature of his deeds in life, his moral character and the mode of his demise have all stimulated public interest. He has been represented a villain, most famously, but not exclusively, by Shakespeare, assisted in the twentieth century by Laurence Olivier, whose iconic performance in film (*Richard III*, 1955) has become a benchmark in modern times. But, from George Buck, writing in the seventeenth century, to the eighteenth-century essayist Horace Walpole and onward to his many modern enthusiasts, he has been romanticised as a hero wronged by the Tudors and by the

The Bones of a King: Richard III Rediscovered, First Edition. The Greyfriars Research Team with Maev Kennedy and Lin Foxhall.
© 2015 University of Leicester. Published 2015 by John Wiley & Sons, Ltd.

fate which relegated him to the losing side in history. The enormous scale of public interest in the discovery of a skeleton in September 2012 that might possibly have been that of Richard III reflects these longstanding controversies and the emotions they provoke even today. In the first instance the identification was far from certain, and the global response was overwhelming for the research team. This book presents the reality behind the many months of complex, painstaking research by highly trained experts from many different fields who sifted through and evaluated the available evidence that allowed them to pin down the identification 'beyond reasonable doubt'.

We still cannot answer the question of whether Richard III was a villain or a hero, probably because that is the wrong question to ask. Although archaeology can uncover a huge amount of information about his life, health, death and the manner of his burial it cannot tell us anything about his personality, his morals or his character. Even written historical documents and texts cannot reliably help us on this most of the time, since even accounts from the time of Richard himself, or those written only shortly after his death, were certainly not objective and were tainted by the turbulent morally and politically charged environment in which they were written.

Compared to that given to the human remains normally recovered by archaeologists, the time, effort and resources devoted to the bones of Richard III has been exceptional. For the academic researchers involved this was not because they were studying the body of a king. Rather, this discovery presented an extraordinary opportunity to find out about the life and death of a very well-documented individual. This allowed the team to set the information obtained from archaeological and scientific analyses into an exceptionally rich and detailed historical context, enabling them to achieve the most from scientific methodologies. It also provides a body of evidence about the lifestyle of an elite, indeed royal, individual, which can be compared to the information we can obtain from the bodies of ordinary people to see what experiences they must have shared and in what aspects their lives differed. This will lead to a much better understanding of the impacts of social and political hierarchies on late medieval society more broadly.

This book is based on the research and publication of the academics and other experts who carried out the investigations, and on conversations with them about how they followed the trails where the evidence led. It covers the progress of the project from its inception to a period shortly before the reinterment of Richard's remains in Leicester Cathedral in March 2015. The initials which appear after chapter and section headings indicate the specific researchers whose work underpins that chapter or section. The book also attempts to set the results of the discovery and the subsequent research findings against the background of England in the time of the Wars of the Roses and to consider the implications for how we now might understand contemporary Tudor and later representations of Richard. That process of reconsideration is only just beginning.

In this book we have tried hard to make clear the difference between actual primary evidence and data on the one hand and interpretations of that evidence by scholars on the other hand. Primary evidence consists of archaeological 'facts' (such as the grave itself) and data (such as the radiocarbon dates for the bones), as well as texts, documents and images from Richard III's time. Inevitably, all of these are fragmentary and incomplete. The job of researchers is to try to assemble the pieces, which do not always fit together smoothly: no single piece of evidence tells the whole story, and the researchers must try to assemble them in a way that gives the best fit on the basis of their expert knowledge of similar material and its wider contexts. This is the case for all academic research. It is often the case that more than one interpretation is possible, and experts do not always agree. Where the experts have come to different conclusions on the basis of the same evidence we have tried to make this clear.

Sometimes the fragmentary nature of our evidence means that questions have to be formulated in appropriate ways to fit the nature and the state of preservation of the primary evidence available. Inevitably there are questions which cannot be answered, and there are questions that cannot be appropriately asked of the available evidence. Hence, we have also tried to explain the processes of research to show how academic experts generate and assemble their primary data and how they form their interpretations. These are not simply rabbits pulled out of a hat by a magician. Rather results, conclusions and interpretations are formed on the basis of many hours of painstaking investigation and the application of carefully formulated and rigorous research methodologies. It is important to present these methodologies and research processes to explain how it is that we think we know something and why we have asked these particular questions in the specific ways that we have asked them.

Although this book is not cluttered with academic referencing, at the end of each chapter we have included a limited selection of items for further reading. Generally, we have kept to those most likely to be easily available.

Wherever possible, we have attempted to make clear the primary sources which have been used to tell this story. Many of the key historical sources are freely available online, and for those that are we have included website addresses. Where appropriate we have also listed useful works of secondary scholarship, some of which are also freely available online. One major source that we have not cited in the further reading items but that many readers of this book will find useful to follow up the lives of several of the historic individuals mentioned in this book is the *Oxford Dictionary of National Biography*, available online through many libraries. The University of Leicester website also has a large amount of information that is regularly updated along with links to academic publications of the project.

We have tried to tell the story of the discovery as it happened, painting in the background as we go along. Chapter 2 covers the Greyfriars excavation and the research that led up to it. Chapter 3 sets the excavation in the wider contexts of the roles of medieval friaries and the medieval town of Leicester. Chapter 4 explains the complex multidisciplinary research on the skeleton. Chapter 5 sets Richard and his life in the context of the Wars of the Roses. Chapter 6 explains the genealogical and genetic research. Chapter 7 explores what Richard might have looked like working from the surviving portraits. Chapter 8 recounts the announcement of the discovery and the world's reaction to it. Chapter 9 considers the implications of the discovery for broader cultural understandings of Richard III from Tudor times until today. Chapter 10 presents the background to the reinterment of Richard III's remains. Alongside what we do and can know – the facts that the archaeological and historical processes uncover – runs so much that we can never know of the small, personal details of lives lived in the past. We have tried to capture something of the inevitable intertwining of these evanescent events with historical record in the short introductory paragraphs at the beginning of chapters that we have headed 'Imagine ...'; they are purely speculative. Interspersed with them, at the head of other chapters, are factual paragraphs in which we have hoped to show something of the tension for the Greyfriars team as Richard's history became part of their own, these are headed 'The Slow Reveal ...'.

Undoubtedly the controversies surrounding Richard III will continue, and it will take many years for the full impact of this momentous discovery to sink in. But, the repercussions are still reverberating, and we await with eagerness the new results and insights still to come. Now, as we write this, we are only beginning the journey of re-evaluating what this discovery means for interpreting the life and death of Richard III.

2

So How Did He Get There?
(RB, MM)

Imagine ... A Walk in the Garden

As the two men strolled down the garden path one afternoon in 1612, Robert Herrick saw his guest staring at the terracotta tiles beneath his feet, some beautifully decorated. 'A splendid path, is it not?' he said to his friend.

'Yes, indeed', came the reply. 'Where did you get them?'

'Why they were here all the time,' Herrick responded: 'from the house of the Grey Friars pulled down on the orders of our good King Henry. Here, come this way and I'll show you something worth seeing'.

And, he hurried his friend off the path, through the maturing gardens toward the lowering sun as the wood pigeons cooed soothingly in the trees.

The 'Lost' Friary

Leicester has been an urban centre since Roman times, and today the centre of Leicester is densely occupied, like any other modern city. This means that finding a place to excavate that does not have buildings on top is a problem. Below the surface lurk 2,000 years of remains from urban construction, demolition and rebuilding, so the archaeology is very complicated as sites were constantly reused and materials from abandoned buildings were recycled. It is difficult and costly to dig in busy urban areas, and it can cause considerable inconvenience. Most archaeological investigation in Britain is carried out as part of the

The Bones of a King: Richard III Rediscovered, First Edition. The Greyfriars Research Team with Maev Kennedy and Lin Foxhall.
© 2015 University of Leicester. Published 2015 by John Wiley & Sons, Ltd.

planning process and is paid for by the developers when new structures are built or modified in a way that could disturb archaeological remains below ground level. This is where the expertise of the University of Leicester Archaeological Services (ULAS) team, and their unparalleled knowledge of the complex urban archaeology and history of Leicester, was invaluable for tracking down with some precision the layout of the church which held Richard III's grave.

How It All Began

In January 2011, Philippa Langley, an enthusiastic member of the Richard III Society based in Edinburgh, approached Richard Buckley, Co-Director, University of Leicester Archaeological Services, with a proposal to search for the remains of Richard III. Langley had been inspired by John Ashdown-Hill's 2010 book *The Last Days of Richard III*. From the outset, she aimed to attract a production company to document the search on film for a television programme.

For Buckley, this was an unusual request. For the reasons mentioned at the beginning of the chapter, very few purely 'research' excavations take place in British cities. And, archaeologists do not, as a rule, set out to search for famous people or named individuals. Indeed, most of the people (and the material remains of buildings and artefacts) discovered by archaeologists are anonymous. Generally, they have no idea of the names or beliefs of the people whose skeletons they unearth, or who made the artefacts or constructed the buildings that they find.

However, Langley's project idea also presented a wonderful opportunity: The friary of the Franciscans, or Greyfriars – thus called from the colour of the robes they wore – was located in the centre of the town in the medieval period. Although an important part of Leicester's archaeology and history, little was known about it, or its role in the life of the urban population. Although Buckley thought it improbable that the project would locate Richard III's remains, or that it would be possible to identify them securely, he agreed to go ahead with it because it offered a chance to reveal new knowledge about this important friary. For Buckley, with 35 years' experience and virtually unmatched expertise in the archaeology of Roman and medieval Leicester, the prospect was enticing.

Langley's enthusiasm captured the imagination of several key people in Leicester City Council. She persuaded them to give permission for investigations to take place on land owned by the City Council and a private developer. Eventually, in the summer of 2012, with promises from the university, the city council, Leicester Shire Promotions and the Richard III Society to contribute some funding towards the initial excavations, the diggers first broke ground. But much hard work was needed before this could happen.

Finding the Friary

Before the university excavation, we knew very little about the layout of Leicester's 'lost' Franciscan friary, which had been decommissioned during the reign of King Henry VIII, in 1538, as part of the dissolution of the monasteries. The buildings were demolished, and there are records of useable building stone and timber beams being sold off as 'architectural salvage', for recycling in other structures. From the time the friars left, the site had three owners before Robert Herrick acquired it in the early seventeenth century. Herrick, a prosperous ironmonger by trade, was also a prominent local politician who served as an alderman (a member of the local council) and was three times mayor of Leicester (1584, 1593, 1603). He represented Leicester in Parliament in 1588.

On the southern part of the land where the Greyfriars precinct had been, close to what is now Friar Lane, Herrick erected a house (Grey Friars House) and garden. Judging from his will, the property seems to have contained a number of buildings. In 1612, Christopher Wren, the father of the famous architect of St Paul's, London, visited Herrick; he wrote that in a part of the garden where the friary had been he was shown 'a handsome Stone Pillar, three Foot high, with this inscription, "Here lies the Body of Richard III. some Time King of England," This he shewed me [Chr. Wren] walking in the Garden, Anno 1612'. We have no idea how accurately placed this marker really was, and no trace of it was found in the archaeological excavations carried out by the University of Leicester.

Grey Friars House stayed in the Herrick family until it was sold in 1711. In the mid eighteenth century the owner at the time ran a new

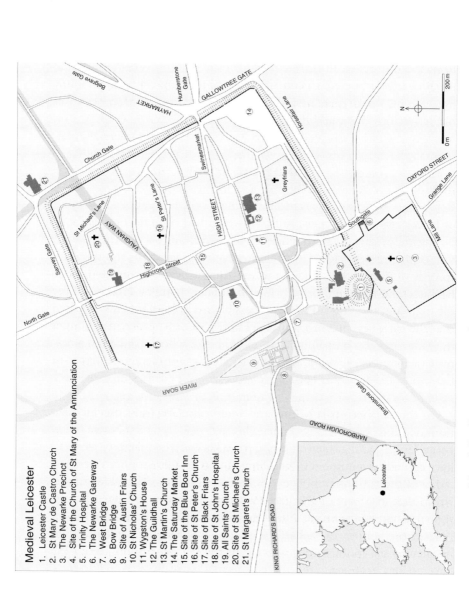

Medieval Leicester

1. Leicester Castle
2. St Mary de Castro Church
3. The Newarke Precinct
4. Site of the Church of St Mary of the Annunciation
5. Trinity Hospital
6. The Newarke Gateway
7. West Bridge
8. Bow Bridge
9. Site of Austin Friars
10. St Nicholas' Church
11. Wygston's House
12. The Guildhall
13. St Martin's Church
14. The Saturday Market
15. Site of the Blue Boar Inn
16. Site of St Peter's Church
17. Site of Black Friars
18. Site of St John's Hospital
19. All Saints' Church
20. Site of St Michael's Church
21. St Margaret's Church

Map 2.1   Reconstruction of the centre of Medieval Leicester.

public street through the property, now New Street, and sold off much of the land in smaller plots. A few years later a different owner of the house sold much of the land close to it. During the later eighteenth and nineteenth centuries many of the buildings and (originally) private houses still standing in the area were constructed. Among them is the Alderman Newton School building, begun in 1864 and presently housing the King Richard III Visitor Centre. Robert Herrick's now old house was demolished in 1871, a new street (Grey Friars Street) was laid out and the rest of the land was sold off for commercial development. So, after many changes of ownership, division of the land into smaller plots, and the addition of two new streets, the process by which the location of Richard III's grave was lost was complete.

Laying the Groundwork

In March 2011, on Buckley's advice (because it is normal practice before planning expensive excavation work), Langley commissioned ULAS to undertake a desk-based survey, carried out by Leon Hunt, to assemble as much information as possible about the precise location of the 'lost' friary. The key information for this was obtained from historic maps (especially that of Thomas Roberts, see Plate 1) which indicated the general location of the friary and from the Leicester Historic Environment Record, which contains details of archaeological find spots. This was essential before any digging could sensibly begin, since to make the most of the archaeologists' time and expensive hired equipment, and to get the right permissions from landowners, the location had to be pinpointed as precisely as possible.

Fortunately, Charles Billson, writing in 1920, and a Leicester scholar, David Baldwin, working in the 1980s, had already laid much of the groundwork, studying the historical sources that pinpointed the location of the tomb. In 1987 Richard Buckley, working from historic maps, had also published a plan of medieval Leicester indicating the location of Greyfriars.

Two historical texts written close in date to the events surrounding the death and burial of Richard provide key evidence. One was the comprehensive history of the kings of England (*Historia Regum Angliae*) by John Rous (d. 1492), an Oxford scholar from Warwickshire and a one-time friend of Richard's. This text was written mostly in Latin shortly after Richard's death. The other was the broad historical work the *Anglica Historia*, written by Polydore Vergil between 1512 and 1555 and published in three editions, obviously some years after Richard's death. He was an Italian scholar serving as the official court historian of Henry VII and must thus be considered something of a 'hostile witness'.

Rous provides the most detailed information, stating that 'tasting what he had more often served to others, he ended his life miserably, and finally he was buried among the Friars Minor [another name for the Franciscans] of Leicester, in the choir' (Figure 2.1). Polydore Vergil may well have been in a position to know details of Richard's burial directly from King Henry VII, the man who ordered it. He confirms Rous's account but gives little more information, stating that Richard was 'buryed two days after [his death] without any pompe or solmne funeral ... in thabbey of monks Franciscanes at Leycester'.

But, where exactly was the friary precinct? John Leland, an antiquarian writing in the mid sixteenth century, located the friary destroyed within his living memory as being 'at the end of the hospital of Mr Wigston'. John Throsby, writing much later, in 1791, suggested that it 'stood on the south side of St Martin's church-yard'. The precinct, he said, was 'spacious and extended from the upper end of the Market Place to the Friar Lane meeting house', though we cannot be sure how he knew this since almost all traces of the friary must have long since vanished by his time.

On the basis of these accounts, and by studying the historic maps and the history of the Herrick property after the friary was closed down, Baldwin came to the conclusion that 'the grave probably lies between the northern (St Martin's) end of Grey Friars Street, or the buildings that face it on either side'. And, how close he turned out to be!

The historic maps found new life in the age of computer technology in the skilled hands of ULAS staff. Using a Geographical Information Systems programme (GIS), they were able digitally to rescale the map made by Thomas Roberts in 1741 (or maybe 1714, since it is possible that the printed date was a typographical error; Plate 1) along with a less accurate seventeenth-century map of Leicester by John Speed to overlay them onto the modern Ordnance

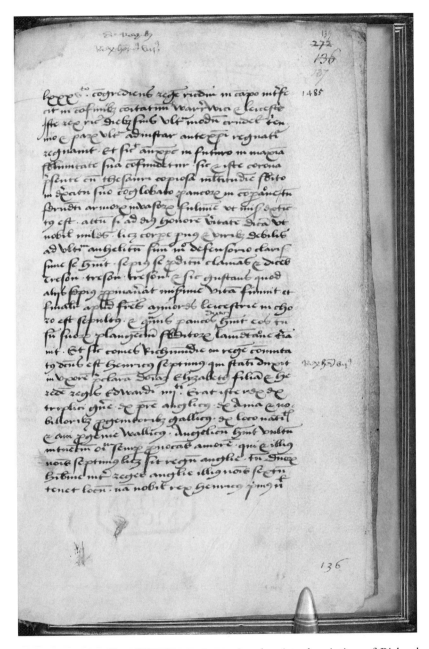

Figure 2.1 Section of the Rous manuscript showing description of Richard III's burial place. British Library, MS Cotton Vespasian A XII, folio 137r. *Source*: Copyright © The British Library Board, MS Cotton Vespasian A XII, folio 137r.

Survey maps. This exercise confirmed Buckley's mapping exercise in 1987, and it suggested that the areas clear of standing buildings in the part of Leicester where the Greyfriars church might have stood consisted of a private car park on New Street, another car park belonging to Leicester City Council Social Services Department and the playground next to the old Alderman Newton School building, then vacant. The private car park on New Street is the largest, and initially it seemed most promising to Buckley. Langley approached the owners, but unfortunately it would have been too expensive to find alternative parking for all the cars. So attention was focused on the car park owned by Leicester City Council and the old school playground, which by extraordinary good luck was already empty and up for sale.

All three areas were surveyed using Ground Penetrating Radar in August 2011 in the hope that the remains of walls might be detected. However, what showed up most clearly were the subterranean utility pipes (water, gas, electric); underground debris in this area of very complex archaeology seemed to mask any preserved archaeological features, if indeed any existed.

There had been few finds and little archaeological work in the area that could provide any clues as to the layout of the friary. In the eighteenth century, builders digging cellars for new houses on St Martins Lane and New Street, opposite St Martin's Church, unearthed many human bones and at least one complete skeleton, which could well have been associated with the friary. A small portion of a stone wall preserved in the New Street car park (the upper brick section visible in Figure 2.2 was added later) might have belonged to the friary. This is quite similar to a section of wall shown in a late nineteenth- or early twentieth-century photograph; it was probably located to the south and west of St Martin's church and demolished in 1928. Again, the lower stone portion is older and likely to be medieval, while the brick was added later. It is possible that both of these walls were associated with the friary, and they may have been boundary walls of some kind. Otherwise, rescue archaeology over the years had revealed only late medieval garden soil and refuse pits, some of which contained broken floor and roof tiles and one frag-ment of a stone coffin, all of which could have originated from the friary, though this was far from certain.

Figure 2.2 Section of medieval stone wall in New Street car park that may have belonged to the friary.

Where to Dig

When Langley commissioned the Ground Penetrating Radar survey of all three areas in the summer of 2011, hoping to discover the remains of walls but instead only revealing the tangled fabric of years of human urban development of the site in the form of multiple utility pipes and general detritus, all combining to obscure what if any archaeological features there were, the project drew to a temporary halt. A lack of funding meant that excavation was postponed to Easter 2012, and put back again to August 2012. Langley was instrumental in persuading the city council as the land owner of the social services car park to give permission for a three-week excavation in August 2012. However, the project was still faltering and on the point of collapse for want of funds. The university stepped in with a substantial contribution, and Langley turned to the Richard III Society for help, rapidly convincing enough individuals to donate money for the dig to go ahead.

Buckley lined up experts in the unlikely event that the project actually found the grave of Richard III. Looking back on his response to Langley's original ideas for the project, including the reinterment of the king's remains, he commented, 'In my head, as the boring archaeologist, I thought "I wouldn't be in too much of a hurry to commission that coffin".'

Back in June 2011, he had emailed Turi King to ask if she would like to be involved. With her background in both archaeology and genetics, her role would be to advise on digging under 'clean' conditions and to undertake any genetic analysis made possible, should a suitable set of remains be found. In July 2012 he emailed Mathew Morris, also from ULAS, asking, 'Would you be interested in running the Greyfriars RIII trial trenching? It will be fairly high profile and will involve some weekend working over the August bank holiday and the following weekend.' Of course, in the event, Morris has done much more 'weekend working' than he ever anticipated. On 17 August he emailed osteoarchaeologist Jo Appleby saying, 'Whilst I think it is rather unlikely that we will actually find the remains of the king given that we are not sure where the church is, where he was buried and whether his remains were exhumed at the Dissolution we need to be prepared!' On 25 August, when sufficient funding had been raised for the initial excavation, ULAS finally broke ground (Plate 2).

Once the dig had started and human remains had been discovered that could be confirmed as located within the church, Buckley, as lead archaeologist, applied to the Ministry of Justice for a licence to exhume up to six skeletons. Medieval churches regularly contain graves, and it was not clear before work started that a grave or a skeleton of Richard III would be identifiable or distinguishable in any way.

The initial plan developed by Buckley (devised originally in 2011) was to lay out two long, narrow trenches, each measuring 30 m × 1.6 m (Trenches 1 and 2) in the social services car park. These were designed to stretch in a north-to-south direction over the longest extent possible within the confined space of the car park. Most Christian churches are oriented east to west, with the altar at the east end. The reasoning behind ULAS's placement of the trenches was that if any portion of the church lay under the site, north–south trenches offered the best chance of cross-cutting it somewhere. To this end, Buckley overlaid scaled plans of a church and cloister based on Leicester's Austin Friars on the Ordnance Survey map, hypothetically locating the church at both north and south. The specific trench locations were chosen to maximise the chance of picking up walls running east–west and to miss known utilities services. Plans were outlined for a third trench, depending on the results from the first two trenches, but the size and shape were not decided at the start.

The modern tarmac surface was carefully removed by machine down to the archaeological levels. Then the digging began in earnest, revealing a jumble of walls from nineteenth-century outbuildings. Clearly the team had come down on structures, but where was the friary? Now they started on their painstaking detective work to make sense of the remains.

The Search for the Friary

In Leicester, supplies of good building stone are scarce. Consequently, in the past when structures were abandoned or dismantled all the useable stone was removed and reused for construction. Because of this recycling habit of many centuries, in Leicester archaeologists often find 'robber trenches' instead of walls; these are the impressions in the ground where there had been a wall or the footings underpinning a wall but the stone has been deliberately removed. Many, though not all, of the walls discovered in the Greyfriars excavation were visible as robber trenches.

In Trenches 1 and 2 the ULAS team struck lucky (See Figure 2.3). At the southern end of one trench and the northern end of the other the footing of a robbed wall about 1 m wide was discovered which appeared to align across both trenches. The section of wall visible in Trench 2 joined to a wall running north–south along the western side of the trench for about 1m to the north and about 7.75 m to the south. A second robbed wall footing running east–west at a distance of 5.65 m to the north of the first one and parallel to it appeared in Trench 1. Mortar on the floor between the east–west walls bore impressions where tiles had been laid in a diamond pattern, though most of the tiles had been removed for reuse. These features clearly added up to prove that this was the remains of building oriented east–west with part of the western wall preserved.

An additional feature revealed the function of this building. Against the inner faces of the two east–west walls in Trench 1 there survived short, narrower walls made of sandstone rubble, 0.4 m wide, with lime plaster coating the surface. Since it was also plaster coated it was clear that the top of one of these was complete; it projected out into the room, making the upper surface 0.5 m wide. The arrangement is most likely to be a room with benches against the walls. In a medieval friary, the kind of building most likely to be furnished in this fashion was the chapter house, a meeting room for the friars. Usually chapter houses are located close to the church, but would traces of the church appear in the trenches?

Another key clue to the layout of the friary precinct appeared in Trench 2. Parallel to the north–south wall to which the chapter house wall is joined runs another wall 3.75 m long and further to the south in the eastern side of the trench. The narrow space between these two north–south walls had a tiled floor – again the impressions in the surviving mortar suggest a diamond pattern. It seems likely that these two walls were part of the eastern cloistral range of buildings typical of friaries (see Chapter 3). This would have been situated to the west of the chapter house.

It was the discovery and recognition of the chapter house, however, a remarkable combination of great skill and good luck, that enabled the

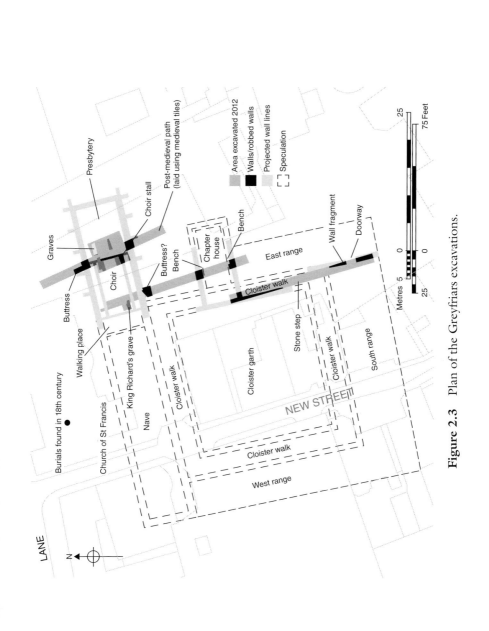

Figure 2.3 Plan of the Greyfriars excavations.

LANE

N

Burials found in 18th century

Graves

Presbytery

Church of St Francis

Buttress

Walking place

King Richard's grave

Nave

Choir

Buttress?

Bench

Choir stall

Post-medieval path
(laid using medieval tiles)

Chapter
house

Bench

Cloister walk

Cloister walk

East range

Cloister garth

Stone step

Wall fragment

Doorway

NEW STREET

Cloister walk

South range

West range

Cloister walk

Area excavated 2012

Walls/robbed walls

Projected wall lines

Speculation

Metres 5   0   25

0   75 Feet

0   25

archaeological team to locate the church. At this point they realised that the church must have been nearby, and located either to the south or the north of the chapter house, but it was difficult to know for certain on which side it was located. Although the layout of medieval friary precincts is relatively standardised, on urban sites variations occur because of the need to accommodate pre-existing buildings and sometimes constrained or oddly shaped plots. So either location was equally possible.

Therefore when, on the first day of the excavation, traces of human remains were exposed in Trench 1, they were left intact and covered up again. At that point it was impossible to be certain where in the friary precinct they were situated. Were they inside or outside a building? Indeed, were they even in the precinct at all?

The northern part of Trenches 1 and 2 were riddled with the remains of eighteenth- and nineteenth-century building activity, which made it difficult to see or interpret the medieval levels. However, a deep linear feature was visible in the section of Trench 1 at the northern end, running east–west. This may have been a robbed-out wall footing, and it was only when Trench 3 was opened that the position of the church was revealed.

On 1 September Trench 3 (30 m × 1.6 m) was opened in the car park of the former Alderman Newton School playground with the aim of finding better-preserved medieval levels and clarifying the complex and confusing picture in Trench 1. It seemed likely by this time that the church was at the north end of the site, but confirmation from the third planned trench was needed. In the new trench, the team discovered two large robbed-out wall footings, up to 1.5 m wide running east–west across the trench and positioned about 7.48 m apart. The northern of these two walls appeared to align with the robbed-out wall footing in Trench 1. It also had a small spur at right angles, heading north. This may have been a buttress or traces of another wall. The two walls were interpreted as the exterior walls of the friary church. These initial results were sufficiently promising that this trench was widened a few days later, on 4 September, to clarify what part of the church had been revealed. At the same time Trench 1 was also widened to allow full excavation of the human remains that had been partially exposed on the first day of the dig, which was by this point known to be in the east end of the church, most likely in the choir.

Immediately over the southern wall of the church, to the south, were a number of the floor tiles, many of them broken, which were originally from inside the church. They had been roughly relaid in a line running north–south. It is possible that this was a garden path from a later period – perhaps during the Herrick family's residence. Excavation in Trench 3 revealed several different floors over the life of the building. Four graves were discovered, three of which cut through the earliest floor levels, but they were not excavated in the 2012 season. The easternmost grave contained a large limestone coffin which was left undisturbed.

A critical discovery was the base of a narrow wall 0.81 m inside the southern wall of the church and running parallel to it. This was built on the second phase of flooring, and the team suspected that it was the support for the southern choir stall. During this second phase of flooring the eastern side was raised to create a step up of about 0.11 m to the east. The boundary between the two areas was indicated by a line of flat slates, extending north across the floor from the eastern end of the choir stall. In the third phase of flooring, the floor was tiled but the tiles on the western side were laid in a diamond pattern, diagonal to the walls, while those on the eastern side were laid in a square pattern, parallel to the walls (Plate 3).

This distinction of space, marked out in these two phases of flooring, almost certainly represents the division between the presbytery, the most sacred and prestigious space in the church – located at the eastern end, closest to the altar – and the choir. The choir, on the western side of the presbytery, was also a prestigious space, but not so highly regarded as the presbytery. Normally only the friars would have had access to the eastern portion of the church, where the services were performed. It would have been separated by a screen from the (western) main body of the church (the nave) where the ordinary people of the congregation stood and listened to the services.

The fact that the team had come down not only on the friary church but on the division between the choir and the presbytery confirmed the working hypothesis developed by Mathew Morris, Richard Buckley and Deidre O'Sullivan. The revelation came even as they were discussing it in relation to the archaeology of Trench 3 with a visiting expert, Glyn Coppack, an authority on medieval religious houses and former English Heritage inspector. The staggering implication was that the grave being excavated at that moment in Trench 1 must have been located in the choir of the church, exactly the place where John Rous said Richard III had been buried. And, just as they were contemplating the impact of their discovery, Morris rushed over to Buckley and whispered to him, 'you have to come see this ...'

Excavating King Richard's Grave

While work progressed on Trench 3, on 5 September Appleby and Morris excavated the grave in Trench 1 to exhume Skeleton 1. Appleby donned a full anti-contamination suit to prevent contamination of any surviving DNA, on one of the hottest days of the summer, to begin the delicate task of removing the skeleton (see Plate 4).

Appleby started excavating the skeleton at the foot (western) end of the grave. In addition, soil samples were taken from beneath the torso and pelvis of the skeleton, from the bottom of the grave, and an additional 'control' sample was taken from outside the grave. This was so that the scientists would be able to test for the remains of parasites and bacterial DNA in the grave and to distinguish the results from 'background' levels of parasites and bacteria outside the grave in an effort to retrieve information about the health of this individual (see Chapter 4).

The feet were missing, and seem to have disappeared long after death, probably as the result of gardening or building activities in later periods. Everything seemed to be proceeding as expected until Appleby reached the middle of the back (the thoracic vertebrae). Suddenly the line of the spine disappeared – was the skeleton only partially preserved? It was only when she explored the area a little to the left of where the spine ought to have been that she discovered the extraordinary curve. And that was when Morris headed off to summon Buckley and O'Sullivan.

As she worked her way around the body from the outside in, Appleby exposed the unusual position of the head, then the arms and hands, before exposing the torso. At the head end, it seemed initially that the skull might belong to a different skeleton since it was not on the same level as the rest of the body (Plate 5). But, it became clear when fully excavated that the fact that the grave was too short at the bottom accounted for its odd position.

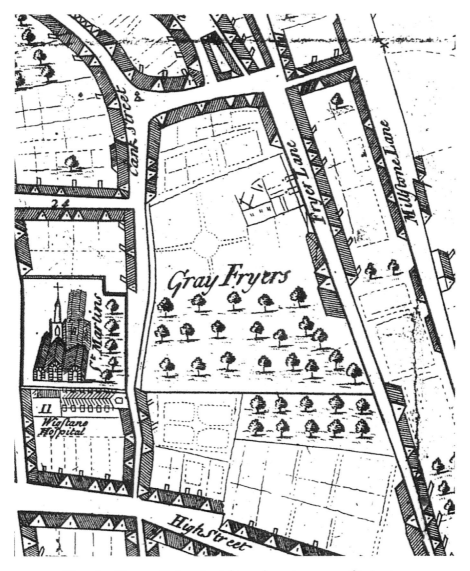

Plate 1   Thomas Roberts's eighteenth-century map of Leicester.

The Bones of a King: Richard III Rediscovered, First Edition. The Greyfriars Research Team with Maev Kennedy and Lin Foxhall.
© 2015 University of Leicester. Published 2015 by John Wiley & Sons, Ltd.

Plate 2 The initial stages of the Greyfriars excavation, August 2012.

Plate 3 Greyfriars excavation, the east end of the church showing the difference in level between presbytery and choir.

Plate 4 Greyfriars excavation, Jo Appleby and Turi King excavating Skeleton 1. The anti-contamination suits they are wearing are designed to prevent modern DNA from coming into contact with the bones.

Plate 5 Greyfriars excavation, the skull emerging from the soil.

Plate 6 Greyfriars excavation, Skeleton 1 in the grave.

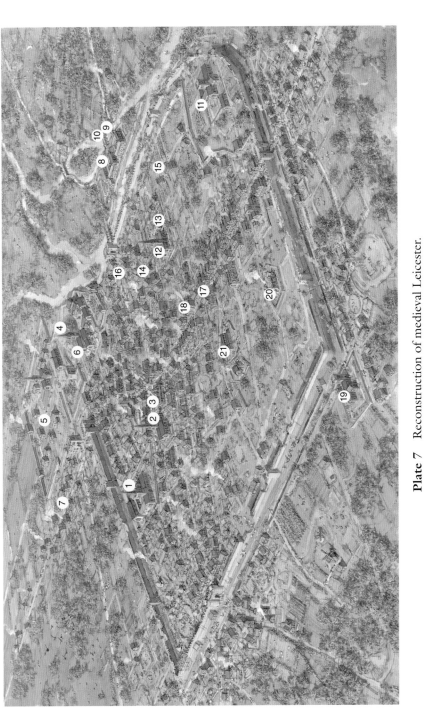

Plate 7 Reconstruction of medieval Leicester.

1. Greyfriars Precinct 2. St Martin's Church 3. Guildhall 4. Leicester Castle 5. The Newarke 6. St Mary de Castro 7. Southern suburb 8. Austin Friars 9. Little Bow Bridge 10. Bow Bridge 11. Blackfriars 12. St Nicholas's 13. Jewry Wall 14. Butchers' area 15. Tanneries 16. Hot Gate 17. The medieval high street (= modern Highcross Street) 18. Blue Boar Inn 19. St Margaret's 20. St Michael's 21. St Peter's

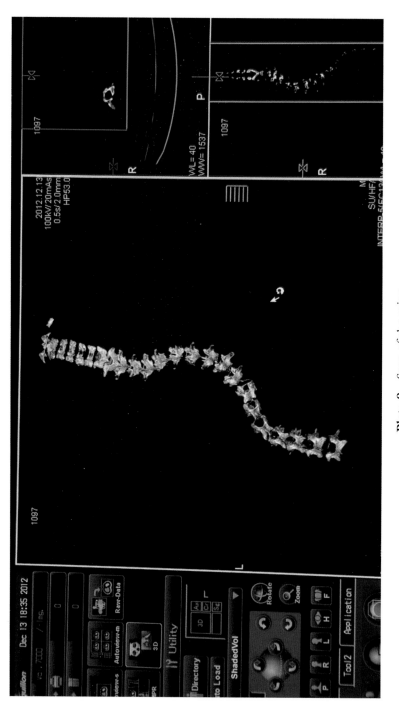

Plate 8 Scan of the spine.

The grave itself was unusual. In Leicester, medieval graves are generally dug very tidily, with neatly squared sides. The other graves discovered in the friary church were like that. This grave, however, had messy, sloping sides and was smaller at the bottom than at the top, as if it had been dug quickly. It may be that the body was lowered feet first into the grave, followed by his torso and head. The body was lying towards one side of the grave, perhaps indicating that someone was standing in the grave to receive it. The peculiar position of the hands could indicate that they were tied together when the body was placed in the grave, but this is not certain (Plate 6).

The position of the skeleton showed that the body had not been tightly wrapped in a shroud – a common medieval burial custom – nor was there any evidence of a coffin (for example, no coffin nails were found). Few artefacts were found in the grave itself, and all seem to have been accidentally incorporated into the grave soil and to have had nothing to do with the burial. It seems inconceivable that the corpse would have been buried naked, and O'Sullivan suggests that the body may have been wrapped in a friar's robe, though of course this cannot be confirmed. As the grave was in consecrated ground within the church, and in a relatively prestigious spot, whoever was buried there would certainly have had a proper Christian funeral, however minimal that might have been. He was almost certainly buried in haste, from the evidence of the grave itself, but the archaeological evidence cannot tell us the degree of respect with which he was (or was not) committed to the earth.

The circumstances of the burial of Skeleton 1 and its condition were sufficient to arouse intense interest, providing possible evidence to support Langley's hope that this could be shown to be Richard III but not proof. The work still to do would extend across many months.

Following Up: The 2013 Excavation

In summer 2013, in the wake of the big announcement identifying Greyfriars Skeleton 1 as Richard III, thousands of visitors watched from the specially erected viewing platform as excavation funded by the University of Leicester continued for a further four weeks. This was essential to clarify the plan of the east end of the church, before the site was covered over as part of the construction of the new visitors centre by Leicester City Council. This time a much bigger area, 17 m × 25 m was opened and excavated. Key aims were to learn more about the plan of the friary church and its architectural development and history, and to investigate other burials inside the building discovered but not excavated in 2012. These excavations confirmed that Richard III had indeed been buried against the southern choir stall at the far western end. Excavations also confirmed the previously discovered wall lines and revealed evidence for the western wall of the choir (the wall dividing it from the nave) and for the northern choir stall. One small area of tiled flooring was found intact and in place – the first to be discovered inside the church. South of the church a substantial structure with large buttressed walls was discovered. This could be a different building associated with the friary. Alternatively, it is possibly the remains of an earlier church building, pre-dating the one in which Richard III was buried.

Three more burials were exhumed. One body was located in the presbytery in a lead casket inside a stone coffin positioned centrally and probably close to where the high altar had been (Plate 3). This would have been an extremely prestigious position, and it was clearly the burial of a high-status, and possibly wealthy, person. The second was located at the eastern end of the choir up against a choir stall while the third was found in a position under the division between the choir and the presbytery meaning that it was probably from an earlier phase of the building before that division had been delineated. The latter two burials were both in wooden coffins, on the evidence of impressions of the wood from the coffin in the soil. Analysis of the skeletons revealed that all three belonged to females who had died in the late thirteenth or fourteenth centuries, 100 years before Richard.

Unfortunately, extensive post medieval disturbance at the western end of the excavation had obliterated evidence of the nave and of the 'walking place' (ambulatory), the area between the choir and the nave typically found in friary churches, which often had a tower above. It appeared from the excavation that the disturbance might have been caused by a major robbing or quarrying event, perhaps removing stones from a substantial feature like a tower base. The excavation revealed that this large-scale disturbance missed Richard's head by millimetres – emphasising yet again how lucky the team was to have found the grave intact.

Why Greyfriars?

Although it must have been King Henry VII who authorised the burial of Richard III in the Greyfriars church, we do not know what motivated his choice. We know that Henry VII venerated St Francis and acted as a patron to the Franciscan order in England. He was also the first English king to have Franciscan friars as his confessors. However, there may have been other factors behind his decision.

There were other monastic foundations in Leicester: Leicester Abbey to the north of the medieval town and two other friaries, the Dominican Blackfriars and the Austin Friars. However, all of these establishments were further from the medieval town centre. The Greyfriars precinct was close to the commercial centre of the town and near to the Guildhall, which by that period was the town's political headquarters (see Chapter 3).

The location of the grave in the choir of Greyfriars church meant that there was limited public access to it. This could be interpreted as discouraging veneration of the deceased king or loyalty to him that might breed future dissent or rebellion, and as preventing the development of a cult of 'miracles' surrounding the tomb. However, it was a place of quite high status and respect within the church, and there are other examples of disgraced aristocracy being buried in the choir of churches. It is probably significant that he was not buried in the most prestigious part of the church, in the presbytery close to the high altar at the eastern end; perhaps this implies that the respect accorded him was grudging, but this is not certain. It is possible that this location would have been a good one for agents of Henry VII – perhaps stationed in the town centre – to keep a close eye on the grave to ensure that it did not become a focus of rebellion against the new king, but this is only one interpretation and far from certain.

The friary had a chequered history of involvement with royal politics some 80 years previously. In 1402, some of its members were involved in a plot to spread rumours that King Richard II (d. 1400) was alive in Scotland and intending to reclaim the throne from the current incumbent, King Henry IV. Eight of the friars were incarcerated in the Tower of London then hanged and beheaded for treason at Tyburn, and their heads were displayed around the country afterwards; two others were executed in Lichfield. What part this earlier, quite dramatic incident might have played in the decision to bury Richard III in the Franciscan church is impossible to know for sure. Perhaps when asked by King Henry VII to undertake the task of laying the deposed king to rest, they felt it was a request they could not refuse, especially in light of their past history. But, there is no firm evidence to confirm or negate this speculation.

King Henry VII's Monument

Although the archaeologists found no evidence of a tomb monument on Richard III's grave, it seems that Henry VII eventually decided to erect a permanent memorial there. Almost certainly, this monument was removed when the monastery was closed in 1538 so that its valuable materials could be sold for reuse. We cannot be sure what form this tomb took. Its size may have been constrained by the somewhat limited space where Richard was buried in the church. And, nobles in this period were buried with a range of different types of monuments.

The most direct and compelling evidence for the tomb comes from the chancery record (TNA C1/206/69) of a legal dispute which arose over its construction by an alabaster sculptor, Walter Hylton, based in Nottingham. Hylton had been commissioned by two of Henry VII's chief agents, Reynold Bray and Thomas Lovell, to construct and install a monument commemorating Richard III in the Greyfriars church in Leicester, and this is specified in the chancery record as background to the court case. The document is dated to 1 July in the eleventh year of Henry VII, that is, 1496. However, the order for the work must have been placed a year or two before this lawsuit occurred, and the memorial was probably installed around 1495.

Although there are several other contemporary historical records that can, with varying degrees of plausibility, be linked to the construction of this tomb, the chancery record over Hylton's lawsuit remains the most secure evidence for the tomb itself. And, although there are many alabaster tomb monuments and effigies dating to this period, these vary considerably in size, configuration and magnificence, so it is impossible to be certain how alabaster carving featured on this particular tomb.

George Buck (d. 1622) provides a description of the tomb in his *The History of the Life and Reigne of Richard the Third*, which attempts to dispel the bad reputation Richard had acquired under the Tudor kings. Buck had an ulterior motive for this: his family had lost property because they had supported Richard III in the Wars of the Roses, and Buck was attempting to claim back some of this property. The earliest copy of Buck's work appears on a partially burned manuscript dating to 1619, but it was not printed as a book until 1646, after his death. Although he could never possibly have seen it himself, Buck asserts that the tomb was 'in the chief Church of Leicester, called Saint Maries, belonging to the Order and Society of the Gray Friars'. There is no primary source contemporary with the friary church that confirms the main saint to which it was dedicated, and it is probable that Buck was wrong about this (see Chapter 3). He may have confused this church (which no longer existed in his time) with other churches in Leicester dedicated to St Mary, perhaps Leicester Abbey or St Mary de Castro (see Chapter 3). Buck goes on to explain that

> the King in short time after causing a fair Tomb of mingled colour'd Marble, adorned with his [Richard III's] statue, to be erected there-upon, to which some grateful pen had also destined an Epitaph, the Copie whereof (never fixt to his stone) I have seen in a recorded Manuscript-Book chained to a Table in a Chamber of the Guild-hall of London

Buck does not explain where he got his information about what Richard's tomb looked like, so it is impossible to judge the accuracy of his account. The detail that 'mingled colour'd Marble' was used prob-ably came from the epitaph (see below), but the text of the inscription does not mention any 'statue' or effigy. John Leland, who visited Leicester sometime in the first half of the sixteenth century, mentions that Richard III was buried in the Greyfriars church, but he does not describe the tomb, which suggests that he did not see it in person.

The Epitaph

The history of the epitaph is very complicated. It is interesting that Buck says exactly where he found the text of the epitaph, though it is not clear why he believed that the epitaph had never been added to the tomb. If he did indeed copy the text from an old manuscript, as he claims, we do not know what manuscript it was.

However, a different text of the epitaph was transmitted via another tradition through the College of Arms. The text is preserved in a manuscript probably written by Thomas Wriothesley, Garter King of Arms at the time of his death in 1534, and earlier in his career pursuivant (an officer of the College of Arms lower in rank than herald) to the sons of Henry VII. It is possible that Wriothesley actually saw the inscription himself, but this is not certain, and in this manuscript version there are errors in the Latin. The text also appears in a different manuscript, copied and slightly changed by another herald, Thomas Hawley (d. 1557). Both of these manuscripts are reproduced by John Ashdown Hill (see 'Further reading'). Eventually this text was published in 1677 by Francis Sanford, also a herald, and it is presented in Philip Schwyzer' s book *Shakespeare and the Remains of Richard III* (see 'Further reading').

A third version of the text appears in a manuscript (Ellesmere 1129) probably dating to the later sixteenth century, so the writer of this manuscript almost certainly could not have seen the original inscription. The manuscript includes Latin verses on all of the monarchs from William I to Elizabeth I, but the author is unknown. (Figure 2.4).

One of the most interesting features of this text is the heading, which claims that it was carved on a bronze plaque next to Richard's tomb, information which appears in none of the other manuscript traditions. If correct, it might suggest that whoever the author had copied it from had seen the inscription in person, but we cannot be certain of this. Perhaps significantly, the Latin text of this manuscript seems to be largely free of errors and often uses words that make more sense than either the Buck or the Wriothesley versions. Although this could indicate that it is a more accurate copy of the original, we cannot be certain – maybe the original copyist was simply better at Latin.

The text of the Latin epitaph, which Buck claims to have corrected, reproduced in the 1647 edition of his book and the rather different texts from Wriothesley (as published by Sanford in 1677 and presented by Philip Schwyzer, see 'Further reading') and Ellesmere 1129 are presented here with translations. It is clear that Buck's version has chosen wording which is more favourable to Richard III than the other two variants of the text.

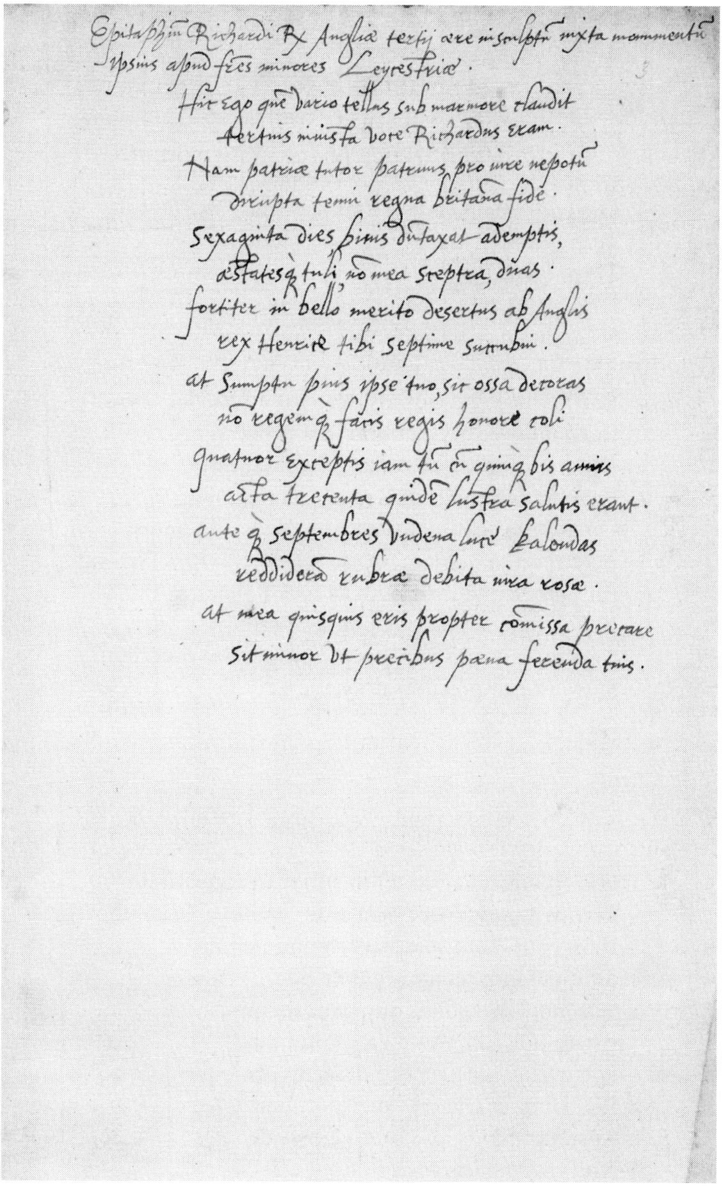

Epitaphium Richardi Rx Angliæ tertij ære inscript[um] iuxta monument[um]
ipsius apud f[rat]res minores Leyrestriæ.

Hic ego que[m] vario tellus sub marmore claudit
   Tertius iniusta voce Richardus eram.
Nam patriæ tutor patru[u]s pro iure nepotu[m]
   Dirupta tenui regna Britana fide.
Sexaginta dies binis du[n]taxat ademptis,
   æstatesq[ue] tuli no[n] mea sceptra, duas.
Fortiter in bello merito desertus ab Anglis
   rex Henrice tibi septime succubui.
At sumptu pius ipse tuo, sic ossa decoras
   no[n] regem q[ue] faris regis honore coli
Quatuor exceptis iam tu o[mn]i quinq[ue] bis annis
   acta trecenta quidem lustra salutis erant.
Ante q[ue] Septembres v[n]dena luce kalendas
   reddideram rubra debita u[n]a rosæ.
At mea quisquis eris propter co[m]missa precare
   Sit minor ut precib[us] pæna ferenda tuis.

Figure 2.4 Epitaph from Richard III's gravestone set up by Henry VII, in Ellesmere 1129 manuscript, written in Latin in late sixteenth-/early seventeenth-century secretary hand on four leaves of paper, folded into folio format. The epitaph to Richard III is the longest verse on the last page. *Source*: This item is reproduced by permission of the Huntington Library, San Marino, California. Ellesmere Manuscript, EL 1129, folio 3r.

The Latin Epitaph

Buck 1647

Hic ego, quem vario Tellus sub Marmore claudit,
Tertius a justa voce Richardus eram;
Tutor eram Patriae, Patrius pro jure Nepotis;
Dirupta, tenui regna Britanna, fide.
Sexaginta dies binis duntaxat ademptis
Ae[s]tatesque, tuli tunc mea Sceptra, duas.
Fortiter in Bello certans desertus ab Anglis,
Rex Henrice, tibi, septime, succubui
At sumptu, pius ipse, tuo, sic ossa dicaras,
Regem olimque facis Regis honore Coli.
Quatuor exceptis jam tantum, quinq, bis annis
Actatrecenta quidem, lustra salutis erant,
Antique Septembris undena luce Kalendas,
Redideram rubrae jura petita Rosae.
At mea, quisquis eris, propter commissa precarem
Sit Minor ut precibus poena levata tuis.

Wriothesley/Sanford 1677

Hic ego quem vario tellus sub marmore claudit
Tertius a multa voce Richardus eram.
Nam patris tutor patrius pro iure nepotis
dirupta tenui regna Britanna fide.
Sexaginta dies, binis duntaxat ademptis
Estatesque tuli non mea sceptra duas.
Fortiter in bello merito desertus ab Anglis
Rex Henrice tibi septime succubui.
At sumptu pius ipse tuo, sic ossa decoras
Non regem facis regis honore coli
Quatuor exceptis jam tantum, quinque bis annis
Acta trecenta quidem lustra salutis erant.
Anteque septembres undena luce kalendas
Reddideram rubrae debita iura rosae.
At mea quisquis eris propter commissa precare
Sit minor ut precibus pena ferenda tuis.

English translations

Buck 1647

Here I, whom Earth has shut under variegated marble,
was called Richard the Third by a just voice;
I was the defender of my fatherland, a fatherly guardian on behalf of a nephew;
I faithfully held the broken British kingdoms.
For sixty days minus two,
and two summers, then I bore my sceptres.
Bravely contesting in war, deserted by the English,
King Henry the Seventh, to you I submitted
And you, a pious man, thus honoured my bones at your expense
And you made a former king to be revered with the honour of a king.
When indeed there had passed three hundred half-decades of our salvation,
With twice five minus four taken away[1]
and eleven days before the Kalends[2] of September
I restored to the red rose the rights which were sought
But I pray, whoever you are, that by your prayers
my punishments on account of my deeds, may be lightened and lessened by
    your prayers.

Wriothesley/Sanford 1677 (translation adapted from Schwyzer)

Here I, whom Earth has shut under variegated marble,
Was by many called Richard III
I was the defender of my fatherland, a fatherly guardian on behalf of a nephew;
I faithfully held the broken British kingdoms.
For sixty days minus two
and two summers, I bore sceptres that were not mine
Bravely in battle, deservedly deserted by the English,
King Henry the Seventh, to you I submitted.
And you, a pious man, thus honoured my bones at your own expense
You made a non-king to be revered with the honour of a king.
When indeed there had passed three hundred half-decades of our salvation,
Then with twice five minus four now taken away
and eleven days before the Kalends of September
I restored to the red rose the rights which were owed
But pray, whoever you are, on account of my deeds,
So that my punishments may be borne by your prayers.

[1]   That is, 1494.
[2]   The first day, eleven days earlier: 22 August, the day of the Battle of Bosworth.

Ellesmere 1129

Epitaphium Richardi Rex [regis] Angliae tertij aere in sculptum iuxta monumentum ipsius apud fratres minores Leycestriae

Hic ego quem vario tellus sub marmore claudit
tertius iniusta voce Richardus eram.
Nam patriae tutor patruus pro jure nepotuum
Dirupta tenui regna Britanna fide.
Sexaginta dies, binis duntaxat ademptis,
Aestatesque tuli non mea sceptra, duas.
fortiter in bello merito desertus ab Anglis
rex Henrice tibi septime succubui.
At sumptu pius ipse tuo, sic ossa decoras
non regemque facis regis honore coli
quatuor exceptis iam tum cum quinque bis annis
acta trecenta quidem lustra salutis erant.
anteque septembres undena luce kalendas
reddideram rubrae debita iura rosae.
at mea quisquis eris propter commissa precare
sit minor ut precibus poena ferenda tuis.

Ellesmere 1129

The epitaph of Richard the Third King of England carved in bronze next to a monument to the same in [the church of] the friars minor in Leicester.

Here I, whom Earth has shut under variegated marble,
was called Richard the Third by an unjust voice;
I was the defender of my fatherland, a paternal uncle on behalf of his nephews;
I faithfully held the broken British kingdoms.
For sixty days minus two,
and two summers, I bore sceptres that were not mine.
Bravely in battle, deservedly deserted by the English,
King Henry the Seventh, to you I submitted
And you, a pious man, thus honoured my bones at your own expense
And you made a non-king to be revered with the honour of a king.
When indeed there had passed three hundred half-decades of our salvation,
Then with twice five minus four now taken away
days before the Kalends of September
I restored to the red rose the rights which were owed
But pray, whoever you are, on account of my deeds,
So that my punishments may be borne by your prayers.

Had this text been carved on a bronze plaque, Henry VII's name, prominently located at the beginning of the central line of the poem, could have been made to stand out visually for viewers. The sentiments expressed are sometimes positive on the surface, but the language is often ambiguous and not fully laudatory, especially in the Wriothesley/Sanford 1677 and Ellesmere 1129 versions. It certainly does not paper over what the Tudors, at least, perceived as his misdeeds. And it clearly validates Henry's rule and Richard's 'submission' to him.

However, the plea at the end to pray for Richard's soul in purgatory could be significant. The fact that it is there at all suggests that Henry VII was not accusing Richard III (at least openly) of killing the princes in the tower or his brother Edward. In terms of the Christian beliefs in England at the time, this could have been an indication that Henry wanted to portray Richard as redeemable. The theological premise behind this passage is that he was not already in hell for the terrible crimes of killing his nephews, the princes in the tower, or his brother, Edward IV of which he had been accused. At the very least this representation implies that he must have repented before his death. Had he been considered to have committed such terrible crimes and not repented, his soul would not have been able to benefit from prayers said for him.

Why did Henry feel it necessary to erect a memorial to Richard at this time? In the 1490s, Henry was faced with an imposter named Perkin Warbeck who claimed to be Richard of Shrewsbury, the youngest son of Edward IV. He became the focus of former supporters of Richard III and the Yorkists in many parts of the country, and the activities of these rebellious groups threatened to destabilise Henry's realm. Moreover, the existence of this imposter was very attractive to Margaret of Burgundy, an aunt of the genuine Richard of Shrewsbury, who was already in conflict with Henry VII. Together with her stepdaughter's husband Maximillian of Austria, who became Holy Roman Emperor in 1493, Margaret encouraged the pretender. By 1495, Maximillian and Margaret were planning an attack on England to install 'Prince Richard' (aka Perkin Warbeck). Assigning the establishment of a tomb for Richard III to the hands of such capable and powerful agents and advisors as Bray and Lovell suggests that Henry thought this was an important task. It may also indicate that he was keen to placate supporters of Richard III and the Plantagenets and to damp down the sparks of rebellion, while staunchly maintaining his right to rule. Henry may also have felt that Richard was owed the honour of a tomb as a tribute to the value and sanctity of the office of king itself.

But, as the archaeological excavation proved, Henry's commemoration of Richard was short-lived, lasting only another 40 years or so until the friary was dissolved and its buildings dismantled in 1538 under Henry VIII.

Further reading

Ashdown-Hill, J. (2008) The epitaph of King Richard III. *Ricardian* 18: 41–44. Available online at http://www.richardiii.net/6_3_1_the_ricardian_archive.php (last accessed 11 November 2014).

Baldwin, David (1986) King Richard's grave in Leicester. *Transactions of the Leicestershire Archaeological and Historical Society* 60: 21–24. Available online at http://www.le.ac.uk/lahs/publications/vol51_60.html (last accessed 11 November 2014).

Buck, George (1646) *The History of the Life and Reigne of Richard the Third. Composed in five books.* London: William Wilson. A 1647 edition is available online at: http://books.google.co.uk/books?id=ZiFEAAAAcAAJ&printsec=frontcover&dq=George+Buck&hl=en&sa=X&ei=B7WFVMS8HceuU_PcgPgP&ved=0CCIQ6AEwAA#v=onepage&q=George%20Buck&f=false (last accessed 9 December 2014).

Buckley, R. and Lucas, J. (1987) *Leicester Town Defences.* Leicester: Leicestershire Museums, Art Galleries and Records Service.

Buckley, R., Morris, M., Appleby, J. *et al.* (2013) 'The king in the car park': new light on the death and burial of Richard III in the Grey Friars church, Leicester, in 1485. *Antiquity* 87: 519–538. Available online at http://antiquity.ac.uk/ant/087/ant0870519.htm (last accessed 11 November 2014).

Morris, M. and Buckley, R. (2013) *Richard III: The King under the Car Park.* Leicester: University of Leicester Archaeological Services.

Polydore Vergil (1555) *Anglica Historiae.* The Latin text and English translation are available online at http://www.philological.bham.ac.uk/polverg/ (last accessed 11 November 2014).

Rous, John [1745] *Historia Regum Angliae.* Oxford: Fletcher and Pote. The Latin text is available online at http://books.google.co.uk/books/about/Joannis_Rossi_antiquarii_Warwicensis_His.html?id=yQw2AAAAMAAJ (last accessed 11 November 2014).

Schwyzer, Philip (2013) *Shakespeare and the Remains of Richard III*. Oxford: Oxford University Press. See pp. 25–28 on the epitaph of Richard III.

Chancery records: images of original documents:

http://aalt.law.uh.edu/AALT7/ChP/C1no206/IMG_0122.htm (last accessed 9 December 2014).
http://aalt.law.uh.edu/AALT7/ChP/C1no206/IMG_0123.htm (last accessed 9 December 2014).

3

The Bigger Picture

Imagine …

Their faded grey robes looking rather the worse for wear, two elderly men peered through the gate, watching the workmen strip the lead from the roof. 'It's over, William', said one to the other with a catch in his throat, 'now who will look after the townsfolk in this world, and what will happen to all those buried there in the next? Who will sing the masses for the relief of their souls?'

Aye', came the reply, 'We took a vow for ourselves and made a promise to them, and now we can't keep either.'

Slowly they turned away and faded into the crowd of waggons, workers and curious onlookers pushing towards the gate.

Friaries in Medieval England and Wales (DOS)

The church of the Greyfriars in Leicester had been entangled with the history of the town and serving its people since its foundation sometime between 1224 and 1231. By the time Henry VII had a memorial placed on Richard III's grave the Franciscans had been a feature of life there for almost three hundred years.

The Christian church played a major role in the life and politics of medieval societies. Although there were many monastic institutions of different kinds in medieval Britain, friaries were distinctive. For a start, they were relative latecomers: the first friaries in England and

The Bones of a King: Richard III Rediscovered, First Edition. The Greyfriars Research Team with Maev Kennedy and Lin Foxhall.
© 2015 University of Leicester. Published 2015 by John Wiley & Sons, Ltd.

Wales were founded by the Dominican and Franciscan orders in the early thirteenth century, many hundreds of years after the earliest monastic establishments emerged. Other orders of friars followed rapidly, establishing their houses later in the thirteenth century and into the fourteenth century. Of the 208 friary foundations established over the medieval period, the Franciscans remained the most numerous (57 establishments known), followed closely by the Dominicans (54 establishments known).

In contrast to earlier monastic orders, the friaries were often located in the growing towns and cities, where they could fulfil their distinctive mission of preaching and ministry and were able to support themselves as they were supposed to as mendicants by begging. The Greyfriars precinct in Leicester was situated right in the heart of the town. Small friaries in more remote locations might have fewer than 10 friars, but the largest friaries, in bigger towns and cities, sometimes had 50 or more. A document dating to 1300 records a request to the Bishop of Lincoln to license 18 friars of Greyfriars Leicester to hear confession. This gives a good idea of the numbers of friars living in Greyfriars, since that request probably covered almost all of them. However, it is clear that the presence of friars was often resented by older and more powerful monastic orders such as the Benedictines, and in places where these older orders were powerful, friaries either were never established (for example, Peterborough) or were chased out (as was the case in Bury St Edmunds). This is part of a wider hostility to the very public activities of the friaries that emanated from some of the more established church institutions and monastic orders by which they were sometimes characterised as lax and sinful.

Many monastic institutions, established according to their rules as self-sufficient communities, accumulated great wealth and large land holdings, often as the result of generous gifts from wealthy patrons. It was not unusual for monks to live like wealthy aristocrats, despite their vows of poverty, chastity and obedience. Many of them might be drawn from the upper orders of society, while in contrast, the men who became friars often seem to have come from families that were well-off but not aristocratic. In most cases these friars seem to have taken their vow of poverty quite seriously, even though they still may have had a higher standard of living than most ordinary people. Inventories made in 1538–9, when the friaries along with other monastic institutions were closed by Henry VIII, demonstrate their modest assets and incomes.

For the most part friaries' incomes seem to have come from fees for burial and donations, including gifts left to the friary by donors in their wills, in contrast to the landed estates and rents which supported many monasteries. Often the donations to friaries paid for prayers and services for the deceased for a number of years. In 1516 Ralph Gells left 10 shillings to Greyfriars in Leicester for 30 masses to be performed after his death. He also bequeathed small sums of money to each individual friar and novice, and left his son, who was one of the friars, a pair of sheets and a blanket.

Friars might be involved in funerals that took place in other churches. In 1524, Robert Staples asked that the Franciscan friars carry his body to St Martin's church (across the street from Greyfriars Leicester) and perform his funeral service there.

In England and Wales, the total of the establishments of each order of friars (Dominicans, Carmelite, etc.) constituted a 'province'. Within each order (province) friaries were loosely organised into roughly geographical groups (called 'custodies' in the case of Franciscans) under the direction of a 'lead' house. Greyfriars Leicester, with Reading, Bedford, Stamford, Nottingham, Northampton and Grantham, was under Oxford. (Friaries were, in fact, important members of the university communities of both Oxford and Cambridge.) Each individual friary also seems to have had a specifically assigned area within which they preached and collected alms: usually friaries of the same order were located at some distance from each other so as not to overlap their territories (called 'limits'). However, they were not under the authority of the local bishop, as other monastic establishments were. And, though local bishops could license friars to preach in parish churches, hear confession and hold funerals, they were not always keen to do so.

Preaching was central to the mission of friars. They regularly travelled out to preach in public spaces such as marketplaces, but they also preached in their own friary churches. This was quite different from some other monastic orders who kept themselves isolated from the wider world. Hence, friary churches were more open to the ordinary lay people who lived in the towns where they were established than were other monastic churches. Sometimes both church and royal authorities would try to mobilise particular orders of friars to spread specific messages in their preaching, for example to publicise crusades or to stir up specific political sentiments. In addition, since friaries had libraries and scribes, they provided education for members of the clergy. By the later medieval period some friaries also developed schools which taught lay people, although it is not clear how common this was.

No friary precincts survive intact with all their buildings, largely as a result of Henry VIII's dissolution of the monasteries. At some sites, however, there are standing remains of fragments of the original buildings, and sometimes portions of friary buildings were incorporated into later churches and other structures. Hence, what we know of the actual layout of friaries comes largely from archaeological evidence, supplemented by evidence from historical documents and texts.

The architecture of friaries, in keeping with their ideals of poverty, is relatively simple compared to that of many other medieval ecclesiastical establishments. Friary churches, like almost all Christian churches, are aligned east–west and generally consisted of a nave at the western end and a choir (which only the friars and other clerics could normally enter) on the eastern side. These two parts of the church were separated by a narrow passage way, often known as the 'walking place', which led to the cloister, an area which was usually private to the friars and other inhabitants of the friary. If the church had a tower or a steeple it was normally set above the walking place. All of these features can be seen clearly in the relatively well-preserved plans of Greyfriars Walsingham in Norfolk (Figure 3.1) and Greyfriars Carmarthen in Wales (Figure 3.2). In the case of Walsingham and Greyfriars Leicester, the choir of the church was subdivided into the western part where the choir sat and sang (and which might be used for small or private services by the friars) and the more prestigious eastern end, sometimes called the presbytery, where the high altar lay and which was the holiest part of the church.

Friaries could include a range of other buildings and structures. Nearly all had one or more cloisters, which were courtyards with covered walkways around the outside, and provided quiet spaces for the friars to walk, converse and think. Most had a chapter house, usually located adjacent to the eastern side of the cloister: these served as meeting rooms for the friars. Chapter houses often had a dormitory above, and if there was a separate refectory (dining room) it was likely to be in close proximity to the chapter house. However some friaries also had separate kitchen blocks (often to the west), infirmaries, hospitals, guest houses and other facilities, some of which appear in the plans of Walsingham and Carmarthen.

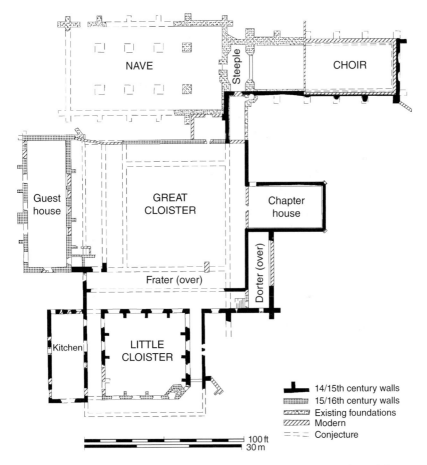

Figure 3.1 Plan of Greyfriars friary, Walsingham. *Source*: Adapted from O'Sullivan 2013: 329, fig. 5.30.

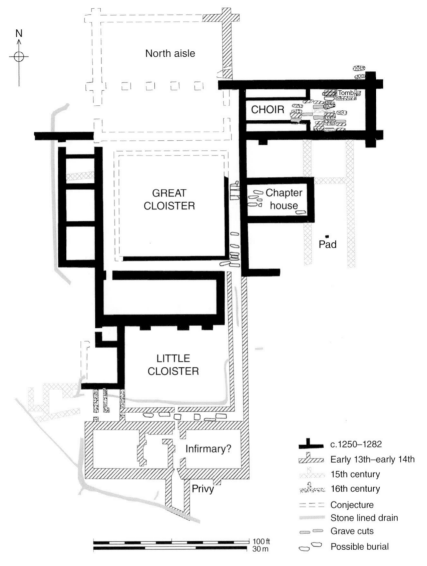

Figure 3.2 Plan of Greyfriars friary, Carmarthen. *Source*: Adapted from O'Sullivan 2013: 103, fig. 2.48.

Most friary churches also had churchyards, which served as cemeteries for the burial of ordinary lay people who wanted, and could pay for, the protection and pastoral care of the friars even in death. These people would have taken a conscious decision to be interred in a friary rather than in a local parish church, though we do not usually understand the reasons for this choice. As noted above, burial was a major source of income for friaries, and one which other monastic establishments sometimes resented. The friars themselves were often buried in the cloister (although secular burials are recorded in cloisters as well), or in the walking place of the church.

The graves of wealthier or higher status individuals might also be located in the church: as a general rule, the closer to the eastern end of the church and the high altar, the more prestigious (and perhaps costly) the location. A register of 1526 for London Greyfriars which is sufficiently detailed to work out who was buried where shows that wealth and social status were prime considerations for the location of an individual's final resting place. In the spaces closest to the altar were the tombs of royalty (King Edward II and his wife Queen Isabella). Side chapels to the north and south of the east end were filled with aristocrats and important clergy. Moving westward, the small chapels at the east end of the nave were occupied by upper-class people, while further west still, in the aisles to the north and south of the nave, wealthy London citizens were buried.

Significantly, in relation to the grave of Richard III, a number of other disgraced or executed political figures are documented as having been buried in friaries. Such burials are documented in London and York, as well as Leicester. These include Perkin Warbeck, who was buried in the church of the Austin Friars in London following his execution by Henry VII in 1499. Other leading unfortunates buried in the Austin Friary London included Richard Fitz Alan (d. 1397), John de Vere (d. 1463), James Tyrell and James Wyndham (d. 1503), and Edward, Duke of Buckingham (d. 1521). The Dominican friary in London held the bodies of John Tiptoft, Earl of Worcester (d. 1470) and Lord Audley (d. 1497). Humphrey de Bohun, John Mowbray and Roger Clifford, who all died in the Battle of Boroughbridge (1322) were buried in the Dominican friary in York, and the executed Thomas Mowbray (d. 1402) was buried in the Franciscan friary there. Given this well-established tradition, burial in a friary might have seemed particularly suitable for a deposed king defeated and killed in battle, in the case of Richard III.

Greyfriars, Leicester (DMO, RB, MM)

The little historical documentation for Greyfriars Leicester that survives and is published has been assembled by Nick Holder (Regent's University, London) for the Greyfriars Project. Its history begins sometime between 1224, when the Franciscans first came to England, and the first mention of a Franciscan friary in Leicester dates from when it was visited by John of Malvern in 1230–1231, as documented by Thomas of Eccleston in his chronicle *De adventu Fratrum Minorum* (The arrival of the Brothers Minor). There is some confusion in the later historical sources over the identity of the founder. The sixteenth-century traveller John Leland thought it was Simon de Montfort, and historians of the eighteenth century suggest several other names, but there is no independent primary evidence to support any of these suggestions. It may be significant that the archdeacon of Leicester at the time of the foundation, Robert Grosseteste, was a supporter of the new friaries, especially the Franciscans. This may at least have provided a sympathetic climate for the establishment of their friary in Leicester.

We do not know the date when the building of the church commenced, but in 1255 King Henry III gave the timber of 18 oak trees from the King's Hay in Alrewas, Staffordshire 'for making their stalls and lining their chapel', in response to a request from his sister Eleanor, who was the wife of Simon de Montfort and countess of Leicester. This must have been done as one of the final tasks in the construction of the eastern end of the building. However, the church seems to have been formally opened and consecrated later, judging from the incentive (10 days fewer in Purgatory) to visit 'the newly consecrated church of the Franciscans in Leicester' offered by the Bishop of Lincoln in July 1290. This same document also suggests that the saints specially venerated in the church were St Mary, St John the Baptist and St John the Evangelist, though whether it was to any of these that the church was primarily dedicated remains uncertain.

Historical documents reveal that from the late thirteenth century onward the friary had become a local landmark. It is regularly mentioned in property transactions to locate plots of land and houses. One of these documents cites the friary's enclosure wall as a property boundary. The wall seems to have had two or more gates, at least one with a gatehouse. Within the walls there seem to have been spacious gardens. One part of the garden, perhaps in the north-west sector of the friary precinct and measuring 115 × 85 ft (35.1 × 25.9 m) was leased in 1520 to Wygston Hospital. But, there were certainly other areas of garden as well, and one document mentions their orchards and vegetable plots.

By the mid thirteenth century historical sources document a lector (teacher) at Greyfriars, suggesting that a library and a school for preparing clerical candidates for further study elsewhere also existed. In 1401 the chapter house (identified in the 2012 excavations) was the setting for the chapter meeting of all the English Franciscan friaries. By 1414, the infirmary and refectory, along with the chapter house, are also recorded as used for political activity. All of these buildings, however, were probably built much earlier than their first mention in historical documents.

Friary buildings were also used for other gatherings and purposes. Tithe assessors are recorded as meeting at the friary in 1332 or 1333. In 1334, Sir William of Harley is documented as holding the banquet following his wife's funeral at the friary; presumably she was also buried there and the funeral took place in the church. In contrast, a confessed murderer, John of Bussby, took sanctuary in the friary church in 1327, but managed to escape after five weeks.

As mentioned in Chapter 2, eighteenth-century modifications to houses then facing St Martin's church unearthed numerous bones in the area between the Greyfriars church and what is now Peacock Lane. This was perhaps the location of the friary's cemetery.

In 1349 Gilbert and Ellen Lavener sought permission from the Crown to donate a plot of land to the friary 'for the enlargement of their house'. Otherwise, few large-scale donors are known by name, although numerous surviving wills indicate that many people left money to all three of Leicester's friaries.

In the fifteenth century, Greyfriars Leicester was in the spotlight several times, including, as mentioned earlier, in the plot of 1402 when the head of the friary (the guardian) and some of the friars allegedly conspired to return the deposed King Richard II to the throne. All were arrested and executed. In 1414, Parliament met several times in the friary's chapter house, rectory and infirmary to deal with members of the Lollard religious reform movement, who initiated an insurrection led by Sir John Oldcastle.

When Greyfriars was closed under King Henry VIII on 10 November 1538, only the guardian and six friars remained. The guardian received a pension, but the friars were left to fend for themselves as best they could. In August 1539 the empty friary precinct was let out in a complex chain of transactions. The Crown gained a tidy income from a combination of the rent paid by the tenants and the sale of architectural salvage, including structural timbers, bronze from the church bell and lead from the roof. The friary was sold in 1545, at which point more building materials, including stone, were sold. During the 2012 excavation, the rubble from the process of dismantling the friary buildings and the foundation trenches robbed of stone confirmed the evidence of the historical documents which testify to the dismemberment and sale of its very fabric.

Life in the Medieval Town (RB, MM)

Although written sources concerning medieval Leicester survive, the archaeology carried out as part of the development of the modern city in the second half of the twentieth century and the twenty-first century has provided us with a wealth of information about the medieval town. Particularly important in this regard was the large-scale redevelopment of the main shopping centre, Highcross, where ULAS's excavations revealed much about the Roman and medieval town.

The medieval town (Plate 7) was walled, though by the later medieval period it seems likely that this may have been more for the purposes of controlling traders and commerce, and to look impressive, than for defence. The course of the medieval walls seems largely to have followed the Roman walls, and the north, west and east gates were situated in the same places as the Roman gates, though this is not certain for the south gate. Historical records from the high and later medieval period suggest that they were locked at night. These gates were demolished in 1714. The castle (Plate 7: 5), built in 1068, shortly after the Norman Conquest, was tucked into the south-western corner of what had been the Roman walls. The ditches around the walls were re-dug at various points, but in some periods seem to have filled up with earth and refuse and become overgrown with vegetation. By the later fifteenth century, stone was being removed from the walls and sections were being dismantled.

Within the walls, the mid fifteenth-century town (Plate 7, recon-struction) was probably not very densely occupied, and there were areas of open space especially in the north-eastern sector. By this time small suburbs had sprung up around the four gates into the town. Outside the walls, there was agricultural land to the east, west and south.

The Southern Area

In Richard III's time the town was a bustling and busy place with a number of prominent monumental buildings. The south-eastern dis-trict, where the Greyfriars precinct (Plate 7: 1) was located, was one of the most lively areas, and many of the surviving streets already existed in Richard III's time. Here the Saturday Market was held, which had been operating since at least 1298 according to historical sources. A wide range of commodities was on sale here including foodstuffs and textiles, and historical sources suggest that there were discrete areas for grain, sheep and pigs. In the thirteenth century, St Martin's church (now Leicester Cathedral; Plate 7: 2) was the wealth-iest parish church in the town, perhaps not surprising in this prosper-ous area. On one side of St Martin's, and opposite Greyfriars, is the Guildhall (Plate 7: 3), built around 1390 as the headquarters of the religious Guild of Corpus Christi, founded by Sir Ralph Ferrars and Geoffrey Kent in 1343. This guild was associated with St Martin's, celebrating religious festivals and helping to support the chantry priests. By the later fifteenth century, however, its activities had become more political, and as its influence over the mayor and bor-ough council grew, the building became the seat of meetings of the borough council. It served as Leicester's town hall until the one pres-ently in use on Horsefair Street was built in the nineteenth century. On the other side of St Martin's was the headquarters of the religious Guild of St George. This guild played a lesser role in the political affairs of Leicester in the later medieval period, and the building no longer survives.

In the southern part of the borough, beyond the castle (Plate 7: 4) and the walls, stood the collegiate church of the Newarke (Plate 7: 5), founded by Henry, Earl of Lancaster in 1330. According to some accounts this Lancastrian church was where Richard's body was dis-played after it was brought back to Leicester after the Battle of

Bosworth, but this is not certain. The church, dedicated to the Virgin Mary, was very beautiful according to historical accounts, though not large. A few arches still survive below ground in the basement of the Hawthorn Building of De Montfort University. The spacious precinct was surrounded by a wall and there was a monumental entrance with a smaller entryway to the castle. It was inhabited by a college of priests and also contained Trinity Hospital (part of the original foundation), for the care of people who were ill or elderly.

From 1107, the castle had been the primary residence of the earls of Leicester, and they patronised the adjacent church of St Mary de Castro (Plate 7: 6). According to historical sources, in 1173, the third earl of Leicester, Robert Blanchmains helped to lead a revolt, and the destruction of the castle was ordered by King Henry II after he captured it. However, archaeological excavation shows the buildings were in fact only partially destroyed, and many, including the Great Hall, survived. The castle, which had reached the peak of its grandeur in the fourteenth century as the residence of the earls (and later the dukes) of Lancaster, was by Richard III's time no longer at its best. In 1399 it had ceased to be a ducal residence when the second duke of Lancaster became King Henry IV. Its rather shabby state in the fifteenth century seems to be one piece of evidence in support of the tradition that Richard III stayed at the Blue Boar Inn before the Battle of Bosworth, rather than in the castle.

We know from archaeological excavation that by the fifteenth century the area beyond the Newarke, in the southern suburb (Plate 7: 7) outside the wall, was where tanners processed animal hides for leather. The area seems to have been quite poor, and these are smelly and dirty activities, so it was almost certainly not a very desirable part of town in Richard III's time.

The Western Side

The River Soar flows along the west side of the town, and in medieval times, its several channels created small islands. In 1254 one of these, just outside the town walls, was occupied by the Augustinian (also known as the Austin) Friars (Plate 7: 8). Historical sources indicate that the church had been built by 1306, though it no longer survives. Archaeological excavation has revealed two cloisters to the north of the church, with a wide drain between them. On the northern side of the larger, southern cloister was the friar's refectory, and on the eastern side their dormitory. The smaller cloister had buildings on three sides but their use is unidentified. There were two bridges over the western channel of the River Soar near this friary. The smaller, Little Bow Bridge (Plate 7: 9), was for the use of the friars and led to St Augustine's Well. The larger, Bow Bridge (Plate 7: 10), joins with the road heading west out of Leicester towards Hinckley, and in the case of Richard III's last fateful journey, also towards Bosworth.

The western side of the town wall has also been discovered in excavations in this area, showing that the 2.5 m thick granite structure still incorporated much of the Roman wall in medieval times. From historical documents, it is known that from the mid thirteenth century the Dominican friars (Blackfriars; Plate 7: 11) based themselves at St Clement's church, which already existed before their arrival but was apparently very poor. It seems that the Blackfriars occupied quite a lot of the land in this sector of the town within the walls. This church, like all the other friary churches in Leicester, did not survive Henry VIII's dissolution of the monasteries and the subsequent dismantling of most monastic churches.

St Nicholas's (Plate 7: 12), the oldest surviving church in Leicester is also located in this part of the town. Archaeological excavation has revealed that it was once attached to the Roman Jewry wall (Plate 7: 13), so it may be very early indeed. However, the oldest parts of the existing building are parts of two windows dating from the tenth century. Historical documents also reveal that the area around this church was inhabited by numerous butchers, and archaeological excavation shows that the complementary trade of tanning and processing animal skins was practised in land near the river south of Blackfriars and west of St Nicholas's (Plate 7: 15). Close to the church, to the south, the Wednesday Market was held at the junction of what is now Highcross Street and the modern High Street. Nearby the ovens of the earl of Leicester had been situated at the so-called Hot Gate, a little to the east of the west gate of the town (Plate 7: 16).

The Northern Sector

The area around what is now Highcross Street and the main modern-day shopping complex, located not far from the area that had been the medieval Wednesday Market towards the northern part of the town, was the medieval high street (Plate 7: 17) and the main trading street. Excavations revealed, most unusually, an entire street front with a line of medieval and post-medieval buildings with long narrow plots of land running back from the street. The earliest of these were simple wooden buildings dating to the later ninth or tenth centuries. By the twelfth century the buildings were timber-framed and set on stone footings, and by the late thirteenth century stone boundary walls separated the properties. The plots were inhabited continuously until the twenty-first century.

Numerous food remains tell us about the diet of the medieval and early post-medieval inhabitants. The bulk of their diet, as is common in pre-modern times, consisted of cereals, including wheat, rye and barley. There is evidence from animal bones for the consumption of beef, lamb, pork, goose and even some rabbit and duck. Among the fish consumed were eel, trout, herring, cod, halibut and one example of a small shark or ray. Plant remains document that people were eating figs, grapes, blackberries, plums, apples, peas, beans and leeks.

The plots behind the buildings contained rubbish pits, external toilets and other small buildings. There was also evidence of animals such as pigs being kept. One property housed a commercial brewery with a stone platform; ovens and kilns for roasting the sprouted barley (malting); and hearths for boiling up the crushed malted barley mixed with water (the mash), for making beer. The boiled mash residue from the brewing process was probably used for feeding animals. Brewing had stopped in this property by the fifteenth century, but many other small breweries like this must have existed to supply the inhabitants, and the inns, with beer.

One particularly notable inn was also located on what is now Highcross Street: the famous Blue Boar Inn (Plate 7: 18) where Richard III is said to have stayed the night before he set out for Bosworth on the morning of the battle. Little is known about the building as it was in Richard's time, and what remained of it was, sadly, demolished in 1836. However, a number of nineteenth-century engravings of the building, especially the wing that Richard was supposed to have stayed in, have survived. A full record of the building made before its demolition made by Leicester architect Henry Goddard, with precise measured drawings and details of the construction of the roof structure, timber joints and mouldings, has recently came to light. This has been translated into a 3D printout through the work of Greyfriars' lead archaeologist Richard Buckley and Steffan Davies at De Montfort University.

It seems likely that the structure Goddard recorded in the nineteenth century was only one wing of what had originally been a much larger building with windows facing the street on one side and the courtyard on the other. The building may have had two wings on either side of a gatehouse with a passage opening onto a court, and entry to the ground floor rooms would have been from somewhere in the court, though where exactly is not known. It may have resembled the layout of the Talbot Inn in Oundle, built with architectural salvage from Richard III's castle in Fotheringhay. According to Goddard's drawings, the ground floor of the building in his time consisted of a single big room (41 × 24 ft or 6.15 × 3.6 m) with a large stone fireplace. There was no external door, but windows looked onto the street on one side and onto the courtyard on the other. The room on the floor above, where Richard III supposedly stayed, projected out towards the street over the ground floor room, with a window looking out to the front. The upper room was probably entered through a door of oak planks from an external gallery off the courtyard at the level of the upper storey. This room too had a large stone fireplace and there was no ceiling – the room was open to the rafters and the timbers were decorated in painted scrollwork in black, red and yellow. On the outside of the upper storey there was a large gable with ornamental barge boards.

By the later medieval period, after the Black Death, the north-eastern sector of the town was not very densely populated and much land was given over to orchards and gardens. St Margaret's church (Plate 7: 19), still standing close to the medieval town wall, now with the modern bus station nearby, was under the jurisdiction of the Bishop of Lincoln, like various other churches in medieval Leicestershire. Historical documents reveal that in this part of town the wall was patched with mud and straw, and this was also the area where archery was practised.

The area just outside the walls beyond the north gate was where dyers and fullers practised their crafts on land close to the river, since a copious water supply was essential for these processes. Like tanning and leatherworking, fulling and dying were smelly and dirty occupations: one of the main components of these processes was human urine. It is hardly surprising, then, that they were relegated to areas away from the town centre.

The low population in the north-eastern part of town may be part of the reason for the late and post medieval destruction of two other churches in the area. St Michael's (Plate 7: 20) had been dismantled by the middle of the fifteenth century and St Peter's was demolished in 1573. Excavation has revealed that St Michael's was established around 1200, later than had been thought. The church was surrounded by a cemetery which was set out carefully around the ruins of a large Roman building. Most of the graves in this cemetery were simple shroud burials, suggesting that this was a poorer parish than that of St Peter's. Since there were no graves in the building, it is possible that the structure was still in use for some purpose associated with the church in the medieval period; possibly it served as a vicarage. Worked stone from the robbed-out Roman ruins under the church had probably been reused in the construction of the buildings at Leicester Abbey, before St Michael's was erected.

St Peter's church (Plate 7: 21) and its cemetery were revealed by archaeological excavation off Vaughan Way, in the location of the present-day John Lewis store. Radiocarbon dating of burials demonstrated that the earliest in the cemetery date to the tenth century. This cemetery has been important for augmenting our knowledge of medieval burial practices in Leicester, and it has provided valuable comparisons for the Greyfriars burials excavated in 2012 and 2013. In particular, this large quantity of cemetery data showed how unusual the grave and burial of 'Skeleton 1' (which was identified as Richard III) was in terms of contemporary practices in the same town.

St Peter's graveyard was in use for a long period, and over time burial practices changed. As is usual with Christian burials, most individuals had no grave goods. A few of the earliest burials were laid on a layer of ash or charcoal. Some graves were stone lined. There were a few stone coffins, probably suggesting wealthier families holding more elaborate funerals. Some of the wealthier parishioners of St Peter's were buried in wooden coffins. Although the wood does not survive the passage of time, the impressions of the wood can be detected in the surrounding soil, and iron nails, which do survive, and their positions in the grave, provide evidence that there was once a coffin.

In the St Peter's cemetery, graves were usually oriented east–west, with the head at the west end. Most were shroud burials. Although the shrouds, cloths which wrapped the body, do not survive, the corpses were wrapped tightly so that an individual who has been buried in a shroud is found in a quite compressed position. In contrast, the very lax position of Greyfriars 'Skeleton 1' provided clear evidence that he, King Richard III, had *not* been wrapped in a shroud.

This cemetery has also provided valuable evidence about the conditions of life and health of the medieval people of Leicester. About 40 per cent of the burials were male and 60 per cent were female. The average height for men was 5 feet 7 inches (1.71 m) and for women it was 5 feet 2 inches (1.59 m). Most people seem to have died between the ages of 32 and 50. Although women seem to have lived a little longer than men on average, more women than men appear to have died as young adults. This may reflect the perils of pregnancy and childbirth in an age before modern medicine. About 25 per cent of the individuals in this cemetery were under the age of 12, reflecting the high rates of child mortality in pre-modern times.

Life was plainly hard for the medieval town folk. Sometimes people died of injuries, such as one woman who suffered a severe blow to the front of her head, a tragedy of which we will never know the full story. Almost half of the adults showed signs of osteoarthritis at life stages when most people would not expect to suffer this condition today. Heavy manual labour was a fact of everyday life for most men and women, and this was demonstrated by the condition of their bodies. Quite a number of people suffered from nutritional deficiencies such as anaemia (from lack of protein, especially meat) and rickets (Vitamin D deficiency, suggesting lack of sunlight and insufficient intake of dairy products). In a time before toothbrushes, toothpaste and modern dentistry, the condition of people's teeth was quite bad. A number of people suffered from dental hypoplasia, a condition in which the tooth enamel does not form properly because of poor nutrition in childhood.

Nearly 10 per cent of the population showed evidence in their bones of infectious diseases such as tuberculosis and syphilis. These are diseases that may have an impact on the bones which would then be detectable in skeletons found by archaeologists. However, there are a number of infectious diseases that leave no trace on the bones for osteoarchaeologists (archaeological human bone specialists) to discover and identify. This was the case with a grave in one corner of the cemetery which contained over 20 individuals all buried at the same time in the second half of the twelfth century. Most of these individuals were under 13 years old, and all showed signs of generally poor health and malnutrition. This suggests that they all died of some kind of epidemic disease, though the specific illness is unknown. They were not victims of bubonic plague as this grave predates the period of the Black Death by 200 years.

St Peter's was a prosperous and substantial parish church, which had been enlarged over the years since it was first constructed sometime in the late tenth or early eleventh centuries. In the twelfth century, the nave was extended, and, a bell tower was added at the west end.

The pit used for casting the bell was discovered under the tower, and the burning of the stones was archaeomagnetically dated to sometime between 1150 and 1180. Archaeomagnetic dating depends on the fact that the earth's magnetic field is constantly shifting, so that the magnetic north pole is not always in the same place. However, when something is burnt, the orientation of the magnetic field is fixed on magnetic north as it was at the time of burning. This allows archaeologists to date the burning event because scientists know the historical sequence of how magnetic north shifted at different time periods.

Subsequently, in the thirteenth century aisles were added to the north and south sides of the nave, and a new, enlarged chancel was added in the fourteenth century. The church was at its most extensive in the fifteenth century. At this time the south aisle was enlarged, and extra rooms had been added to the north and south of the chancel, including a small charnel house for the storage of bones. The remains of at least 80 individuals were found neatly kept in this room. It seems probable that these were skeletons that had been found by later grave-diggers, and the bones were carefully gathered and deposited here.

Historical sources record that St Peter's had a vicarage as early as 1226. It is possible that excavated buildings located to the east of the church can be identified with the vicarage, but this is not certain. These date to the period between the eleventh and late thirteenth/early fourteenth centuries. At first they were built in wood, but a stone hall was added in the twelfth century. The buildings may have been dismantled when the new chancel of the church was built in the four-teenth century. After this time a series of timber and mud-walled buildings were constructed which were abandoned in the late sixteenth century, presumably following the demolition of the church.

The Leicester that Richard saw was a thriving late medieval town, not densely populated but with a lively commercial centre, a range of crafts and industries, and a number of beautiful churches and other buildings. The piety of the town and its religious orders would probably have pleased him. The town's shape and line of the walls that surrounded it were still based on those the Romans had built. A few of the inhabitants were prosperous; most worked hard to survive. The place that Richard beheld was perhaps, metaphorically, in the last few moments of a medieval way of life, soon about to change, gradually not suddenly, over the course of the new Tudor regime.

Richard's Arrival in Leicester, His Departure ... and His Return

In the summer of 1485 Richard had based himself in Nottingham. For the previous 18 months or so he had been travelling all over the Midlands and the north of England gathering support, and making many promises of favours, lands, pardons and charitable donations to a wide range of institutions and individuals, especially potential allies and their underlings (see Map 5.1). These are all carefully recorded in a manuscript now in the British Library (Harley 433), which has been edited by the great Richard III scholar Rosemary Horrox. They included the notorious college of priests for a chantry chapel at York, which has been interpreted by some scholars as indicating his funerary wishes but can equally plausibly be interpreted in other ways. (Figure 3.3)

On 11 August word reached Richard of Henry Tudor's landing a few days earlier at Milford Haven in Wales. Richard remained in Nottingham waiting for his northern supporters, some of whom, including the powerful but fickle Lord Stanley and his family from the northwest of England, never arrived. He ordered his southern and East Anglian supporters to meet him in Leicester, about 30 miles to the south. Leicester's central location on several important routes meant that it was well placed to intercept Henry's approaching forces from Wales, and to join with any forces that might have come from the north.

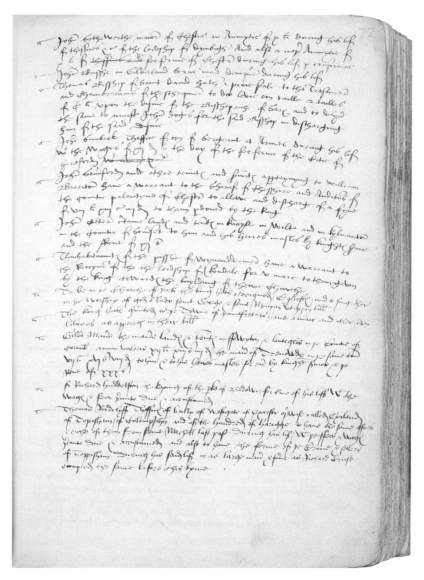

Figure 3.3   Section of Harley manuscript 433, showing the promise of a chantry college of 100 priests to York Minster. *Source*: Copyright © The British Library Board, MS Harley 433, folio 72.

Richard arrived in Leicester late on either 19 or 20 August, just before sunset. According to one historical source he entered the town with great ceremony after dark, almost certainly through the north gate. It seems likely that his troops camped outside the town, perhaps on some of the open ground near Leicester Abbey, while Richard allegedly enjoyed the comfort of the Blue Boar Inn.

Henry had moved through the Midlands from Wales along Watling Street, the still-functioning Roman road which is now the A5. He arrived at the border between Warwickshire and Leicestershire on 21 August.

Richard departed from Leicester on 21 August, again, according to one of the historical sources, in grand style, attended by John Howard, Duke of Norfolk and Henry Percy, Earl of Northumberland, with a throng of lesser nobles and commoners. Richard probably rode along the medieval high street (the modern Highcross Street) and then moved west along Hot Gate and Applegate, heading for the West Bridge across the eastern arm of the River Soar. He would then have crossed Bow Bridge, spanning the western arm of the Soar near the Austin Friars, perhaps close to where the majority of his troops were camped. The road over Bow Bridge led west towards Hinckley and, of course, Bosworth, where Richard's and Henry's forces met.

Accounts of the fate of Richard's body after the Battle of Bosworth differ in detail, but all agree that the corpse was carried back into Leicester (according to Polydore Vergil, slung across the back of a horse) and put on public display there so that everyone could see for themselves that king was genuinely dead. For this reason it was important for Henry that Richard's face was recognisable in death (see Chapter 4).

Both Polydore Vergil and Fabyan's Chronicle of 1553 specify that he was taken straight to Greyfriars, in the centre of town, where he was ultimately buried. Several accounts simply specify the venue as 'a church', which could also conceivably refer to Greyfriars. Only one source, the popular song *Battle of Bosworth Field*, specifies the Newarke, just outside the walls of the southern part of the town near the castle, as the location. *Battle of Bosworth Field* may be close in date to these momentous events, but the text is not easily datable, and given its genre, it may not in any case be reliable. The earliest extant copy of this ballad, in a seventeenth-century manuscript (British Library Additional

MS 27879), is much later than the events it describes, though the song could be older than the manuscript or, indeed, the date at which it was first written down if the two are different. The collection of popular songs contained in this manuscript was further edited by Bishop Thomas Percy in the eighteenth century, and his collection was in turn republished by John Hales and Frederick Furnival in three volumes in 1867.

So, Richard had returned to Leicester, not at all in the style in which he departed as a king, and there he was to remain, under the floor of Greyfriars, for the next 500 years.

Further reading

Horrox, R. (1995) *Fifteenth Century Attitudes: Perceptions of Society in Late Medieval England.* Cambridge: Cambridge University Press.

Morris, M., Buckley, R. and Codd, M. (2011) *Visions of Ancient Leicester: Reconstructing Life in the Roman and Medieval Town from the Archaeology of the Highcross Leicester Excavations.* Leicester: School of Archaeology and Ancient History, University of Leicester.

O'Sullivan, D. (2013) *In the Company of Preachers: The Archaeology of Medieval Friaries in England and Wales.* Leicester Archaeology Monographs 23. Leicester: School of Archaeology and Ancient History, University of Leicester.

4

THE BONES TELL
THEIR TALE

The Slow Reveal ...

Anyone else caught in the evening traffic in Leicester city centre would just have seen a tired couple at the end of a long day, the man giving his colleague a lift home from work, the woman with a box on her lap.

It would be hours before Mathew Morris and Jo Appleby got back to their homes. As they drove away from the site, their urgent priority was how to protect the bones both from accidental contamination with modern DNA, which would make the possibility of recovering uncompromised DNA evidence even more remote, and from the avid curiosity of the outside world.

The archaeologists had always made it quite clear that they were embarking on a research excavation and that the most likely outcome was some interesting new evidence about religious foundations in medieval Leicester.

That was never how the media saw it. Before the first digger blade hit the tarmac, the only story was the hunt for the king under the car park. If the news leaked of the discovery of so much as a knuckle bone, still less an entire skeleton with a twisted spine and a gaping war wound in the skull, it would inevitably provoke a feeding frenzy. On her lap, in the plastic box, as months of research would ultimately prove, Appleby held the skull of a king.

Finding a Home: Preparing for Analysis

The low, flat-roofed Archaeology and Ancient History building at the university, where the ULAS offices are housed, was never going to be a suitable long-term storage space for the bones. It is a busy place,

The Bones of a King: Richard III Rediscovered, First Edition. The Greyfriars Research Team with Maev Kennedy and Lin Foxhall.
© 2015 University of Leicester. Published 2015 by John Wiley & Sons, Ltd.

heavily used by students and staff for teaching and research. The laboratories are open and generally occupied, so there is no safe storage or private work space in them. Only the team directly involved knew what had been found in the car park. Officially they were still only the bones of a nameless individual, which would be treated with the respect given by archaeologists to all human remains. Once the story leaked out, however, they would be at real risk of being targeted by souvenir hunters or worse. Finding a secure space to keep and study the skeleton was crucial.

While the hunt began for lab space, Lin Foxhall, as then head of department, took responsibility for keeping the bones safe. She found a temporary and well-hidden resting place in the Archaeology and Ancient History building, but this was not suitable for longer-term work or storage. In answer to this need, the head of the College of Medicine, Biological Sciences and Psychology alerted the team to a couple of departments which might have spare lab space. Medical schools and research facilities are highly regulated by the government and are housed in secure buildings with carefully monitored access. The Department of Cell Physiology and Pharmacology generously provided a safe and private lab where the bones could be cleaned and the skeleton laid out for several months.

The next problem was finding the right storage for the selected bones and teeth, which might yield DNA evidence that Appleby and the archaeologically trained geneticist Turi King had so carefully excavated wearing full forensic gear. They had been kept fully wrapped and chilled to preserve their DNA and prevent contamination from modern DNA.

The secure university building housing Genetics might have seemed the obvious place to take the remains, but in fact would have been the worst possible location for these precious samples. Much modern genetics research, and general biological research, involves making many millions of copies of sections of our DNA (much like photocopying a page of a book many, many times) in order to make them easier to analyse. With so many studies going on in the department, copies of sections of the DNA of thousands of people would have been made over the years the department had been in existence. Invisible to the naked eye, many of these copied fragments remain in the labs, on bench tops, in fridge and freezers, on lab coats, any number of which could transfer onto the sample through handling and confuse the DNA analysis. Therefore, King could not store the samples in any lab which had already been used for modern DNA research.

The improbable solution came from the Space Research Centre, part of the Department of Physics. The kind of clean-room lab that is needed to prevent contamination of samples from Mars is exactly what King needed for storing the samples for DNA testing. Anyone entering the lab must change first into full forensic cover suits in a sealed ante-room, while the lab itself has sophisticated air filtering systems, positive air pressure, and a fully sealed door to prevent even the tiniest particles entering from outside.

Most importantly, no biological samples were stored there, and contamination-control systems already existed that would prevent DNA contamination from the modern DNA of the staff there. Despite all these precautions, anyone closely involved with the project was DNA-tested so that – as in all forensic investigations – should their DNA have contaminated the remains it could be eliminated from the analysis.

The samples for DNA analysis of the skeleton were taken from the teeth and the thigh bone. Teeth are often particularly well-preserved parts of the remains and are therefore more likely to yield useable DNA. There was also a reasonable chance that this could be obtained from the thick femur bone. If the two samples yielded the same DNA this would also help rule out the possibility of contamination, since in the absence of contamination, the same results could be expected from each sample. Furthermore, the DNA analysis would be carried out in two separate labs to ensure replication of results and rule out contamination.

Skeletal Analysis: Unlocking the Secrets of the Bones (JA, GR, BM, SH, RW-S)

Shakespeare gave his Richard III a hunchback and a withered arm, which many dismissed as a propagandist view drawing on accounts by his enemies after his death. However, the chronicler John Rous, who knew Richard, said he had 'unequal shoulders, the right higher and the left lower'. The team, though, set out not to prove that the skeleton had these features and therefore must be Richard but to consider, as in any modern forensic case, the characteristics of this individual to assist in identification and how he had died.

Before the bones were even washed, they were all scanned at the Leicester Royal Infirmary under the supervision of imaging specialist Bruno Morgan, with forensic pathologist Guy Rutty and Appleby observing. The Post Mortem Computed Tomography (PMCT) scanning was done by Claire Robinson, an experienced forensic radiographer, outside normal hospital hours, since modern people take priority over a medieval skeleton, and on one occasion the work had to be postponed because the equipment was needed for casualties from a road traffic accident.

The equipment which creates computed tomograph (CT) images is basically a three-dimensional X-ray which also creates three-dimensional images of slices across the bones to reveal their internal structure without cutting them open. By scanning the whole skeleton as soon as possible after excavation, and before washing, the team created a permanent digital record of the bones as they came out of the ground. These initial digital files were also used to make some of the 3D printouts of the entire skeleton using cutting-edge techniques developed by Russell Harris, Professor of Medical Engineering and Advanced Manufacturing, Loughborough University, as discussed later in this chapter.

The bones were scanned first laid out flat. Then, after cleaning, they were scanned again on a specially designed polystyrene mould which held them in a more anatomically correct position. The limbs, pelvis, spine and head were also scanned separately (Plate 8). After scanning, they were brought back to the lab in the medical school, where ULAS staff carefully and painstakingly washed every bone. The skeleton was then ready for a full examination by Appleby (Plate 9).

An expert human osteologist – an archaeologist specialising in bones – can detect many features which reveal much about the life, health and death of an individual. A typical skeletal analysis seeks to establish the sex, approximate age, physique and build of the individual. Some diseases, such as tuberculosis or severe infections, can leave their mark on the bones, as can injury earlier in life, chronic, congenital or genetic conditions, or injuries around the time of death; however, many injuries and diseases that can affect people during their lifetime leave no mark on their bones. In this case the sex was determined through the distinctive masculine features of the pubic bones and skull and the presence of a Y chromosome in the preliminary DNA analysis.

Appleby began her minute bone by bone study of the skeleton, and identified most of the wounds, without consulting any of the historical accounts of Richard's death. She then brought the bones to the East Midlands Forensic Pathology Unit for examination by the forensic pathology team directed by Rutty. The team included Mike Biggs and Stuart Hamilton (Home Office pathologists) and Alison Brough (CT imaging expert). Rutty identified the cause of death, wrote the official autopsy report and provided it to the coroner, because the processes that had been undertaken required the coroner to be informed so that a decision could be taken about whether or not to open an inquest. In this case, as the skeleton had clearly been excavated in an archaeological context that was almost 500 years old, an inquest was not deemed to be necessary.

Two experts on the injuries inflicted by edged weapons, ancient and modern, also joined the team to add their insights. Sarah Hainsworth, an engineer and Professor of Material and Forensic Engineering at Leicester, is also an expert in identifying the weapons used to inflict an injury from the distinctive cut marks (tool marks) left in human bone. Robert Woosnam-Savage is the curator of European Edged Weapons at the Royal Armouries. Shining in glass cases for visitors to study at the museum in Leeds and the Tower of London are the beautiful but ferocious weapons – swords and daggers, halberds and poleaxes, bills and war hammers – which inflicted grievous injuries in medieval warfare.

Like the other members of the team, Hainsworth, who has contributed her expertise to many modern murder cases, was careful not to study the historical accounts of Richard's death before examining the bones. Woosnam-Savage, however, was very aware of the accounts of the Battle of Bosworth. He has studied the damage inflicted by weapons similar to those in his care, through the marks left on battered armour and bone. The human remains invariably came from anonymous war dead, such as the mass graves for those who died at the Battle of Wisby in 1361, the Battle of Towton in 1461 and the Battle of Dornach in 1499.

As soon as he heard that the Leicester team had found a battle-scarred medieval skeleton which could just possibly be Richard's, he contacted Richard Buckley offering to help. He was less excited at the idea of identifying a lost king than at the exceptionally rare possibility of potentially studying a named individual whose history in battle was known. Buckley told Woosnam-Savage that he had actually intended to contact him, but he had beaten him to making the call!

He went to Leicester in November 2012 with as open a mind as he could manage, but after a long day poring over every bone with Appleby – at one point they thought it was probably time to break for lunch and then realised it was already late afternoon – he was convinced of the identity. 'I said later I was sorry I hadn't cashed in my life savings and put the lot on the skeleton being that of Richard,' he recalled. 'We already knew we had a man of approximately the right age, in the place Richard was recorded as having been buried, a man who had died a particularly violent death with injuries that, to me, matched some of the historical records of the battle. I don't believe in coincidences – so who else could it be?'

The bones were examined in normal light and under multi-spectrum lighting, which helped identify wounds not easily visible. Together the team identified all the bones with apparent signs of injury, including one wound to the skull, identified by Rutty, that had been previously missed, and a cut on one of the vertebrae. Richard's physical courage was noted by several contemporary and near contemporary chroniclers: Rous wrote that he carried himself 'like a noble soldier' – '*nobilis miles*'. However, until his last battle Richard had been fortunate: although he first fought as a teenager there were no traces of earlier healed injuries, something that Woosnam-Savage was keen to look for as it was well known that Richard had been wounded during the Battle of Barnet in 1471. It seems, therefore, that on that occasion, he must have suffered soft tissue damage, which would have left no traces on the bones.

The team was interested not just in the cut marks of swords and the penetrative straight-edged V stab marks of daggers but also in where on the body they had been inflicted. Hainsworth had Foxhall kneel on the floor of her lab at the Department of Engineering, neck stretched and head bent forward, to demonstrate the position she and Woosnam-Savage believe Richard must have been in when the injuries to the back of the skull were inflicted.

Ten bones were selected and brought to Hainsworth's lab for much more detailed microscopic and microCT analysis, techniques she usually uses to help in police investigations. Scanning at this resolution can reveal both external and internal injury where a weapon has punched right through the bone, but it is a very slow process. The turntable on which the sample is set moves less than a hundredth of a millimetre after each scan: it took up to eight hours to complete the process on the larger bones and an entire day for the skull. Each morning one bone was brought to the lab, and for security and monitoring, members of the team took it in turn to spend long hours watching over the equipment and the bone turning invisibly slowly inside the scanner.

When the scans were analysed, the striations – the marks left on the bone by the edge of the sharp metal blade, each unique to the weapon that made it – revealed what had been used to inflict each injury. This analysis showed that the same sharp dagger probably caused the two shallow stab wounds to the face and also the top of the skull.

The 3D Printouts

Russell Harris first encountered the Greyfriars project when he and his family attended one of the open days at the excavation site in Leicester. Imagine his surprise when, a few days later, he received a call from the lead archaeologist, Buckley, asking him about the possibility of building a 3D printout of the skeleton to serve as a permanent record. A full printout of the skeleton and a high-resolution printout of the skull are now on display in the King Richard III Visitor Centre.

Harris's main research is in medical engineering. He regularly builds anatomical models and devices to provide custom-made bone implants, prosthetics such as artificial ears, as well as models of organs for use in training doctors and planning surgical procedures. Harris, then, with his knowledge of anatomy as well as engineering was precisely the person for this job.

The initial printout from CT scans was made before the bones were even cleaned to provide a record of their original state, before washing, although the soil still adhering to them at that stage is clearly evident in the rather lumpy model, obscuring some of the detail. The second, clearer printout was made using the cleaned bones. Both of these models used a technique called selective laser sintering, in which the sequential layers of the model, derived from digital images provided by the

CT scans, are generated by the scanning of an infrared laser to join particles of a nylon powder. This results in a plastic model, normally white in colour. However, because the CT scans of the entire skeleton were made on a scanner designed for living patients, some detail is lost. This is because these scanners have to scan a relatively large scan volume reasonably quickly, so the maximum spatial detail of the images is based on 0.5 mm boxes or voxels.

For smaller volumes, such as an individual bone, or the skull, the alternative technique of microCT can be used. The images created by Hainsworth in the Department of Engineering in Leicester could be made at a much higher magnification and higher resolution, because in microCT the sample can be placed nearer to the X-ray source than in PMCT. Subsequently, Harris was able to reconstruct these images to make impressively detailed models of the skull and the other bones that particularly highlighted the areas of trauma. Some of these high-resolution models were made using laser sintering. However, Harris made one copy of the skull using a different, even more sensitive technique called stereolithography. In this method, an ultraviolet laser produces the layers of the model from a photosensitive polymer liquid. The resulting clear plastic model, dubbed 'the crystal skull', was so accurate that the growth rings in the bone are visible.

The Towton Mass Grave

Comparison with the bones of men who died in a near contemporary English medieval battle could reveal similarities to the injuries suffered by the Greyfriars skeleton, but also possible differences indicative of how a king would be treated in battle.

The Battle of Towton was fought on 29 March 1461, a few miles south of the market town of Tadcaster in North Yorkshire, and it was reputedly one of the bloodiest battles in the Wars of the Roses. The Yorkists inflicted a crushing defeat on the Lancastrians. In July 1996 a roughly rectangular mass grave was discovered during construction work on the edge of the battlefield. In a pit some 6 m east–west and 2 m north–south, the remains of at least 61 people had been buried. The skeletons disturbed by the construction workers were removed and reburied, but a team from the University of Bradford excavated and analysed the undisturbed part of the pit, recovering the remains of 38 individuals, all male and aged between 16 and 50 years.

Appleby and Woosnam-Savage examined a number of these remains, now kept at the Bioarchaeology Research Centre at Bradford, and discussed them with the Bradford archaeologists, including Jo Buckberry, comparing the injuries they had found with Appleby's analysis of the Greyfriars skeleton. The comparisons were striking: evidence of battle wounds was discovered on almost all the skeletons, some certainly fatal. Twenty-seven skulls (98 per cent) showed major head wounds of the kind suffered by Richard. There were between 1 and 13 wounds per individual, though only two had more than 10 injuries. As with Richard, some were major injuries, while others were relatively superficial. Sharp force trauma from a bladed weapon was much more common than blunt force trauma or puncture wounds. There were many instances of sharp force trauma to the face, especially to the left side, indicating that they were inflicted in face-to-face combat by a right-handed opponent. The blunt force injuries were also mostly to the left. Square-shaped puncture wounds, similar to those on Richard's skull (discussed in this chapter under 'Battle Wounds'), were also found on several of the Towton skulls.

Many of the injuries could only be defined as 'perimortem', that is, inflicted around the time of death, as it was impossible to say with certainty whether they were sustained when the man was still alive, or shortly after death – often thought of as 'insult injuries', intended to humiliate the corpse of a dead enemy. A significant difference between Richard's skull and a number of the Towton skulls was apparent to Appleby and Woosnam-Savage: some of the Towton skulls had suffered a series of savage blows, probably immediately after death, which would have seriously disfigured the faces, probably making them unrecognisable – this had not happened to Richard.

Battle Wounds (JA, R-WS, SH, GR)

When the bones and the high resolution scans of the Greyfriars skeleton were studied, they revealed 11 injuries from a variety of weapons (Figure 4.1). Another area of damage to the skull, separation of the sutures below the right eye, could have been caused by a blow, but also

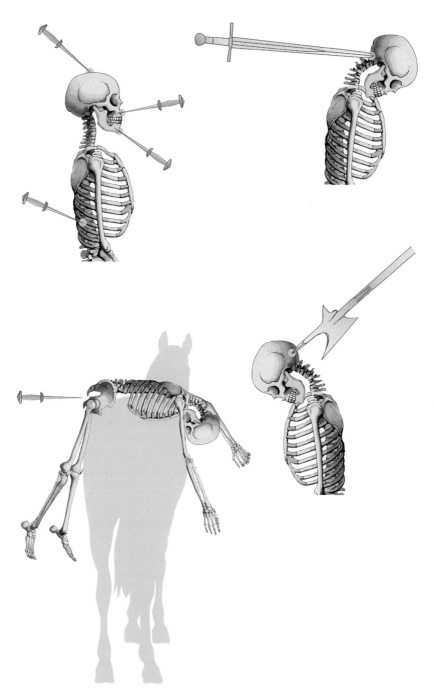

Figure 4.1 Diagram showing the angle of entry of the weapons used in attacking Richard III. *Source*: Appleby *et al.* (2014b).

by the result of the pressure of the soil in the grave as the bones decayed – the experts disagreed on this one.

It was clear to the expert team that Richard died a very violent death. Each of the injuries was distinct, unlike the overlapping blows often found in battle injuries and on some of the skeletons from Towton. This made it impossible to establish the sequence of injuries: either of the blows to the back of the head would have proved fatal.

The team were able to reject several previous suggestions about what happened to Richard in the last minutes of the battle. They found no evidence of an attempt to scalp him – Hainsworth believes anyone trying it would have started from the brow and worked towards the back of the head, but all the injuries to the top and back of the skull came from behind.

Most of the injuries were to the head. Around his face and jaw there were three wounds, none of which would have been fatal. A 10 mm square hole in the right maxilla (the right upper jaw), lines up with another hole through the back of the jaw, suggesting a stab wound from very close quarters perhaps with an edged weapon like a rondel dagger – a type of dagger that had a round or disc-shaped guard (hence its name), that could bear a domed pommel and that often had a stiff, square-section blade (Plate 10; the entry wound but not the exit wound is shown on Figure 4.1). There was also a 10 mm cut to the right of the mandible (the lower jaw), a smooth, narrow, v-shaped cut made by a slender, fine-edged knife or dagger. Another injury, also to the lower jaw, was made by a sharp blade, but this one was too indistinct for the weapon to be identified.

There were three shallow injuries to the dome of the skull, all inflicted with a sharp blade which sliced and removed part of the scalp and cut into the bone (Plate 11; not shown on Figure 4.1). The striation marks had the same pattern in the three injuries, but there wasn't a match over a sufficient length to prove definitively that they were all caused by the same weapon. All of these wounds would have bled profusely, and could eventually have caused death from loss of blood or infection if left untreated, but they would not have been immediately fatal.

At the saggital suture, the point where the bones join at the top of the skull, there was a depressed keyhole shaped injury measuring 9 mm × 10 mm (Plate 12). The blow, delivered from above and at an angle, was violent enough to push two flaps of bone inwards towards the brain yet not strong enough to separate the flaps completely. Though it could have caused extensive internal and external bleeding, this would not have killed him immediately either. The shape of the injury was too small for a blow from a war hammer or mace and lacked any radiating fractures that may have resulted from an arrow strike. It was, again, probably caused by the square-sectioned tip of the blade of a rondel dagger – possibly the same weapon used to inflict the cheek injuries.

Woosnam-Savage's interpretation was that it could suggest a possible attempted *coup-de-grâce*, a final blow to finish off a dying man, with the point of the dagger placed right over the skull and the attacker then punching down on the domed end of the hilt. A late fifteenth-century illuminated manuscript illustration depicting the death of Wat Tyler shows a rondel dagger being used in exactly this manner. Alternatively, Woosnam-Savage suggests it is possibly an example of 'overkill', a phenomenon seen on many skulls from various medieval battlefields. The near contemporary chronicler Polydore Vergil describes the Battle of Bosworth as lasting only some two hours, and Woosnam-Savage believes that most of the sustained man-to-man fighting was probably over in possibly as little as 40 minutes.

There were two massive injuries to the lower side of the back of the skull (Plate 13). One was a 65 mm × 55 mm hole in the bone, with the straight smooth edges of sharp force trauma. It was caused by a large bladed weapon, possibly a sword but more likely by a blade mounted on a long wooden haft (staff) such as a halberd or bill. When Woosnam-Savage first examined this massive trauma he immediately noted the one description of the death of Richard that makes any mention of a weapon that was used to kill him. Molinet's Chronicles, of about 1490, states, 'One of the Welshmen then came after him [Richard], and struck him dead with a halberd (*d'une halebarde*). The other injury, to the lower left side, was a 32 mm × 17 mm hole with a radiating fracture. This injury lined up with further damage to the inner surface of the skull and to the atlas vertebra, the bone that supports the head, which had a distinct cut mark. These were probably caused by a stabbing blow from a sword tip, or possibly, the top spike of a bill or halberd that pierced right through bone and brain to the inside of the opposite side of the skull. Either of these injuries would have caused severe bleeding inside the skull and injury to the brain, and would have been fatal.

The sequence of these injuries cannot be proved, and it is unknown which of the two killed him. Hainsworth and Woosnam-Savage believe the larger of the two was delivered with the axe-blade of a halberd-like weapon which sliced through the skull to leave a hanging flap of bone. The smaller injury was probably the stabbing blow from a sword which penetrated the skull and went right through the brain: 'Lights out immediately', as Woosnam-Savage said grimly.

Near contemporary accounts of Bosworth record Richard fighting in the thick of the battle to the last. John Rous, who had known Richard, recorded, 'though he was slight in body and weak in strength, to his last breath he held himself nobly in a defending manner, often crying that he was betrayed and saying, "treason, treason, treason"'. The anonymous author of the Croyland Chronicle, writing in 1486, gave this description of his death: 'in the thick of the fight, and not in the act of flight, King Richard fell in the field, struck by many mortal wounds, as a bold and most valiant prince'. The Italian historian Polydore Vergil, no friend to Richard as he was writing for the Tudors 20 years after the battle, is believed to have based his account on eye-witness reports. He too wrote that Richard was killed 'fighting man-fully in the thickest press of his enemies'.

The three skull injuries bore out these accounts, suggesting that by this final stage of the battle Richard had lost his horse and then quite likely his footing, and must also have lost his helmet or had it forcibly ripped off him. There were no defensive wounds to the bones of his arms or hands, suggesting that up to the point of his death he was still wearing all his armour apart from his helmet, and that it was working effectively.

Woosnam-Savage is also an expert on the protection aristocratic soldiers had in war (he possesses his own replica suit of late fifteenth-century armour, and indeed wore it to his wedding). At this time, Richard would have gone into battle probably protected by plate armour together with elements of mail armour. He would have worn a helmet with a visor, and although the whole armour would have been custom-made for him particular attention would have probably been given to his breast- and backplates, which were worn over a heavily padded jacket, giving good protection to the vulnerable head and torso. He also probably wore a deep skirt of hooped steel plates protecting his lower body and beneath this a short mail skirt or breeches. On horseback his pelvis would have had some further protection from the war saddle.

The team was particularly interested in injuries that could not have been dealt while Richard was still in armour. Their conclusion was that – as in the despairing cry Shakespeare gives the character, 'a horse, a horse, my kingdom for a horse!' – he was most likely unhorsed and without his helmet when the fatal head injuries were inflicted. It would appear, therefore, that he was then stripped of his remaining armour, which is in accordance with the historical accounts, and was almost certainly already dead, when he suffered these wounds.

There was one small injury, a v-shaped wound, in the right tenth rib, probably from a dagger blade (Plate 14). The shape of the cuts shows that the blade moved, either as the ribs twisted or because it became stuck and had to be jerked clear. The injury would not have been fatal, and it was the only one to the ribs. Richard's armour would have been highly effective, and this blow could really only have been delivered after his body armour, including the backplate, had been removed.

He had one more grievous injury that also could probably not have realistically occurred while he was fully armoured. His pelvis was reconstructed to show how the bone-piercing injury 30 mm in length could have been caused. A fine-bladed weapon penetrated the right buttock, and passed right through the pelvic cavity (Plate 15). In life this would have damaged the internal pelvic organs including the bowel and caused massive bleeding. However, the injury seems to match those accounts which describe Richard's stripped body being humiliatingly treated and slung over the back of a horse. With his arms on one side and his legs on the other this would have presented a perfect target and opportunity to inflict such a wound. 'From the historical accounts alone I had perhaps expected to see evidence of humiliation injuries – and there they were before me, in the bones', Woosnam-Savage said. Such humiliation or insult injuries are not unique, for he had also noted how mobile-phone footage of the killing of the deposed Libyan president Muammar Gaddafi, in Libya in 2011 showed an identical injury being inflicted in exactly the same location on the body, with what appeared to be a bayonet. The only difference was that Gaddafi was definitely alive when the injury was delivered. He continued 'There could have been further soft-tissue damage but that evidence no longer survives.'

The team was also struck by how the wounds to the face, none fatal, caused very little damage to the underlying bone structure: indeed Woosnam-Savage speculates that the stab wound through the cheek may have been the result of somebody aiming at the eye socket in an attempt to make a quick killing and, in the process, missing. However, other team members do not think that it is possible to establish with certainty the direction from which the attack was made from the evidence of the wounds.

'These injuries are very interesting', Hainsworth said. 'In the thick of battle, with tempers high and adrenaline surging, you have to imagine somebody in the most senior position of authority shouting orders to hold back and not to destroy his face – the obvious conclusion is that Richard had to remain recognisable after his death.' Woosnam-Savage pointed out that Henry VII himself had specifically stated in a proclamation of 22–3 August 1485 that Richard was to be 'laid openly, that every man might see and look upon him', which by implication meant the corpse of Richard had to be recognisable.

Modelling the Bones (JA, RB, RH, BM, PM)

Back in September 2012, as soon as Appleby exposed the bones in the shallow grave, the most startling revelation was the severe scoliosis – abnormal side-to-side bending of the spine. Her later work confirmed that although the upper cervical spine and lower lumbar spine were straight, there was an S-shaped bend in the mid and upper back, from the fourth thoracic to the first lumbar vertebra. Since the bones were supported by the soil when he was buried, and the spinal ligaments are among the last in the body to decompose after death, the grave had preserved the shape of his spine for more than 500 years.

To work out how the scoliosis might have affected Richard's appearance and mobility, Bruno Morgan, an expert in medical imaging, reconstructed the spine as a three-dimensional plastic model. This meant the spine could be manipulated and studied without risk of damaging the original bones. The model was made by computed tomography, using a Toshiba Aquilion 64×0.5mm detector scanner. The scan images were reconstructed into 3D data sets of each bone, which were then used to make a polymer replica of each vertebra using a laser 3D printer at Loughborough University. Each of these model bones was next drilled through the centre and connected by being threaded on a flexible steel cable. The facet joints at the back of the vertebrae were tied together with fishing twine by Morgan. Felt spacers of varying thickness were used to mimic the cartilage that would have separated the bones in life. The facet joint ties allowed some movement where the bones appeared normal, but were fixed in position where arthritic degenerative changes forced them close together. The result was a three-dimensional model of the spine as it was in Richard's life. It was made without referring back to the excavation photographs, but when it was finished it closely matched the position of the spine in the grave.

It was important for the team, led by Piers Mitchell, an expert on scoliosis who is also a children's orthopaedic surgeon and osteoarchaeologist, to try to work out what caused the scoliosis, when it developed and how it would have affected Richard.

Apart from the twisted spine they found no other abnormalities. The shape of the vertebrae suggested he was born with a normal spine, with the vertebrae properly formed and separated – making it unlikely that it was a congenital condition. Neuromuscular causes such as cerebral palsy were also ruled out. His pelvis and limbs were normal, and there was nothing in the bones to suggest a genetic syndrome such as Marfans, with its typical high, arched palate and tall stature. The scientists concluded that Richard's problems began in adolescence, probably after his tenth birthday. The cause is unknown – as in most cases of adolescent-onset scoliosis, though, there could have been a genetic element. Once the spine began to twist, it put additional stresses on vertebrae in the middle of his back. Some bones grew in an asymmetrical shape because of the curved spine, and some at the most curved section showed signs of osteoarthritis (Plate 16).

It is impossible to know for certain whether Richard's back caused him pain. Studies have shown that the risk of back pain in people with this degree of scoliosis is about double that of the general population with a normal spine. However, many sufferers, including the Olympic athlete Usain Bolt, report that by working hard to maintain core strength, they are almost unaffected by the condition.

When Richard was clothed, little of the truth would have been apparent. The S-shaped curve was well balanced, leaving the upper and lower spine still aligned, and his leg bones were well formed so he would not have walked with a limp.

The curve, of 65–80 degrees, would not have reduced his lung capacity, and up to the time of his death would not have prevented him from taking vigorous physical exercise – or fighting a battle. Without the twisted spine, which made his trunk shorter relative to the length of his arms and legs, he would have stood at around 5 ft 8 in (1.7 m), in line with the medieval average of 1.71 m. However, with the scoliosis he would have been about 2 inches shorter (5 ft 6 in). His right shoulder would have been a little higher – but the thick layers of aristocratic fifteenth-century clothing, and custom-made armour may have disguised this almost entirely. Probably only his tailor, his armourer and his most intimate circle –including John Rous, his one-time friend, whose description of the king's raised shoulder was vindicated after more than 500 years – would have been aware that Richard's back was curved.

Dating Richard III and Tracking His Life: Radiocarbon Dating and E Isotope Analysis (RB, AL JE, JA)

Despite the circumstantial evidence of finding a man with a crooked spine buried in the choir of the Greyfriars church, there could be no proving that it was Richard without establishing the age of the bones. If tests showed that they were centuries older than his day, or more recent, it could not be him. Scientific analysis of samples gave a secure date, however, and also revealed much about his diet and lifestyle.

Samples of a rib were sent to two different radiocarbon labs, at Oxford and Glasgow. Radiocarbon dating measures different carbon isotopes. Most of the carbon in the world – and in us, and all living things – is carbon-12, but there are also tiny amounts of other isotopes, including carbon-13 and radioactive carbon-14. Once an organism dies it stops taking in carbon from the environment, and the decaying carbon is not replaced. Carbon-14 decays relatively quickly, and at a known rate, and so measuring the relative proportions of carbon-12/ carbon-13/ carbon-14 in an archaeological sample can determine the sample's age within a range of years.

There are, however, some complications. The proportion of different carbon isotopes has not been constant over all time but has varied in different periods of history and prehistory. The development of the science of radiocarbon calibration allows dated samples to be compared against known proportions of carbon isotopes in different period so that dates can be corrected to prevent a result which would be too new or too old. Furthermore, the proportion of different carbon isotopes in bone can be affected by several other factors, including diet. Radiocarbon labs now routinely also undertake basic stable isotope analysis when dating bone, so they can correct for distortions caused by diet. In this case, both labs found from the isotope analysis that the bones belonged to a man who had probably had a highly varied protein-rich diet, including meat and marine fish and other seafood. This would be appropriate were the bones Richard's since it was a rich man's diet, not a peasant's, but it is a complication in dating as eating lots of fish makes carbon dated bones seem older than that they really are.

When corrected for all these factors, the dates that the two labs came back with were very similar. The uncorrected dates from Glasgow came out at AD 1430–1460, and Oxford at 1412–1449, both at a 95 per cent probability. Correcting for the dietary factors, and using the standard radiocarbon calibration, refined using Bayesian statistical modelling, in which the parameters of a target are updated in the light of new data and which is now becoming standard in radiocarbon dating, the dates were pinned down to 1475–1530 at a 68.2 per cent probability, or 1430–1530 at a 96 per cent probability. The radiocarbon dating did not prove that the bones were Richard's, but the analysis did show that they had come from around the period of his lifetime, not from a far earlier period in the history of the friary. The parameters of the latest possible date were clear: they had to be from earlier than 1538, since there were no new burials in the Grey Friars church after the friary was destroyed in that year on Henry VIII's orders.

Much more detailed isotope analysis was carried out by Angela Lamb and Jane Evans of the British Geological Survey. They took tiny samples from different parts of the skeleton which would have developed at different stages of his life. These included samples from two teeth, representing his childhood and early adolescence; from his femur, representing full adulthood; and from part of a rib. To test for oxygen isotopes they took slices just 1.5 mm thick and weighing only 0.3 mg from the teeth. A small amount (only 0.6 mg in weight) of collagen, the organic, protein component of bone was used to test for carbon and nitrogen; this had to be extracted from very small bone samples. These samples were run through dedicated mass spectrometers, calibrated to detect the isotope ratios of specific elements. Their results corresponded closely with the known facts of Richard's life from written sources, and they revealed important information about his diet over the course of his life.

The oxygen and strontium isotopes in tooth enamel, fixed in childhood as the teeth grow, come from drinking water and food grown in the area where the person lived – and they bear traces of the distinctive isotopic signatures of the geology of the landscape through which water flowed and from the soils in which food crops were raised and animal grazed. These distinctive isotopic signatures can reveal where an individual grew up, and if, as a child, they moved from one place to another. In this case, the samples from an area of tooth formed at about the age of three matched the water of eastern England, but the sample from the tooth from about the age of seven revealed that by then this individual was living somewhere in western Britain. Richard was born in Fotheringhay in Northamptonshire in 1452, and he lived there as a small child, but by 1459 he was living at Ludlow Castle in the Welsh Marches. The isotope results closely matched this history.

A relatively high amount of lead was also detected in his teeth. This was typical in Roman times and continued to be so into the medieval period. The lead came from water pipes, cosmetics, food additives, medicines (none of which now contain lead) and even pewter drinking vessels which contained a higher percentage of lead than is common today.

Changes in carbon and nitrogen isotopes, found in both the teeth and bones and an indicator of protein in the diet, were analysed to reveal what the individual ate over the course of his lifetime. The analysis of his teeth suggests that even by the age of three he was eating a diet rich in protein. However, his life obviously changed drastically and may have been less agreeable when he moved west: the samples show a sharp drop in protein at about the age of five, around the time when Richard moved to Ludlow. Life clearly improved quite quickly: the protein levels began to rise again to reach a maximum at the age of 14.

They then probably – on the evidence of the sample from the femur – decreased a little in adulthood, though the levels are still at the top of the range for medieval adults and represent someone eating a substantial quantity of marine and freshwater fish.

The rib sample, from an area of bone that formed late in life, revealed that his diet changed dramatically in his last years. At that point he was eating larger quantities of exceptionally high status foods, including freshwater fish, wild fowl and pigs. There was more: a substantial change in the oxygen isotopes also suggests that he was drinking more wine than ever before in his life. This was truly a diet fit for a king with many banquets to attend. However, there was no indication that at the time he died, as a relatively young man aged 32, this rich and potentially unhealthy diet had affected his health or fitness, though had he lived longer and survived into his fifties, it might have taken its toll. As far as researchers could determine from the skeleton, he was fit and healthy at the time of his death.

Parasites (PM)

Richard's bones revealed one more small, poignant story of human frailty. When the skeleton was excavated, soil samples were collected from the area of the grave around his pelvis and his skull. For comparison, soil samples were also collected from nearby but outside the pit of the grave.

A team led by Piers Mitchell, of the Department of Archaeology and Anthropology at Cambridge University, studied these samples under powerful microscopes. There were no parasites in the sample from the skull and only a few from the surrounding soil outside the grave. However, the sample from his pelvis, where the intestines would have been, revealed that he was infested with roundworms, on the evidence of their eggs preserved in the soil. This type of parasitic worm is about one foot long, and lives inside the intestines. It is spread when its eggs, mixed in with human faeces, are inadvertently ingested by another person when they eat their food.

The ingredients of his rich diet, including pork, beef and fish did carry parasites in the medieval period. However, his food was obviously well cooked, since there was no evidence of the tapeworms that could have been spread from these animals. The roundworms could have come from crops grown in soil using human faeces as a fertiliser – or more simply because the cooks who prepared his grand meals did not wash their hands after using the toilet.

Further reading

Appleby, J., Mitchell, P.D., Robinson, C. *et al.*(2014) The scoliosis of King Richard III, last Plantagenet king of England: diagnosis and clinical significance. *The Lancet* 383 (9932) (31 May–6 June): 1944. Available online at http://www.thelancet.com/pdfs/journals/lancet/PIIS0140-6736(14)60762-5.pdf (last accessed 4 February 2015).

Appleby, J., Rutty, G., Hainsworth, S.V. *et al.* (2015) Perimortem trauma in King Richard III: a skeletal analysis. *The Lancet* 385 (9932) (17 January 2015): 253–9. Available online at http://www.thelancet.com/journals/lancet/article/PIIS0140-6736(14)60804-7/fulltext (last accessed 4 February 2015).

Fiorato, V., Boylston, A. and Knüsel, C. (eds) (2007) *Blood Red Roses: The Archaeology of a Mass Grave from the Battle of Towton AD 1461*. Oxford: Oxbow Books.

Lamb, A.L., Evans, J. E., Buckley, R. and Appleby, J. (2014) Multi-isotope analysis demonstrates significant lifestyle changes in King Richard III. *Journal of Archaeological Science*, XXX (2014) p. 1–7. Available online at http://www.sciencedirect.com/science/article/pii/S0305440314002428 (last accessed 9 December 2014).

Mitchell, P.D., Yeh, Hui-Yuan, Appleby, J., Buckley, R. (2013) The intestinal parasites of King Richard III. *The Lancet* 382 (9895) (7–13 September): 888. Available online at http://www.thelancet.com/journals/lancet/article/PIIS0140-6736(13)61757-2/fulltext (last accessed 4 February 2015).

5

Who was Richard?

Imagine ...

The strangers met at the top of the steep mound, its slopes worn ragged by burrowing rabbits and the feet of tourists, rising above the lumps and bumps in the grass marking the lines of the lost buildings. Together they looked across the roof of the farm whose buildings incorporated a few much older walls, past the bridge built from recycled stones, towards the spiky grandeur of the tall tower now quite out of proportion with the surviving stump of the church.

The last of the late summer sunlight was fading fast.

'Do you find it a sad place?' the man asked. 'Does such a tragic death cast a shadow? You know, some say the village is haunted.'

They scrambled down the slope again, towards the one chunk of masonry remaining on the riverbank, surrounded by elaborate railings with small cast-iron notices marking the two occasions when this sleepy location carved out its place in the country's history.

The man, taking a tartan ribbon from his pocket to tie onto the railings, saw that the woman had brought a white rose. 'Ah,' she said, 'you came for Mary. It is the 22nd of August – I came for Richard.'

Richard's Early Years

Richard's mother gave birth to him at Fotheringhay Castle on 2 October 1452. He was born into a fractured kingdom, and his own family had been major contributors to its instability (Figure 5.1, Figure 5.2).

The Bones of a King: Richard III Rediscovered, First Edition. The Greyfriars Research Team with Maev Kennedy and Lin Foxhall.
© 2015 University of Leicester. Published 2015 by John Wiley & Sons, Ltd.

Fotheringhay in Northamptonshire is now a prosperous, pretty village with an excellent pub, but its population has declined sharply since the medieval period. Over time the collegiate college established to pray for the souls of the Plantagenet dead, then the largest part of church, and finally the castle itself, where Mary, Queen of Scots was later tried and executed, were demolished. The loss of the college, which would have had scores of servants to wait on its wealthy priests, and the castle with its large household and rich visitors, tore the heart out of the village.

Romantic legend insists that one of the first acts of James I as king of England was to raze to the ground the castle where his mother, Mary, was imprisoned and killed in 1587. This was clearly not true: a survey made after James died in 1625 recorded the castle as having 'a goodly fair court'. It was obviously still roofed and furnished, since it included 'a large room at this present well furnished with pictures'. The great hall, where Mary had been tried, still stood, and though the castle had undergone much rebuilding and modernising over the 140 years since Richard's death, it was probably still a space he would have recognised.

By the time Richard was born in Fotheringhay, a succession of kings had come and gone and many battles had been fought since Henry Bolingbroke had forced the abdication of his cousin Richard II in 1399, initiating a series of conflicts that would finally escalate into the Wars of the Roses. Power had shifted between different families and factions. History has judged some of the monarchs strong, like Henry V with his string of conquests in France, or weak and mentally unstable like Henry VI, who lost most of his father's overseas lands. For most of the people of England, however, it scarcely mattered who was on the throne, unless they were dragged into war in the wake of their lord. The success of the next harvest was far more important, and the dread of a return of the Black Death, which had killed up to half the population during the thirteenth century and left the country littered with abandoned farms and villages, was far more terrifying than any regime change.

Since then, wages had gone up because labour was scarce, agriculture was recovering, wool was making regions like the Cotswolds and towns like Halifax and Leeds rich, and London, by far the biggest city, was ever expanding and booming on commerce and trade. In the countryside, the great monasteries functioned virtually as aristocratic estates, made rich by rents and tithes. Some orders cared for the sick

Figure 5.1 Fotheringhay castle mound, with the church in the background.

Figure 5.2 Fotheringhay church.

and ran hospitals, though these were more like today's hospices for the elderly and incurable. In the towns, orders of mendicant friars, like the Grey Friars in Leicester, operated more modestly, living among the people by begging for alms, preaching, burying the dead and praying for their souls (see Chapter 3).

A growing number of people could read and write, not just aristocracy like the ancestor of the Plantagenets known as Henry Beauclerc but also shopkeepers and small traders. New centres of education were being created, including Eton in 1440 and King's College Cambridge in 1441, both founded by Henry VI. Craftworkers such as stone carvers, weavers, painters and printers brought Continental skills and fashions from the Netherlands, France and Italy.

If the ebb and flow of national politics, and the distant wars rumbling on in Europe for many lifetimes, were far from the lives of most people, for the great families caught up in the Wars of the Roses there had been decades of turmoil.

The power struggle was never a regional war of north against south – the 'Yorkists', with their castles and lands in Yorkshire and the North, were notably popular and enthusiastically supported in Kent and London, and both Scottish and Continental kings were happy to meddle, making and breaking alliances with Yorkists, Lancastrians and Tudors, as it suited their own domestic politics. This was rather a clash between different branches of a royal family and their followers, with supporters of both sides located in every county, city and town. (Map 5.1)

Nor was it the white rose of Yorkshire pitted across the Pennines against the red rose of Lancashire. Indeed, those involved would have been surprised by the term Wars of the Roses. Shakespeare immortalised the image when, in *Henry VI Part I*, he depicted the Lancastrians and Plantagenets quarrelling in the Temple gardens by the Inns of Court in London, still planted with red and white roses. Richard of York plucks a white rose and invites his supporters to follow his example. The duke of Somerset plucks a red rose. The earl of Warwick plucks a white rose declaring 'I love no colours'. The image is wonderfully memorable but it cannot be historically correct as some of the main players, including Richard, were not in London at the time. However, the idea of the white and red roses as symbols of tribal alliance was certainly established by the time of Henry VII, who married the two flowers in his Tudor rose emblem.

Map 5.1 Key places in the Wars of the Roses.

The shifting tangle of alliances and opposition was as tortuous as the shifting ownership of the ducal titles, and the crowds of Richards and Edwards in each generation, which have tormented centuries of audiences of Shakespeare's history plays. The political instability of the period led to plots and counterplots, oaths of allegiance sworn and broken, strategic marriages and disputed legitimacy, executions and assassinations, skirmishes like the half-hour Battle of Northampton – a short sharp Yorkist victory in which Henry VI was taken prisoner – or the carnage of Towton, the bloodiest battle ever fought on English soil.

The houses of York and Lancaster were cousins through the sons of Edward III, and related too to the royal families of France – the land of the Plantagenet ancestors – and Scotland (Figure 5.3). Both the Yorkists and Lancastrians were cousins, too, to the upstart Welsh family the Tudors, whose shaky claim to the throne came as descendants of the Beauforts, children only legitimised after the third marriage of one of those sons, John of Gaunt.

Edward III gave the title Duke of Lancaster to John, his third son, and John's first wife, Blanche. The Lancastrian descendants included Henry Bolingbroke – who became Henry IV when he deposed Richard II – his son Henry V and his grandson Henry VI. After Blanche and his second wife, Constance of Castile had both died, Gaunt eventually married Katherine Swynford, but by then they already had several children. These, including the worldly and powerful Cardinal Henry Beaufort, were retrospectively legitimised by Richard II, but specifically barred from making a claim on the throne – an attempt to check their power that was never likely to hold in such an aspirant family. Their ambition grew after Gaunt's great-granddaughter Margaret Beaufort married into the Tudors. The Welsh family had joined a rebellion against Henry IV in 1400, and their dynastic ambitions increased when Catherine of Valois, the widow of Henry V, married Owen Tudor – or possibly just bore him several children in a long relationship. Their sons, Jasper, Earl of Pembroke and Edmund, Earl of Richmond, whom Margaret Beaufort married, were half-brothers to Henry VI.

The Yorkists felt they had a better claim to the throne than either. They were descended from Edward of Langley, first duke of York and fourth son of Edward III, but their royal connections were strengthened when his son Richard married Anne Mortimer, the great-granddaughter of Edward. Her son was Richard, the third duke of York, father of our Richard.

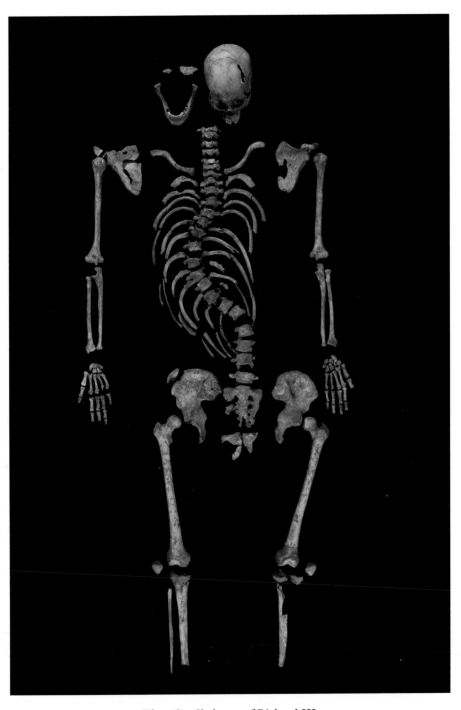

Plate 9 Skeleton of Richard III.

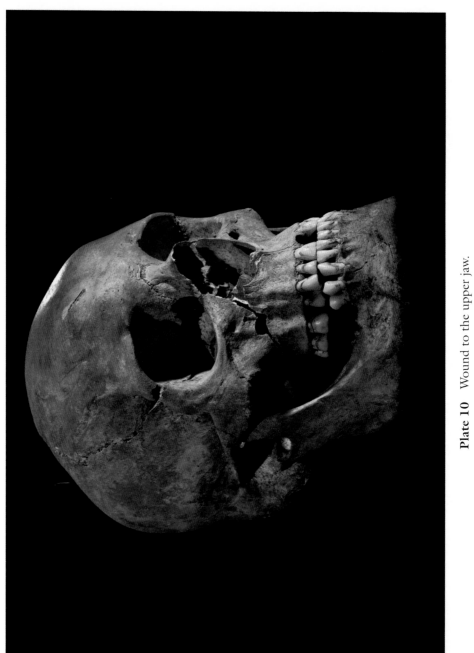

Plate 10 Wound to the upper jaw.

Plate 11 Injuries on the dome of the skull.

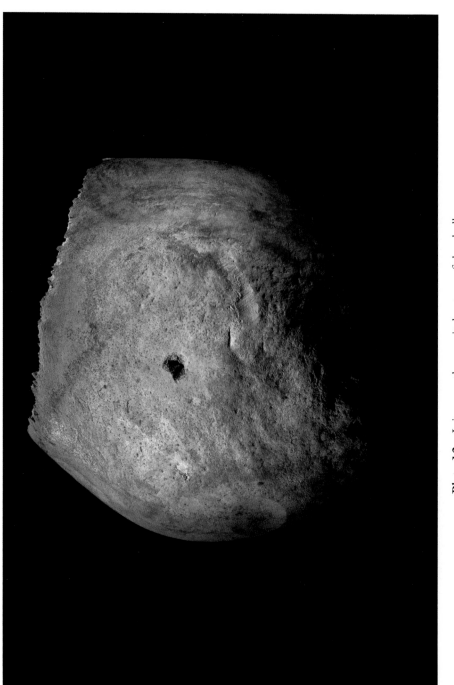

Plate 12 Injury on the saggital suture of the skull.

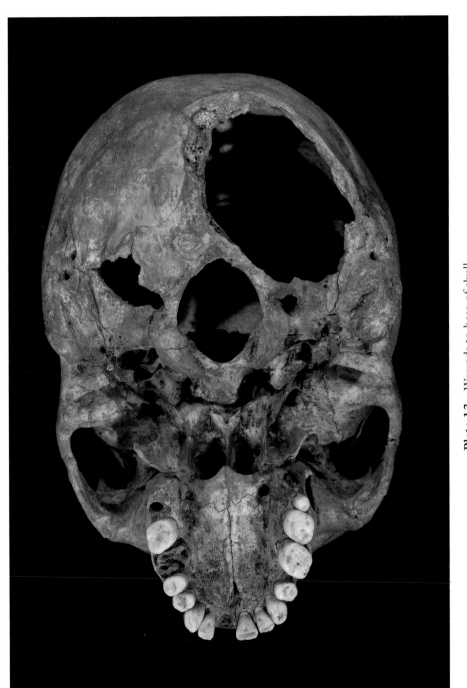

Plate 13 Wounds to base of skull.

Plate 14 Cut injury to rib.

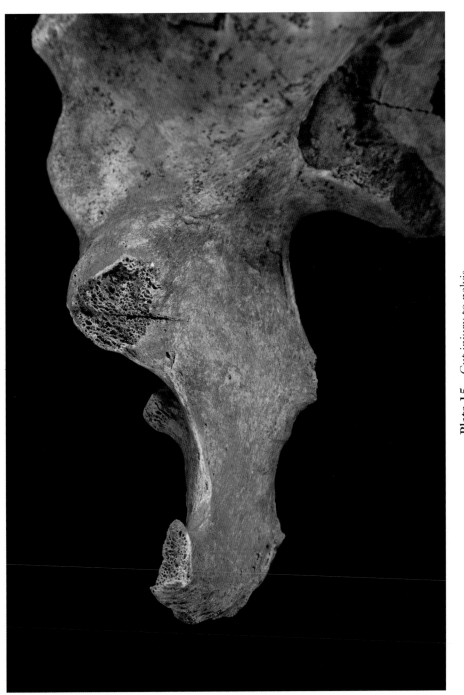

Plate 15 Cut injury to pelvis.

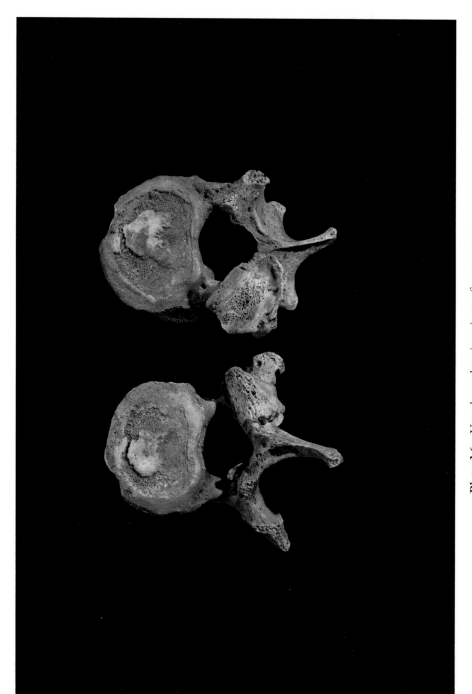

Plate 16 Vertrebrae showing signs of asymmetry.

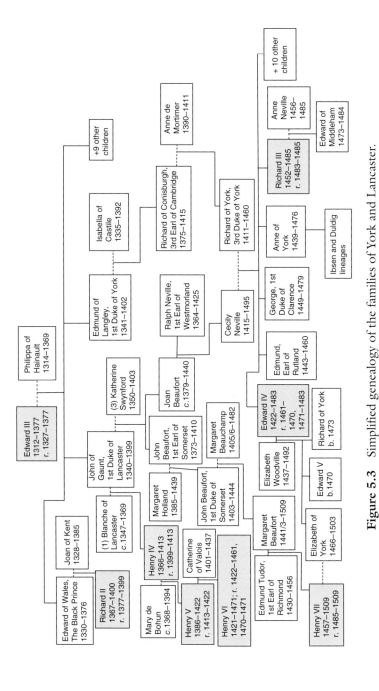

Figure 5.3 Simplified genealogy of the families of York and Lancaster.

The royal family had been nicknamed Plantagenists for centuries, after the broom flower, *planta genista*, which an Anjou ancestor wore in his hat, and which generations after him wore as emblems in battle. However, Richard was the first formally to adopt the name: the Great Chronicle of London referred to him as 'Richard Plantagenet duke of Yorke'. He wanted perhaps to reinforce the message that he was now only a hair's breadth from the throne.

A Baby Comes to the Throne

This rivalry might just have provoked bitter squabbles over precedence at great events at court, had it not been for the power vacuum after 1422, when Henry V died suddenly in France from dysentery, leaving his baby son to succeed as Henry VI at the age of nine months. Crowned at the age of eight, Henry grew into a shy, pious and fragile man without the necessary traits to attract support, and his unpopularity greatly increased when, in 1445, he married Margaret of Anjou, a niece of Charles VII of France. Public dislike of the marriage grew when it was learned that far from gaining extra lands as her dowry, the common pattern in the strategic marriages of the aristocracy, he had actually surrendered land in France to secure the match. She proved as hungry for power, and as willing to lead an army or contrive a diplomatic alliance on behalf of first her husband and then her son, as any of the other contenders for the throne.

The struggle among the various factions at court increased after Humphrey, Duke of Gloucester, an uncle of the king, who had held the title Protector – effectively regent – during Henry's childhood, was accused of treason at the instigation of enemies, including the Beauforts. He died before he could be tried, leaving Richard of York, who also held the title of Lord Protector on three occasions, heir apparent, unless Henry could produce a son.

Richard was packed off to Ireland as governor, exiled from influence at court. However, a string of defeats for the English in France – where Henry had also been crowned king – dramatically changed the situation. Joan of Arc, the Maid of Orleans, had made her startling intervention in history to strengthen the French nerve. Rouen was lost in 1449, Normandy in 1450 (in which year a serious rebellion by Jack

Cade and his supporters in Kent and Sussex was also suppressed), Bordeaux and Gascony in 1451, and finally, in July 1453, came the decisive French victory at the Battle of Castillon which ended the Hundred Years' War. Henry VI had a nervous breakdown when told of the scale of this last defeat, and toppled into a strange trance-like state which lasted for more than a year, and from which not even the birth of his son and heir could rouse him. Inevitably, as with so many of the players in this story, there were questions about the baby's paternity.

By this time, Richard of York was back in England, years short of the decade he was supposed to stay away: the next chapter of the story was about to begin. Richard only inherited the castle at Fotheringhay on the banks of the river Nene because his uncle Edward and father Richard, earls of Rutland and Cambridge respectively, were dead. Richard of Cambridge had been beheaded for joining his brother-in-law in a conspiracy against Henry V known as the Southampton Plot. Edward died supporting Henry at the battle of Agincourt, apparently by toppling or being knocked over onto his face in full armour and being suffocated. According to one account of the battle 'being a fatte man he was smouldered to death'.

As with the Tudors, powerful marriages hardened ambitions: Richard of York married Cecily Neville, a marriage arranged when the children were 9 and 14. The Nevilles were one of the wealthiest and most powerful families in the land, and Cecily was known as the Rose of Raby for her beauty and her birthplace, Raby Castle in Durham – but a later nickname, Proud Cis, suggests that some thought her good looks were not her most memorable feature.

A Disrupted Childhood

The birthplaces of the children of Cecily and Richard tracked the complexity of their lives. Our Richard, born at Fotheringhay, was the youngest son of the 8 of their 13 children who survived infancy. He was followed by another Fotheringhay daughter, Ursula. The first children, a daughter and a son, both died before their first birthdays. Anne of York, the oldest surviving daughter, whose bloodline would prove crucial in identifying the remains from the Leicester car park, was born at

Fotheringhay in 1439. George, the closest brother to Richard in age, was born in Dublin in 1449. The oldest surviving son, Edward, was born in Rouen, like Edmund and Elizabeth; Cecily had followed her husband there when military service took him to France. Historians still argue over claims, first made in Edward's lifetime, that he was not in fact his father's true son, as Richard of York was supposedly with the army far from his wife at the assumed time of conception.

Little is recorded of Richard III's earliest years: as a youngest son he was unlikely to bother history much. However, the archaeology matches the known facts: the tests on his bones and teeth show that his early years were well nourished and healthy (see Chapter 4). He was living with his clever mother, and had young siblings to play with in beautiful countryside. Home was a handsome castle, unrecognisable from its origins as a simple twelfth-century timber motte and bailey. His father had recently spent a fortune on improvements to make it worthy of a claimant to the throne: Proud Cis earned her nickname at this time.

The cold grey stone walls of ruined medieval castles give little impression of life there for the wealthy. When the great families arrived, they brought with them wall hangings, curtains and bed covers, furs, woollens, velvets and tapestries, beds, stools and chairs, chests of gold and silver plate. The recreated medieval interiors at the Tower of London and Dover Castle, though dated to an earlier period, vividly convey the colour and luxury of life indoors for the elite.

Richard must have been a slight boy, but strong and without a trace yet of the scoliosis which would begin to twist his spine in adolescence. He would have had tutors to teach him to read and write, rough and tumble games and toys to encourage the manly arts of war, and he would have been trained to sit on a horse almost as soon as he could walk.

The endless conflict scattered the family for months or even years at a time. In 1454, when Henry recovered the throne, Richard's father was stripped of much of his power, only to win it back at the first Battle of St Albans in May 1455, generally considered the first battle of the Wars of the Roses, when his enemy and the queen's great ally, the duke of Somerset, was killed, and the king slightly wounded. A precarious peace was cobbled together.

In 1459 his father moved Cecily and the younger children to the greater strength of Ludlow Castle – which may be where the lad first met his big brothers Edward and Edmund. A week after Richard's seventh birthday, life changed dramatically for the worse. The Yorkists were defeated at nearby Ludford Bridge, an episode which scarcely became a battle as they were so heavily outnumbered that they recognised the inevitable before the fighting really started. His father escaped to Ireland with Edmund, while Edward fled to France with other Yorkist leaders, leaving Cecily and the youngest children to seek refuge with various friends and allies. Again the story of family trouble is written in Richard's bones: they show that around this period he was eating a much poorer diet (see Chapter 4).

The following year brought initial triumph, then tragedy and humiliation to the family. The Battle of Northampton in July 1460 was a notable Yorkist victory, with Edward and his most powerful ally, his cousin Richard Neville, Earl of Warwick back from France leading the Yorkist side. Warwick, known as 'the Kingmaker' from his political influence as leader of one of the wealthiest families in the country, was, like Edward, related to all the claimants to the throne. Some of Henry's army deserted within the first half hour of the fighting and several of his closest supporters died. The king himself was captured and brought to London. Richard of York and Edmund returned in September, joined up with their supporters and marched on London, which remained a strongly Yorkist city. The Croyland Chronicles, written at Crowland Abbey in Lincolnshire, twice extended by anonymous authors to cover Yorkist politics right up to the Battle of Bosworth, described the dramatic events that followed: 'The duke of York came over from Ireland; and repairing to Westminster while the Parliament was there assembled, entered the sitting; after which, going up to the royal throne, he claimed the right of sitting there as belonging solely to himself'.

As the chronicler wrote, in October Richard briefly actually claimed the throne for himself – surely the proudest moment for Proud Cis – but after negotiations this was scaled down to recognising him as heir, disinheriting Henry's son, Edward. The resulting Act of Accord was a settlement that there was absolutely no chance the determined Queen Margaret would accept. She ordered her Scottish troops south. In early December Richard, apparently seriously underestimating the size of the assembled Lancastrian forces, marched north with a small army. At the Battle of Wakefield, on 30 December, he was killed on the field, and the 17-year-old Edmund was slain as he attempted to escape. Their heads were stuck on spikes over the gates of York, Richard's bearing a mocking paper crown.

Edward, still only 19, was now the leader of the Yorkist cause, while his younger brothers and sister found a variety of temporary shelters with allies, including a period in Burgundy in France. Their status as politically awkward and not particularly welcome guests changed spectacularly in 1461.

The Yorkists were defeated at the second Battle of St Albans in February, but although Henry was freed, the Lancastrians did not take back London, leaving the city a Yorkist power base. Then came the slaughter of Lancastrians at the Battle of Towton, fought in a blizzard on Palm Sunday, 29 March 1461. Edward ordered no quarter given, and his command was carried out with devastating results. The Croyland Chronicle again gave a vivid account of the day, almost certainly based on eyewitness reports:

> Those who helped to inter the bodies, piled up in pits and in trenches prepared for the purpose, bear witness that eight-and-thirty thousand warriors fell on that day, besides those who were drowned in the river before alluded to, whose numbers we have no means of ascertaining. The blood, too, of the slain, mingling with the snow which at this time covered the whole surface of the earth, afterwards ran down in the furrows and ditches along with the melted snow, in a most shocking manner, for a distance of two or three miles.

After months in hiding, Henry was recaptured and back in the Tower of London. Edward was proclaimed king by Warwick, who earned the epithet 'Kingmaker' in the process, and on 28 June 1461 he was crowned Edward IV in Westminster Abbey.

The fortunes of Richard and George were transformed: upon Edward's coronation both were made Knights of the Bath, and George became duke of Clarence. On 1 November, at the age of nine, Richard became duke of Gloucester (he was never Richard of York, the title held by his father). The brothers were soon on the move again, this time sent to another Neville stronghold, the palatial Middleham Castle in Yorkshire, where their education continued under the guardianship of Warwick.

At Middleham – massively extended a generation earlier to hold the 23 children of the two marriages of Ralph Neville – the boys completed their courtly education and military training and grew to be young men. Both also married Neville daughters they first met there, George marrying Isabel in 1469 and Richard, Anne in 1472. Although Anne was the younger sister, she was already widowed, having been briefly married to Henry VI's son, Edward. The York and Neville marriages tied the two families even closer together – but not the brothers. Edward had opposed George's marriage, and George bitterly opposed Richard's: the sisters were heiresses to the great wealth of their mother, and the brothers became entangled in a long dispute about their inheritance. Anne and Richard's relationship can only be glimpsed occasionally through the dry official records, but accounts survive for his orders of silks and furs 'delivered … to his most beloved consort'.

Richard, rewarded with titles and estates forfeited by Edward's defeated enemies, remained loyal to his brother throughout the successes and reverses of the two phases of his reign. In 1464, when the family was ripped apart yet again, and Richard was forced to choose between his brothers, Edward or George – Shakespeare's 'false, fleeting, perjure'd Clarence' – he stayed by Edward.

That was the year in which Edward married Elizabeth Woodville, a match regarded as a catastrophe by many of his closest advisers including Warwick. Elizabeth was famously beautiful; however, she was not only a subject but also a woman whose family had been prominent supporters of Henry VI, and a widow whose first husband had died in battle against Edward. Contemporary gossip said that Edward tried to make her his mistress but that she held out successfully for marriage, and the king's former friends and allies observed her horde of needy and ambitious relatives with horror. Their two sons, Edward and Richard, the heir and the spare, would never live to breed or reign, and their deaths would cast a shadow which has never lifted.

By the time Edward was born in November 1470, Elizabeth was in sanctuary in Westminster Abbey. Her husband and brother-in-law, Edward and Richard, were back in France, and Henry was king again – but not for long. Edward and Richard returned to England in 1471, and their victories at the battles of Barnet in April and Tewkesbury in May followed. Richard was recorded as brave in battle. He was evidently lucky too, as he survived at least one injury, and no injuries seem to have damaged his bones in any of the fights before his final confrontation at Bosworth. A German merchant wrote in a letter after Barnet that Richard 'was slightly wounded but, thanks be to God, suffered no further harm', but any wound raised the risk of the dangers of infection in a world without modern medicine.

Warwick died in the Battle of Barnet. Clarence survived until 1478, but after evidence that he was conspiring again, was then executed for treason. He is said to have suffered one of history's most gruesomely unforgettable deaths. There is no proof that he died in the Tower of London by being drowned in a barrel of sweet Malmsey wine, but the story was repeated by several early historians including Polydore Vergil. Henry VI died imprisoned in the Wakefield Tower of the Tower of London in May 1471. His son, Edward, Prince of Wales, was already dead, killed at the Battle of Tewkesbury, widowing Anne Neville and leaving her free to marry Richard.

One account said that Henry died of melancholy, another that he was murdered while kneeling at prayer. Thomas More said Richard killed him. The Croyland Chronicle was clear that it was murder, and suggested it was Richard without naming him: 'He who perpetrated this has justly earned the title of tyrant while he who thus suffered had gained that of a glorious martyr. The body was exhibited for days in St Paul's church in London, and was carried thence by the river Thames to the conventual church of the monks at Chertsey'. When Richard became king he had Henry's body reburied at St George's Chapel, Windsor, where the dead king later became the centre of a minor cult, credited with several miracles, including curing pilgrims who put on his hat, kept by the tomb, of migraine.

With Henry VI dead, and his widow, Margaret, in exile in France, where she died in 1482 aged just 52, and with Henry Tudor also living in exile, Edward was now beyond challenge as king of England. Richard, who had been granted land and titles in Wales in Edward's first reign, was now rewarded with estates and titles confiscated from the losers, which allowed him to build up a major power base in the North, and appointments including constable and admiral of England. After the death of the Kingmaker, Edward gave Middleham to Richard. It became his favourite home, the base from which he ruled the North for Edward, and where his son, Edward, was born in 1476. In that same year Richard joined the king in a great ceremony at Fotheringhay, to undo the evidence of one of their family's greatest humiliations.

The bodies of their father, and their brother Edmund, whose heads had been stuck on spikes over the Micklegate in York, were exhumed from their modest graves in Pontefract and brought in a magnificent week-long procession to the church at Fotheringhay. A contemporary account by the Chester Herald, Thomas Whiting, described Richard leading the procession with other lords dressed in mourning. The body of his father was dressed in an ermine-trimmed gown and covered with a cloth of gold, carried on a hearse guarded by a silver angel carrying a golden crown. They were met at the church by the king, who put his hand on his father's body, 'crying all the time'. They were buried after solemn masses the following day. The public was admitted after the service and treated to a magnificent banquet, served – to thousands of people according to the account – in the castle and in tents and specially erected pavilions. How could anyone who had attended such a spectacular act of public mourning doubt Edward's royal status or true paternity – which was almost certainly the point of the display.

Time for Another Boy King?

In April 1483 Edward IV died, a few weeks short of his forty-second birthday: various accounts said that he caught a chill while fishing, or that he was unhealthy because he ate too much and had become so fat. Pneumonia has also been suggested, or typhoid. Polydore Vergil suggested foul play, 'either poison or sorcery', without any apparent evidence. The death was obviously sudden, as his brother Richard and Edward, his elder son, were far from his side, and both hurried towards London, travelling from Middleham and Ludlow respectively; his other son, Richard, seems to have been with his mother, who took sanctuary in Westminster at the end of the month. The king was buried at St George's Chapel in Windsor, leaving the 12-year-old, Edward, as the heir apparent.

The events of that summer, and of the two years which followed, have been argued over ever since. Richard intercepted the prince's party at Stony Stratford and arrested some of the more prominent members of the Woodville clan, including the queen's brother Earl Rivers, claiming that they were threatening to take power by force. By the time they reached London in early May, Richard was clearly in charge of both his nephew and the kingdom. The queen once again sought sanctuary at Westminster Abbey.

The coronation was scheduled for 22 June, and for a few weeks the crisis appeared to be economic rather than political, with the council of state meeting to discuss how to pay for the ceremony. However, events were moving fast. Friends, councillors, relations of the queen and supporters of Edward's were arrested on the grounds that they were conspiring against Richard. Richard sent a messenger with a letter to his supporters in York, appealing for urgent aid to deal with 'the Queen, her blood adherents, and affinity', and troops were duly sent south. There were no details about the plot in the letter, but the messenger would probably have given more details verbally about the gathering storm clouds in London.

On 13 June William Hastings, Edward's chamberlain and close friend, who weeks earlier had attended the king's funeral at Westminster and Windsor, was called to a council meeting at the Tower of London. According to the accounts of various chroniclers, including the Croyland Chronicle and the Great Chronicle of London, he was beheaded at the Tower on that same day – without 'processe of any lawe or lawfully examynacion' according to the Great Chronicle. Hastings, like all the other major players a descendant of Edward III and therefore a distant cousin of Richard's, was a well-liked and respected man, and the evidence of his plotting against Richard was shaky at best – although Polydore Vergil does claim that he met with others at St Paul's to express concern over Richard's blatant control of his nephew, recording their view that the young king was '*utterly oppressyd and wrongyd*' by Richard. Hasting's abrupt execution, reportedly so hasty that he had to lay his head on an improvised block, without any public trial, shocked many and may have marked a turning point in popular feeling for Richard. On Monday, 16 June the queen was persuaded to hand over her younger son, 10-year-old Richard, supposedly to attend his brother's coronation. With both boys in his care, Richard changed the date of the coronation to November and lodged them in the Tower. The Tower, then a royal residence as well as a prison, was a perfectly proper place for them, but almost certainly they never left it. On 22 June, the day young Edward should have been crowned, the citizens of London instead heard a sermon read at St Paul's Cross, proclaiming that the boy and his brother were illegitimate. Although the question of the late king's legitimacy had inevitably been raised again, the challenge over his sons was based on a claim that the marriage between Edward and Elizabeth Woodville was invalid because the king had already been contracted to marry Lady Eleanor Butler.

The two boys were seen playing in the Tower gardens for some weeks, and then never seen again, a murder mystery unresolved to this day that has inspired myriad scholarly studies, pantomimes and novels. Tudor propaganda and popular history laid the blame squarely on their uncle, but several others, including Henry Stafford, Duke of Buckingham, have been suggested as potentially responsible for their deaths, acting on Richard's behalf or their own initiative. It has even been proposed that Henry VII killed them two years later, after deposing Richard, though it seems unlikely that they were still alive by that time.

Dominic Mancini, an Italian friar, scholar and probable French spy, who was in London in 1482 and in the summer of 1483, wrote an account in Latin of Richard's rise to the throne, *De Occupatione Regni Anglie per Riccardum Tercium*. He admitted he was not sure what had happened to the princes, or even that they were dead, but he left a touching account of their last days, believed to be based on reports from their doctor, one of the last outsiders to see them:

> He and his brother were withdrawn into the inner apartments of the Tower proper, and day by day began to be seen more rarely behind the bars and windows, till at length they ceased to appear altogether. A Strasbourg doctor, the last of his attendants, whose services the King enjoyed, reported that the young King, like a victim prepared for sacrifice, sought remission of his sins by daily confession and penance, because he believed that death was facing him.

Though writing 40 years later, and without the benefit of knowing many people who were alive at the time, Sir Thomas More wrote the most detailed account of their fate. He named both Richard's agent – Sir James Tyrrell, according to his account – who managed to get the keys to their room, and his henchmen, the actual killers, who smothered the boys under a feather mattress. They were buried at the foot of the stairs, More wrote.

In the seventeenth century workmen at the Tower found bones, said to be of two children, buried in an elm chest beneath the stairs of the White Tower. The accounts are confusing because the workmen apparently first threw away the bones with the building rubble, and then gathered them up again when their potential significance was suggested. Charles II obviously thought they were important, as he ordered the remains to be reburied in a marble tomb at Westminster Abbey. The spot at the White Tower where the bones were allegedly found is still pointed out to tourists.

Whatever happened to the boys, in 1483, as far as the public was concerned, suddenly there was no king, and no younger heir presumptive. The consequence was inevitable. On 6 July Richard, with Anne as his queen in a gown made of 27 yards of white cloth of gold, was crowned at Westminster Abbey. They set off on a royal progress, ending in a ceremony at York investing their son as Prince of Wales, but the first revolt against his reign was already on the horizon.

His former supporter, the duke of Buckingham, clearly feeling that he was left out of the tight circle of favourites of the king, joined a rebellion against him centred on the South and the West Country. It was quickly suppressed, but it led Richard to rely even more on his intimates and his supporters in the North. Henry Tudor stayed in France, spending almost two years planning his invasion of England, but he became a focus for the growing opposition to Richard. In December Tudor made an announcement intended to attract even more of the disaffected: when he became king, he promised, he would marry Elizabeth, the eldest daughter of Edward IV and Elizabeth Woodville.

The new year saw the opening of Richard's only parliament, in January 1484, on which much of his reputation as a good and just law maker rests. Apart from the urgent business of letting the king get his hands on some official funds, and confirming the confiscation of the lands and wealth of rebels, a series of property, trade and taxation law reforms were passed, and although there were regulations against foreign traders and imports, the book and printing trades were protected.

On a personal level, the year would bring the king and queen tragedy when their only child, 10-year-old Edward, died at Middleham. He seems always to have been delicate – possibly suffering from tuberculosis – and had spent most of his life at the castle. He had not attended his parents' coronation, and some accounts say that in the previous year he had been carried into his own investiture as Prince of Wales. His parents, as so often in his short life, were away when he was taken ill. According to the Croyland Chronicle he died in April 'after an illness of but short duration'. 'On hearing the news of this, at Nottingham, where they were then residing, you might have seen his father and mother in a state almost bordering on madness, by reason of their sudden grief.'

The boy is believed to have been buried among his Neville ancestors at the church in Sheriff Hutton, where a battered alabaster carving of a child has traditionally been identified as Edward: it is now believed to be part of an earlier monument. Anne outlived her son by less than a year, dying in March 1485 in Westminster, possibly also of tuberculosis. She was buried in the Abbey. Richard is said to have wept publicly at her funeral, though by then his reputation was already so blackened that rumours rapidly spread that he had poisoned her, clearing the way to pre-empt Henry Tudor's proposed marriage by marrying his niece Elizabeth himself. In Shakespeare's play, Anne makes a last appearance as one of the procession of ghosts which appear to Richard on the eve of Bosworth: she calls herself 'that wretched Anne thy wife, that never slept a quiet hour with thee'.

Throughout 1484 resentment of the king had grown: in July somebody pinned a few vivid lines of doggerel verse to the door of St Paul's Cathedral: "the Catte, the Ratte, and Lovell Our Dogge, rulyth all Englande under a Hogge". The Cat was William Catesby, Speaker of the House of Commons, and widely believed to be a spy for Richard in political circles. He was captured at Bosworth and executed three days later. The Rat was Richard Ratcliffe, who would also die at Bosworth. Francis Lovell, nicknamed the Dog for his family's crest, was another newly rewarded favourite, a friend since childhood who had spent several years with Richard at Middleham, and would fight at Bosworth but survive. The Hogge, of course, was Richard himself, with his white boar emblem.

Given that Richard executed his enemies on the mere hint of conspiracy, the author was courageous. The snarl of abuse expressed an increasingly common view that over the past year Edward's mob of avaricious Woodvilles had merely been replaced by a new band of richly rewarded favourites, the tight group of intimates and confidantes around the new king. Richard ordered the author hunted down, and his revenge was fearful. Suspicion fell on Sir William Collingbourne, who had an unfortunate reputation for writing and pinning up scurrilous verses. In October he was accused of 'rhyme in derision of the king and his council', as well as conspiring to bring Henry Tudor to England to claim the throne. He was hanged, drawn and quartered, and one account says that with his last breath he gasped '*Oh Lord Jesus, yet more trouble!*'.

There was certainly yet more trouble to come for Richard.

Richard's Accomplishments

Although Richard was king for only two years, some of his accomplishments lasted well beyond his lifetime. He founded the College of Arms, which remains responsible for designing and recording coats of arms today. He instituted reforms to the penal system and to the legal system widening access to the courts. He was also a generous benefactor of the universities, providing endowments to Queens' College, Cambridge and a major donation to King's College, Cambridge, to continue the interrupted construction of their magnificent, and now world-famous, chapel.

The Last Battle

On 7 August 1485 Henry Tudor finally made his move. He landed at Milford Haven in Pembrokeshire and marched towards England with his uncle Jasper and an experienced military commander, the earl of Oxford, John de Vere. De Vere's father had been executed by Edward IV, and despite a reconciliation, he had joined Clarence in further rebellion and had spent a period in prison before escaping. Oxford would have one of the longest lives and careers of any of the players in the story, taking a leading role in the Battle at Bosworth, receiving handsome rewards when the Tudors came to power and living on into the reign of Henry VIII.

Henry moved quickly, gathering troops as he went. The two armies converged on the low hills, ploughed farm fields and stretches of marshy land south of the Leicestershire town of Market Bosworth. Richard's troops may have spent the eve of the battle on Ambion Hill, long considered to be the traditional site of the battle – known to Richard's contemporaries as Redemore, not Bosworth.

In 2009, however, extensive research was carried out by Glen Foard and the Battlefields Trust, incorporating maps and place names, field walking and metal detecting over the whole area around Bosworth (Map 5.2). This project produced the largest number of cannon balls and shot from any medieval battlefield, as well as numerous coins (many foreign) and the silver boar badge reproduced on the cover of this book. As a result of Foard's archaeological research, it now seems clear that instead of being a 'set-piece' battle at a single location, the Battle of Bosworth more likely consisted of a series of skirmishes fought by different groups over a wide area. The particularly high concentration of metal remains in the marshy area around Fenn Hole, on either side of Fenn Lane (an ancient Roman road), about two miles away to the south-west of Ambion Hill, suggest that it was here that Richard met his end. The badge, also found here, is particularly significant, as this precious object is likely to have been worn, and lost, by one of Richard's close companions in the final desperate hand-to-hand fighting.

When Richard rode out from Leicester on 21 August he had a far larger army than Henry, but it was still not clear which side the powerful Stanley family and their troops would take. In the Wars of the Roses William Stanley fought with the Yorkists at Blore Heath, his brother Thomas with the Lancastrians at Northampton. Thomas, by now married to Henry Tudor's mother, Margaret Beaufort, was briefly accused of treason and imprisoned after Hastings was executed, but later he was given high office again – though Richard clearly did not entirely trust either Stanley or his wife, since by the time of the battle he was holding his son as a hostage. Polydore Vergil claims that Thomas stayed away from Bosworth but that William brought the Stanley troops to the field – and very late in the two-hour battle, when the tide was turning against Richard, threw his troops in on Henry Tudor's side.

Richard, with his vanguard under Norfolk in serious trouble, led a charge right across the battlefield in an attempt to kill Henry, and the historical accounts which indicate that he managed to kill his enemy's standard bearer, Sir William Brandon, suggest that he came very close to Henry himself, as Brandon would have stuck close by Henry's side.

The research on the site and the evidence of the bones combined to confirm the earliest accounts of the battle and the despairing cry Shakespeare later gave Richard: 'A horse! A horse! My kingdom for a horse!' It is certainly possible that Richard's horse became bogged down in the marshy ground, and it is clear from the evidence of the

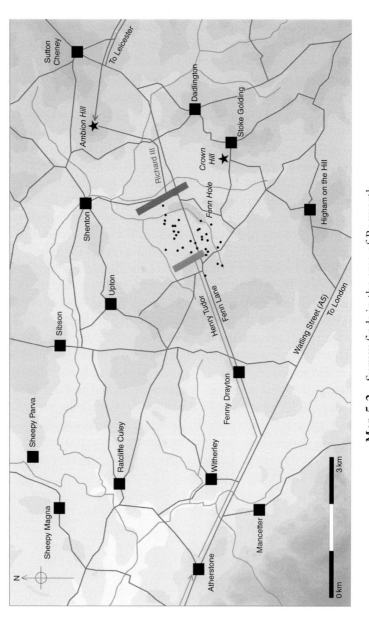

Map 5.2 Survey finds in the area of Bosworth.

wounds presented in Chapter 4 that by the time the fatal blows were struck he was dismounted and his helmet had been lost. Indeed, the forensic evidence of the wounds on the skeleton suggest that Richard may not have been simply a casualty in battle, his 'body found among the other slain', as some of the contemporary accounts claimed. The analysis of the angle of the wounds may suggest that Richard was on his knees, without his helmet, and with his head bent forward when they were inflicted. This could be interpreted as a scenario in which Richard had been captured alive and was deliberately executed while in a posture of submission, though this is not certain. That two of the head wounds were most likely blows from the same weapon may suggest that a limited number of people were directly involved in his death.

According to legend, the crown – which could have been a narrow fillet of gold worn on his helmet, detached when that was wrenched off by his killers – rolled from the dying king's head and was picked up from under a thorn bush and placed on Henry Tudor's head. Richard was dead, and the ambitious Welsh cousins had arrived. The new king rode away from Bosworth towards his role in history as the head of a new royal dynasty, while Richard's body was slung over the back of a horse and lugged back towards his roughly dug grave in Leicester.

After Richard

Anne of York, Richard's sister, had died in 1476, aged 37. She was first married aged just eight to Henry Holland, Duke of Exeter, a political move of her father's which went badly wrong when Holland sided with the Lancastrians in the wars. The couple had a daughter, separated and divorced, and she remarried Thomas St Leger, a friend and supporter of her brother Edward (Plate 17). She did not live to see her second husband also take arms against a brother, when St Leger joined a rebellion against Richard. Anne died in childbirth, but the daughter she had with St Leger, Anne, lived, and her bloodline continued to Michael Ibsen and his siblings and to Wendy Duldig to produce the DNA match with Richard's bones.

Richard's mother, Cecily, outlived most of the main players, and she lived to see the warring Yorkists and Tudor families united when Henry VII married her granddaughter Elizabeth, the eldest child of Edward IV and Elizabeth Woodville: their second son would reign as Henry

VIII. Cecily died finally at Berkhampstead in 1495, but at her request her body was brought back to Fotheringhay, to lie with her husband within sight of their fine castle, now in Tudor hands. Proud Cis had a suitably grand funeral, very different from either her husband's first burial at Pontefact, or her son Richard's in the Greyfriars in Leicester. In her will she left the Fotheringhay college costly books and vessels for the altar, rich cloths and vestments including 'three copes of blue velvet', all presumably used at her requiem service.

The pragmatic decision was taken in the sixteenth century to demolish the entire collegiate chapel end of the church instead of repairing it, and when Elizabeth I visited she was shocked to find the royal tombs – holding the Plantagenets, who through the web of cousins were her ancestors too – exposed to the weather and decaying. The traditional story is that Elizabeth ordered that the bodies be reburied in imposing new monuments flanking the altar, one standing on top of the original marble slab so that a few fragments of the intricate carving and an inch of brass tassle are just visible at its foot, and that she paid for the work. The tombs look more impressive from a distance than when studied close up, when the rather crude carving and finish are obvious. Recent research suggests they may in fact have been built, fairly quickly and cheaply, by a local nobleman as a royal favour. (Figure 5.4, Figure 5.5, Figure 5.6)

When the old York coffins were opened, according to an account written a century later in the 1600s but, it claims, based on an eyewitness report, Proud Cis was found with a silver ribbon around her neck, holding a pardon from the Pope, still perfectly legible 'as fair and fresh as if it had been written yesterday', for any sins committed in her lifetime: the question over the legitimacy of Edward IV perhaps needed to be tackled once again in death.

The boards high on the walls above the monuments carry what are said to be eighteenth-century copies of the original inscriptions painted on the tombs. Two sons of Richard of York became kings of England: the inscriptions mention only Edward. By the time the castle was demolished and its timbers and stone sold off as building materials, the main antiquarian interest in Fotheringhay was in Mary Queen of Scots. Visitors to the Talbot Inn in nearby Oundle are still shown the imposing wooden staircase, down which the queen is said to have walked to her death, and some of the stonework may have come from castle buildings of Richard's day (Figure 5.7). Sir Robert Cotton, founder of

Figure 5.4 Fotheringhay church, the monuments of Duke Richard (L) and Duke Edward (R), either side of the high altar.

Figure 5.5 Fotheringhay church, monument of Duke Edward.

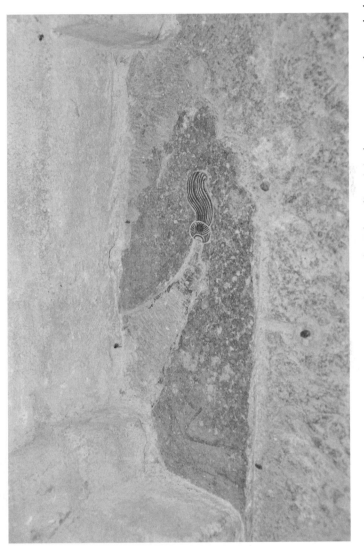

Figure 5.6 Fotheringhay church, bronze tassel on Duke Edward's original monument, underneath the Elizabethan monument.

Figure 5.7 Talbot Inn, Oundle, the staircase down which Mary Queen of Scots is said to have walked.

the Cottonian Library, now housed at the British Library, bought some of the impressive carved stone from the great hall to incorporate in his Conington mansion.

By the late nineteenth century Fotheringhay was a sad place. The clergyman, novelist and local historian Edward Bradley, writing as Cuthbert Bede in 1885, quoted a resident: 'The place is gradually becoming of smaller importance and population. In my early days Fotheringhay could boast of two respectable inns and a cattle and horse fair of considerable importance was held here. Now it has not a beer shop or house of entertainment where a belated traveller or visitor can rest or refresh himself with a glass of home brew.' Bede, suffused with a romantic Victorian's view of history, wrote that the history of the village 'was written in characters of blood. It would appear in every age to have brought its princely possessors a heritage of blood and misery.'

In the twentieth century the fortunes of the village would change radically, its history an asset rather than the curse Bede imagined. The castle ruins and the church would attract a steady stream of tourists interested in the stories of both Mary and Richard, and the church would gain many gifts from the Richard III Society, including a memorial stained-glass window. The beautiful wooden pulpit, said to be a gift from Edward IV himself, has been repainted in the brilliant colours beloved of the Middle Ages, and in the porch there is a charmingly smiley heraldic stone lion, recovered from a pub in Oundle, which is said to have come from the castle of Richard's day.

And in the twenty-first century the story of Richard would take a turn which would have astounded Bede.

Further reading

Bede, Cuthbert (1886) *Fotheringhay and Mary Queen of Scots*. Available online at http://archive.org/stream/fotheringhaymary00bederich/fotheringhaymary00bederich_djvu.txt (last accessed 17 November 2014).

Foard, G., and Curry, A. (2013). *Bosworth 1485: A Battlefield Rediscovered*. Oxford: Oxbow Books.

Foard, G. and Morris, R. (2012) *The Archaeology of English Battlefields: Conflict in the Pre-industrial Landscape*. York: Council for British Archaeology.

Fotheringhay in British History Online. Available online at http://www.british-history.ac.uk/report.aspx?compid=126242 (last accessed 17 November 2014).

Horrox, R. (1989) *Richard III: A Study of Service.* Cambridge: Cambridge University Press.

Matich, S. and Alexander, J. (2011) Creating and recreating the Yorkist tombs in Fotheringhay church (Northamptonshire). *Church Monuments* 26: 82–103.

Ross, Charles (1999) *Richard III*, 2nd edn, Yale University Press: New Haven CT.

6

THE COUSINS IN THE SWABS (TK, KS)

The Slow Reveal ...

From his office at the university, Kevin Schürer dialled the number of a woman he had sought across half the world and finally tracked down to south-west London. He spoke briefly to her, then handed his mobile phone to his guest. After a slightly awkward start, an intense conversation began. Schürer sat politely waiting for his phone to be returned. After 10 minutes he pulled over the pile of files on his desk and carried on with other work. After twenty minutes the Canadian-born furniture maker Michael Ibsen and the Australian-born researcher Wendy Duldig, were still deep in conversation.

Who is Related to Richard III?

The strangers had just learned something extraordinary: that Ibsen was Richard's nephew 16 times removed, and Duldig Richard's niece 18 times removed. Ibsen and Duldig were fourteenth cousins twice removed, and after 528 years, the closest traced relatives of Richard III.

In the spring of 1484 a 10-year-old boy, who had been ill for much of his short life, died at Middleham Castle in Yorkshire. When his parents learned the news, they shut themselves up in their rooms in faraway Nottingham Castle to grieve. Anne Neville, dead a year later, would have no more children. Edward Prince of Wales had been the only legitimate child of Richard III.

The Bones of a King: Richard III Rediscovered, First Edition. The Greyfriars Research Team with Maev Kennedy and Lin Foxhall.
© 2015 University of Leicester. Published 2015 by John Wiley & Sons, Ltd.

There are sketchy accounts of Richard having an illegitimate son and daughter, probably born before his marriage. There are no records of either having any children: John of Gloucester presumably continued the family tradition of rebelliousness, since he was executed by order of Henry VII in 1499, and Katherine Plantagenet seems to have died soon after her marriage to William Herbert, Earl of Huntingdon, in 1484, a year before Richard's death. When young Edward died, Richard's direct male line died with him. The attempt to trace an unbroken line of descent, from a close relative to somebody living in the twenty-first century who might be prepared to give a DNA sample, would depend upon looking among other branches of his family.

Millions of people across the world can claim distant kinship with Richard III. Turi King, the geneticist who led the DNA analysis and who would attempt to extract the DNA from the bones of 'Skeleton 1' from the car park, observed: "We are all related to Richard III. It's just a matter of degree."

Family history is a contemporary passion and hobby, but there is nothing new about tracing ancestors: it has always been crucial not just for family pride but for settling inheritance disputes. The descendants of the aristocracy and royalty have held a particular fascination for professional and amateur genealogists and historians poring through old records and registers. Elaborate family trees and copies of *Burke's Peerage* – founded in 1826, and boasting to be 'the definitive guide to the ancestry and heraldry of the Peerage, Baronetage, Knightage and Landed Gentry' – are to be found somewhere in every stately home.

DNA and the Identification of Richard

The ability to extract scientific evidence of biological relationship, by matching ancient and modern DNA, is comparatively recent. Without this evidence, some sceptics would never have accepted the identification of the Greyfriars bones, whatever the weight of historical and archaeological evidence. Indeed, Richard III is the oldest individual with whom scientists have been able to find a genetic match with a modern relative for identification purposes. And, had the discovery of his bones not occurred for another half century, the opportunity to make the match with a living female-line relative would have been lost forever, since after the present generation, it seems that the line will come to an end.

Some had suggested that even if the skeleton was of the right age and date, had a twisted spine, and was found in the exact location where historians had long claimed Richard was buried, it could easily be another man of the late fifteenth century. Schürer, a specialist in historical demography (the study of populations) calculated that given the total population of Richard's England and Wales of about 2.4 million, and the accepted male to female ratio suggesting somewhere under 1.2 million males, there were approximately 177,206 contemporary men in Richard's 25–34 year-old age range.

True, the skull from the car park displayed gaping war wounds, but the sceptics suggested the grave could even hold another victim of the Battle of Bosworth. Casualty figures for the battle vary wildly, but of perhaps 1,000 dead from among 17,000 who fought, Schürer calculated that a maximum of 400 men would have been in Richard's age range – those who fight and die in war tend to be younger than the king's 32 years. Statistically it was not at all likely that the body in the narrow grave just happened to be another casualty from the battlefield. Long before King's DNA work was complete, the Greyfriars team was persuaded of – if astounded by – the identity of their discovery: the outside world would take more convincing.

Tracing the Lines

To establish a genetic link between Richard III and a modern relative for purposes of comparison, it would be necessary to find individuals who were related to Richard through an unbroken male or an unbroken female line. This is because to demonstrate a match, specific types of genetic material that are inherited in a simple way from only one parent must be compared. Genetic analysis from any random relative where the lines crossed from male to female would not work, because if the lines were broken, no match could be found.

Schürer himself turned to *Burke's Peerage* to trace individuals related to Richard descended through the male line. He managed to identify and contact five living individuals, distant cousins of the current Duke of Beaufort, whose direct line of descent goes back to John Beaufort, Earl of Somerset, the son of John of Gaunt and Katherine Swynford – at the time of the birth Gaunt's mistress but later his wife – and on further to his and Richard's common ancestor, Edward III. (See Figure 5.3)

Men, especially rich men, are usually far easier to trace through history than women: the details of their lives are seen as more significant than the women whose lives are barely noted in the historical record, if at all, as births, marriages and deaths. However, establishing true paternity is much more uncertain. With very few exceptions – there was a royal scandal long after Richard's day when it was claimed a living baby was substituted for a stillborn boy by being smuggled in a bed-pan into the bed of Mary of Modena, wife of James II – it is quite clear who a child's mother is. The same is not true of fathers: there were contemporary accusations that several members of Richard's extended family were illegitimate, including his brother Edward. Schürer points out that one twentieth-century study, the National Survey of Sexual Attitudes and Lifestyles in the 1990s – which by strange coincidence Wendy Duldig had worked on as a researcher – found that 4.5 per cent of married men and 1.9 per cent of married women reported more than one sexual partner over the previous year: 'No reason to suggest that should be massively different historically,' he commented. So, although tracing through the female lineage is more difficult, it is more likely to be a true record of ancestry, and there is another advantage when it comes to DNA: mitochondrial DNA, inherited by all of a mother's children from the egg, but only passed on via her daughters through their eggs, is far more plentiful and easier to extract from ancient bones.

If a true line of descent could be confirmed, mitochondrial DNA offered the best chance of finding a match between Skeleton 1 in the car park and a living relative. Richard and his sisters would have shared their mother Cecily Neville's mitochondrial DNA, but Richard, being male, could not have passed it on. However, a living male or female, descended through an unbroken chain of daughters from one of Richard's sisters, would share his mitochondrial DNA.

Some nineteenth-century genealogists had made heroic efforts with Richard's lineage, including the Marquis of Ruvigny and Raineval, whose own ancestry was slightly more tangled than his splendid titles, and whose interest in royalty stretched to two periods as president of the

Legitimist Jacobite League of Great Britain and Ireland. In the many volumes of *The Plantagenet Roll of the Blood Royal*, Ruvigny set out to trace every descendant of Edward III, Richard's great-great-grandfather. He traced the line of Anne of York, Richard's sister, down as far as a Barbara Gough – one of many daughters called Barbara down the centuries – who married Isaac Spooner and died in 1826.

As far back as 2003 the historian John Ashdown-Hill was working on a project to identify remains thought to be those of Richard's sister Margaret. Margaret of York was only 8 when her father opened negotiations for her to marry Charles the Bold of Burgundy, and 20 when her brother Edward finally arranged the match with Charles, who was by then a widower. Her beautiful crown, enamelled with Yorkist white roses, survives in the treasury at Aachen, Germany. Margaret outlived all her brothers, became a patron of the arts and a considerable political operator as a widow, her interests including backing the claims of Perkin Warbeck that he was a true son, and therefore heir, of Edward IV. She died in 1503, and was buried in another Greyfriars church, this one at Mechelen in modern Belgium: the town bells are said to have tolled for 10 days mourning her. Like the Leicester Greyfriars, the church and its monuments were broken up in the religious wars of the sixteenth century.

Margaret had no children, so Ashdown-Hill set about tracing a female line of descent through one of her sisters. Her sister Elizabeth had many children, but the line died out. However, although Anne of York had only one surviving daughter, and died soon after she was born, that line does continue to this day. Ashdown-Hill bridged the gap from Ruvigny's work to the twenty-first century when he identified a living descendant of Anne in Joyce Ibsen.

Finding the Modern Relatives

Ibsen, known as Joy, was born in London in 1926, one of three children of Muriel Brown, and emigrated to Canada with her mother on the SS *Mauretania* in 1948. She worked as a journalist in Canada and married a fellow journalist Norm Ibsen. He recalled her astonishment and delight when Ashdown-Hill phoned in 2006 to reveal the news of her ancestry: 'it meant quite a bit to her, she was a monarchist', he told their local paper. She gave a DNA sample, but it turned out that none of the disturbed medieval bones found at the Mechelen church site matched. Margaret of York had not been found, and it looked like the end of the story – until six years later the hunt began for Richard himself.

Joy Ibsen died in 2008, but she left three children, Jeff, Leslie and Michael, who, because the DNA typing done on Joy was at low resolution, gave the new DNA sample to the Richard project to allow this project to start from scratch. This line ends with them: Leslie does not have any children.

Schürer thought it was essential for the project not just to check every line of Ibsen's claimed lineage but if possible to find a second lineage, a second line to a living descendant of one of Richard III's close maternal relatives who would have shared his mitochondrial DNA. His team of researchers identified the Duldig family, like the Ibsens descended from Richard's sister Anne. As it turned out, Wendy Duldig's family had emigrated to New Zealand in the 1870s, and she was born in Australia, but she was finally tracked down living in south-west London, a few miles from Ibsen's Islington furniture workshop. Like the Ibsen siblings, the line stopped with her: she has a half-sister from her father's first marriage (who would not, of course, share Richard III's or her mitochondrial DNA) no other siblings, and no children.

Although the public knew of Michael Ibsen from the earliest days of the project, Duldig's lineage was not confirmed until some weeks later, and her name was still not publicly identified until a photograph by Carl Vivian of the two distant cousins standing by a bed of white roses was included in the new visitor centre in Leicester. The photograph is the very last exhibit, and most visitors, hastening towards a welcome cup of tea in the cafe, walk straight past it. At one point, when she remained an anonymous descendant, Duldig and Ibsen stood together at a function in Leicester listening to their neighbours speculate on who might be the descendant through the second lineage: they had to stop themselves from laughing out loud. (Plate 18)

Duldig first learned of her possible connection with Richard through an email from Schürer that was forwarded by a puzzled former work colleague who had at first assumed it was spam but then decided it sounded intriguing enough to send on. King then phoned to invite her to give a DNA sample, and both recall the conversation as slightly surreal. 'I'm a researcher myself, it's what I do – I had to be sure that there was real research being done, and that I could make a real contribution to it', Duldig said.

'I think I had to convince her that I wasn't some complete nutter phoning out of the blue, and that there really was a legitimate scientific reason why a DNA sample from her could be so valuable', King recalled. King, a Canadian geneticist at Leicester University, first trained in archaeology in Canada and at Cambridge and so was ideal to tackle the project. Also, and unknown to Richard Buckley when he invited her to join the team – 'he assured me that there was only the most remote chance my services would ever be needed, because obviously they weren't going to find Richard', King remembered – she had for years been interested in Richard III. When she had first come to England, her aunt, an ardent Ricardian, had taken her to Bosworth and told her the whole story of the last Plantagenet. She had also given her Josephine Tey's 1951 novel, *The Daughter of Time*. The book, in which a modern police officer investigates the life of Richard III, and concludes that he was innocent of the murder of the princes in the Tower, was credited as part of the revival of popular interest in Richard in the twentieth century.

As King settled to live, work and rear her young family in Leicestershire, she was struck by how many reminders of Richard she encountered in daily life. Although she had a mass of other work on her lab bench, the opportunity to join the project, she said, was 'a no brainer'.

She used the same method she had already used on her research on English surnames to collect the Y-chromosome samples from the male relatives Schürer had identified, sending them out swab packs which they returned through the post. Schürer and King had worked together previously as part of her PhD, having met over 10 years earlier when King asked Schürer for information on historical surname distributions. King gave Schürer a sample pack to give to Wendy, which he gave to her personally as they poured over her family tree in the British Library in December 2012. However, King took the DNA sample from Ibsen herself, when they met standing in the car park in Leicester in August 2012, at the launch of the project on the day before the digging started. She told him that since it was most unlikely his DNA would ever be needed to identify a king, she would run a Y-chromosome test which could reveal information about his male-line ancestry as a sort of consolation prize.

On 4 September she helped Appleby and Morris begin the job of uncovering the bones in the narrow grave, but the following day had to attend a conference. When she arrived in Innsbruck for the conference she texted Jo to find out how the excavation was going. She was stunned when a text came back from Appleby with the news of the twisted spine and the skull with the gaping war wounds: 'I missed the whole darn thing'. Over the following week, until the press conference on 12 September, she had to keep the news quiet, not even telling her children – who, in any case, were now thoroughly bored with the subject of Richard III – or her partner. When the news broke, friends and some colleagues helpfully reminded her that the search for the ancient DNA meant her career was on the line as she would never have a higher profile case to deal with.

In fact King already had experience of the intense media interest and passionate, even disturbing, public reaction which her science could spark. Her doctoral work, on the previously unguessed African ancestry of a group of English men who shared the same surname, also became front page news in the UK, which had in turn provoked racist abuse. Her work on the genetic legacy of the Vikings in England had formed part of two of the historian Michael Wood's, television series.

After the announcement on 12 September of the discovery of human remains and the twisted spine, her work and mobile phones began to ring off the hook. In order to be able do any work, after a while she only answered calls from numbers she recognised: 'I didn't need friends to tell me my job was on the line with this one. I knew I would have to double check and then double double check again, because every single thing I did would be examined and challenged.' What was more, she was clear about the key question: 'My first job was going to be to answer the question "is it a boy?". He was quite a gracile chap, and while Jo's analysis of the remains suggested these were the remains of a male, we could confirm it using DNA, if DNA could even be retrieved from the skeleton. I had no idea going into this whether it was going to be possible. Conditions in the car park were far from ideal. DNA preservation is best under cold, dry, conditions, whereas the Leicestershire clay was damp and fluctuating in temperature.'

The modern samples were relatively simple, she could carry out the tests in her own genetics laboratory at Leicester, but for the ancient DNA, with the crucial importance of protecting the samples from contamination and the difficulty of extracting it, she needed to find two separate specialist laboratories where she could carry out identical tests, and hopefully produce identical results.

The Initial DNA Results

DNA sequencing was carried out in two stages. In the first stage, completed before the February 2013 press conference, analysis focused on two elements: (i) determining the sex of Skeleton 1 using genetic markers and (ii) analysing the 'control region' highly variable section of the mitochondrial DNA in all three DNA donors – two living people and one long-dead individual. The amplification of fragments of DNA in the skeleton indicated the presence of a Y-chromosome, confirming the results of Appleby's examination of the skeletal features, to demonstrate definitively that this was a male individual.

The latter investigations of the 'control region' would give relatively speedy preliminary results to indicate whether further, more detailed, genetic testing was warranted. If the Ibsen and Duldig genealogies had been wrong or flawed, this analysis would have shown that the mitochondrial DNA (mtDNA) of the two modern maternal-line relatives did not match each other. If neither of these two modern individuals were related to Skeleton 1 down the female line that would also have resulted in a mismatch between the ancient and the modern DNA samples. The methodology had to be rigorous and meticulous in order to reduce or eliminate the possibility of error or sample contamination which would invalidate the analyses.

To be as certain as possible of the results, duplicate sequences were analysed for each modern individual, Ibsen and Duldig. Not only did the duplicates match up exactly within each individual, but Ibsen's and Duldig's samples match each other perfectly, indicating that the two of them must be related via the female line.

Working in two separate ancient DNA laboratories, in York and Toulouse, and using a well-established methodology for profiling degraded DNA in forensics, King analysed three hypervariable sections of the mtDNA control region of Skeleton 1. As with the radiocarbon dating (see Chapter 4), for which two separate labs performing independent analyses were also used, this strengthens the validity of the analyses. If both come up with the same results, it is unlikely that individual lab practices or conditions have produced errors.

Skeleton 1 was a perfect match with Ibsen, consistent with all three individuals being matrilineal relatives over many generations. King was in the ancient DNA laboratory in Toulouse in December, working with Patricia Balaresque and Laure Tonasso, when these initial results came in, showing the perfect match between Ibsen's DNA and that from Richard's bones. 'I did get up and do a little "oh my God!" dance', she recalls. However, she still had a lot of work to do to be certain and so she tried not to be too excited. 'To have been interested in Richard for so long, for 20 years, and then … I went "Wow, we found him". I still think it's amazing. It has been one of the most stressful things I have ever worked on, but unquestionably, the most interesting.' (Plate 19)

Checking the Lines

Before King made any attempt to work on the DNA, the claimed lineage had to be scrupulously checked. (See Figure 5.3)

Although the genealogies stretching down the centuries looked convincing, particularly the four volumes on Yorkshire families compiled in the nineteenth century by Joseph Foster and Ruvigny's epic publications, they contained little if any supporting evidence. They were based heavily on visitation records; these are documents compiled in the sixteenth and seventeenth centuries by researchers who checked both the social status and the right to bear arms of the county families. The original written records and notes of the visitors are lodged in the College of Arms in London.

Schürer set out to double check every single line and link of the claimed Ibsen pedigree, and to repeat the process when the second line of descent to another living carrier of Cecily Neville's mitochondrial DNA was identified. He contacted friends and colleagues in the genealogy world and recruited two independent experts: David Annal, former principal family history specialist at the family records centre in The National Archives, who set about burrowing through wills and other documents in the Archives and at the British Library; and Morris Bierbrier, a fellow of the Society of Genealogists specialising in royal lineage, who had access to the mass of material in the Society's library.

All the detective work paid dividends, not just confirming the line of descent but also turning up a wealth of information that lay behind the bare list of names and dates: many fascinating historical links emerged, and the exact day one daughter was born was finally confirmed by an entry in her father's diary.

The second lineage was indeed traced, and when the trail seemed to lead to New Zealand, Schürer brought in Bob Matthews, as only New Zealand citizens or registered researchers have easy access to the contemporary records there. Their work identified Wendy Duldig. Like Ibsen she was descended from Anne of York and Anne St Leger, through Anne of York's granddaughter Catherine Manners. Catherine married Robert Constable, a soldier who did well out of fighting against the Scots for Henry VIII, and became a Member of Parliament and the Sheriff of Yorkshire. Among their 11 children were Michael Ibsen's 12 times great-grandmother Barbara, and her sister Everhilda, Wendy Duldig's ancestor. Barbara married Sir William Babthorpe, a county landowner who was suspected of Roman Catholic sympathies and attempted to prove his loyalty to Elizabeth I by also taking up arms against the Scots, helping suppress the 1569 rebellion in favour of her cousin Mary Queen of Scots. Nonetheless, the suspicions about his true faith were almost certainly correct since their daughter Margaret was a devout Catholic, though she and her husband later converted to Protestantism.

Politics – and political dissent – weave in and out of the story of the two lineages for generations. Barbara Belasyse, daughter of Barbara Cholmley and Thomas Belasyse, Viscount Fauconberg, an ardent royalist in the Civil War, married an equally ardent royalist in Henry Slingsby who fought in the Battle of Naseby in 1645 was beheaded in 1658. Two generations further on, Barbara Talbot, who lived to be 98, had seven children; one of them, Barbara Yelverton, married Reynolds Calthorpe, a Whig Member of Parliament and High Sheriff of Suffolk.

From the early nineteenth century there is a charming portrait of yet another Barbara. This one married the anti-slavery campaigner William Wilberforce, though it was through her sister Ann that the Ibsen line continued. Ann's son Edward, whose father was Edward Vansittart-Neale, the rector of Taplow in Buckinghamshire, became a pioneer of education for working-class men, and one of the founders of the Co-Operative Society.

Among Duldig's ancestors, the wealthy brewer Sir Benjamin Truman commissioned the eighteenth-century artist William Gainsborough, one of the most admired and expensive of society portraitists, to create a whole group of family portraits, including full-length paintings of his two granddaughters, Frances and Henrietta Read. When Frances posed for Gainsborough, stately in a superb sky-blue, white-silk and silver-lace masquerade gown, she had recently made a match that may not have pleased her grandfather: she married William Villebois, her French dancing master. However, the marriage did result in the birth of two sons, John and Henry, who so delighted their great-grandfather that he also commissioned a particularly charming portrait of the two little boys playing at building card houses. Frances was Duldig's great-great-great-great-great-grandmother. Her portrait has long since passed out of the family and been hung on several aristocratic walls, including a Rothschild mansion and Cowdray Park in West Sussex. It was sold at auction in 2011 for £6,500,000.

Duldig's ancestors emigrated to New Zealand in 1873, and her great-grandparents' meeting was a romantic family tale. The Lysaght daughters, children of her great-great-grandmother Frances Gardiner and James Lysaght, befriended the sons of the Moore family on the long voyage on board the ship *Crusader*. The result was two marriages, including that of her great-grandmother Sophia Lysaght to Francis Moore.

The young couple first tried farming in the windswept Chatham Islands, where her grandmother Marjorie was born in the family homestead, before settling as landowners and sheep farmers at Taranaki back on the North Island. Her mother, Gabrielle, was born in Wellington, but after Duldig's grandparents divorced, her grandmother brought the nine-year-old girl to London, just a few years before Joy Brown's mother took her across the Atlantic to Canada. They were dauntless women, Duldig says.

Her grandmother supported the family by running a bed and breakfast in Hampstead, doing well enough to encourage her daughter's exceptional promise as a pianist and singer: she studied at the Royal Academy of Music, celebrating her twenty-first birthday in the Royal Albert Hall. In her twenties she returned to New Zealand, and then moved to Australia, where she taught music, married an accountant, Milton Duldig, and gave birth to her daughter, Wendy, before they moved again to London. Duldig herself has repeated the family's pattern of travel, working as a social policy researcher in New Zealand, Australia and England, which was partly why Schürer's researchers found it so hard to track her down.

Cousins in the Swabs

Duldig knew only scraps of her family history, from the anecdotes of her mother and aunt Josephine: they assured her that she was descended from the victor of Bosworth, Henry VII – but through the Moores, her great-grandfather's family, a lineage through the male line that Schürer has also checked and confirmed. Like Michael Ibsen, she only learned the results of the DNA test on the eve of its announcement to the world, when the newfound cousins spoke for the first time on Schürer's phone. 'When Kevin told me the results,' Duldig said, 'I thought immediately that Mum and my aunt, had they been alive, would have been giddy with excitement at the news in the most innocent and joyful way.'

Knowing his strong-minded sister, mother and forceful grand-mother, the woman who had decided to take her family to Canada from the bleakness of postwar London, he was not surprised to learn that he, too, came of a line of formidable women. When he heard the news, he thought of his female relatives, of his mother and sister and their shared passion for horses, and it struck him how many fine animals must have been owned and ridden by his female ancestors. Though they both loved horses, it was his sister for whom they had become a vocation; his equally motivated mother had pursued a writing career, beginning by working as a secretary in a newspaper office in Canada until her talent was spotted and she carved out a successful life as a journalist, eventually writing for the same paper in London, Ontario as her journalist husband, Norman Ibsen.

The irony of the discovery in Leicester, Ibsen said, was that his mother had been proud of her British ancestry and very interested in her family background, and so had done a considerable amount of genealogical research herself. 'She had it all in a great book, tracing the line on the paternal side right back to the fourteenth century, and turning up some very interesting people.' The Ibsen line went back to

Scandinavian sheep farmers, but his distant Brown cousins included the prime ministers William Pitt the Elder and Pitt the Younger, and a former High Commissioner of Southern Africa and fellow of the Royal Society, Sir Bartle Frere, who is buried in St Paul's Cathedral and commemorated by a statue on the Thames Embankment and a mountain in Queensland, Mount Bartle Frere. 'She did have a look at the female line,' Ibsen recalled, 'but she only went back a few generations. She just didn't think they were likely to be very interesting.' The Christmas after she learned from Ashdown-Hill that the women were in fact extremely interesting, her amused and impressed family made her a little crown to wear at dinner.

Ibsen came to London in his first career as a classical musician, a freelance orchestral French horn player, before turning to cabinetmaking in the 1980s after helping a friend work on a chapel conversion. He did not think that the search for Richard's remains was remotely likely to succeed, but he agreed to come to Leicester for the launch of the project in August 2012. He was standing quietly watching everything going on in the car park, when King came over to introduce herself as a fellow Canadian and ask if she could have a DNA sample from him: 'I didn't mind', he said. 'It might have been different if I'd had children, but I knew the line stopped with me. And it made no difference to me: what was she going to do, clone me? But she was overheard, and suddenly, whoosh, there were about 10 camera crews around us, and that was really when I first realised the extent of the public interest there could be in this.'

He was working on a site in Hampstead when King phoned to tell him of the discovery of the human remains, the startling possibility that they really had found Richard, and that the sample he had given so casually could be crucial. He was so astonished he dropped his screwdriver: anyone who has seen his immaculate workshop will understand how unusual this was.

Since the September 2012 press conference, it has never stopped. His workplace is not easy to find, hidden away in a warren of craft workshops behind a quiet side road in north London. To his amazement, and the hilarity of his fellow workers, there has been a constant procession of journalists from all over the world to his door. Whenever he visits Leicester he is recognised and stopped in the street by strangers. Although he is by nature a quiet, reserved man, he says he is touched by their interest and enthusiasm, and happy to speak.

Duldig has been taken by surprise by an intense feeling of a personal connection: 'It's as if I have discovered some long-lost relative, such as a great-grandfather, that I would love to have known. I am grateful that he is going to be buried in Leicester because I know the approach they are taking is very dignified and very honourable. If this was a member of your family, that is what you would want for them.'

Although Ibsen was fascinated by the whole research process, he said it all felt quite remote from him until early on the morning of 4 February 2013, before the mayhem of the press conference which announced the identification to the world. King brought him into the quiet room where Richard's bones were laid out on a black velvet cloth, alone apart from a security guard. 'It was a haunting moment, overwhelming. I looked at the bones, inches away from me, with their terrible, terrible injuries, and suddenly there was the real man, a fifteenth-century king of England. I felt, really for the first time, "I am related to this man, I share his mitochondrial DNA, there is a part of him that is a part of me." It was a profoundly moving moment, and I shall never forget it.'

The Final DNA Results

King had always made it clear, even before the initial DNA results were announced at the press conference in February 2013, that these were only preliminary findings and that far more work remained to be done. She, like the rest of the team, had also consistently maintained that DNA was not the touchstone that would secure the identification of Skeleton 1 as Richard III but was one line of evidence among many. Indeed, many archaeologists long remained sceptical of the preliminary genetic results presented at the press conference because they had not yet been published in a peer-reviewed journal, and because there lingered a widespread belief, even among academics, that somehow the DNA offered 'more secure' or 'more valid' proof of identity.

King immediately set to completing and publishing the rest of the genetic analysis. She managed to secure funding from both the Wellcome Trust and the Leverhulme Trust to support this intensive research, which took an additional 22 months to reach publication, in December 2014. Further work on Richard III's full genome is underway, with more scientific publications to follow.

For these extended DNA analyses, two full mitochondrial sequences were produced for each of the modern donors, Ibsen and Duldig. Simultaneously, a whole-genome sequence of the mitochondrial DNA of Skeleton 1 was painstakingly assembled from the fragmented DNA preserved in the archaeological samples from the teeth and femur. As previously, this was done in labs in Leicester and York and Toulouse, working with eminent ancient DNA expert, Michael Hofreiter and his post-doc, Gloria Gonzales Fortes, and the team in Toulouse.

The results strongly confirmed the preliminary findings: Skeleton 1 was an exact match with Ibsen and differed from Duldig in only one single base. This is again consistent with a matrilineal relationship shared among all three of these individuals. To check the possibility that this very close mitochondrial DNA match was not a chance coincidence, the observed sequences were checked against a highly respected European database of 21,176 mtDNA complete control sequences and a smaller, lower-resolution database of 1,832 mtDNA samples from the British Isles covering only limited positions in the mtDNA sequence. No matches were found with the Ibsen/Duldig/Skeleton 1 type, suggesting that it is a very rare haplotype, and that the possibility of a match occurring by chance was very small indeed.

In contrast with these results, when the fragmented Y-chromosome DNA of Skeleton 1 was amplified and sequenced, it did not match with DNA samples donated by five patrilineal relatives of Richard III descended from the fifth Duke of Beaufort (1744–1803), who ought, according to the published genealogies, to have shared the same Y-chromosome haplotype as Richard III (see Figure 6.1, and Appendix 2). Although four of the modern relatives matched with each other, one of them did not. And, none were the same Y-chromosome haplotype as Skeleton 1. This is almost certainly because of false-paternity events somewhere in the male line, at least one of which occurred after the time of Richard III as indicated by the fact that one of the five modern samples did not match the other four.

In addition, the DNA sequencing gave an indication of Skeleton 1's hair and eye colour: there is a 96 per cent probability that he had blue eyes and a 77 per cent probability that he had blonde hair, though it may have remained blonde only in childhood (see Chapter 7).

These results of the DNA sequencing were also the subject of a broader statistical analysis of the probability that Skeleton 1 was, or

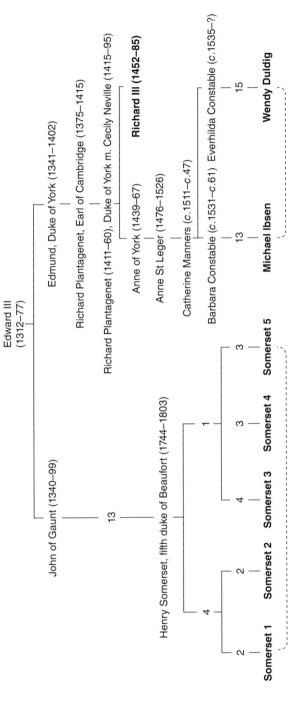

Figure 6.1 Genealogical links between Richard III and modern-day relatives who participated in the project.
Source: Adapted from King *et al.* 2014: 3, fig. 1.

was not, to be identified with Richard III. This analysis, carried out with Mark Thomas and David Balding at UCL, also factored in the non-genetic data, including the radiocarbon dating, the estimated age at death, sex, presence of scoliosis, and the presence of the perimortem traumas. The results suggest that the probability that Skeleton 1 is Richard III is somewhere between 99.9994 and 99.99999 per cent, clearly 'beyond reasonable doubt'.

Further reading

King, T.E., Gonzalez Fortes, G., Balaresque, P. *et al.* (2014) Identification of the remains of King Richard III. *Nature Communications* 5 (5631): 1–8. Available online at http://www.nature.com/ncomms/2014/141202/ncomms6631/abs/ncomms6631.html (last accessed 8 December 2014).

7

WHAT DID RICHARD LOOK LIKE?

Imagine ...

The host flung open the door and led his guest into the room in which he took most pride: his long gallery. Secretly the visitor preferred the silvery stone and cool, dim interiors of the old house, but the new brick mansion with the modish acres of expensive glass was undeniably impressive, and at his first, startled, glance the gallery seemed to stretch to the far horizon.

'Walk with me and see my pictures', his host invited. They strolled past the portraits of remarkably plain family and ancestors, and stopped at a more interesting face, a pale, narrow-featured man, wearing a magnificent golden collar and a velvet gown in the antique style.

'Your grandfather?' the guest hazarded.

'No indeed,' his offended host snapped, 'surely you know the likeness of Richard Crookback?'

Representing Richard

Portraits of that pale man hung on the walls of many great houses in the late sixteenth and seventeenth centuries. When the rich adopted the fashion for long, narrow picture galleries, spaces which provided both an indoor exercise area and an opportunity for a display of opulent good taste, their walls were often hung with processions of portraits of the kings and queens of England turned out in multiple copies by specialist workshops. And whatever the politics of the household, Richard

The Bones of a King: Richard III Rediscovered, First Edition. The Greyfriars Research Team with Maev Kennedy and Lin Foxhall.
© 2015 University of Leicester. Published 2015 by John Wiley & Sons, Ltd.

took his place among these crowned heads. Many such portraits survive: one dating from the late sixteenth century and now in the collection of the National Portrait Gallery is believed to come from such a set. But would anyone who knew the man in life recognise him from these copies of copies, painted years or even centuries after his death?

What did Richard really look like? The evidence from his DNA suggests a strong probability that he was blue eyed and fair, like his brother Edward, startlingly unlike the swarthy villain of so many later images. Was he the scuttling, twisted figure of so many films and stage productions or a slight, handsome man, his deformed back completely hidden under a well-tailored, lined and padded jacket, a man strong enough to have been a redoubtable soldier into the last minutes of his life on the battlefield?

Shakespeare, looking back across more than a century through the fog of Tudor monarchy, created one of his most unforgettable characters, but made him a monster. Richard, in the first lines of the play, describes himself as 'curtailed of this fair proportion, cheated of feature by dissembling nature, deformed, unfinished, sent before my time into this breathing world scarce half made up – and that so lamely and unfashionable that dogs bark at me as I halt by them'.

Descriptions of Richard in Life (sk, mal)

There are only tantalising scraps of eyewitness description to set against these enigmatic portraits, even though so many literate people, family and friends, commoners and courtiers, visiting dignitaries and mortal enemies, met Richard.

The eighteenth-century author and collector Horace Walpole attributes an enchanting description of him to the ancient Katherine, Countess of Desmond. She 'had danced with Richard,' he wrote in his *Historic Doubts on the Life and Reign of King Richard the Third*, and 'declared that he was the handsomest man in the room except his brother Edward, and was very well made'. Since Katherine was claimed to have lived to the age of 140, dying in 1604, she could certainly have danced with generations of Plantagenets, but Walpole was writing almost 300 years after Richard's death, and he was notoriously unable to resist colourful anecdotes or claimed memorabilia of medieval royalty.

Sarah Knight and Mary Ann Lund, experts in literature and historical sources who have studied all the earliest portrayals of Richard, have traced how the descriptions in contemporary or slightly later accounts of a slight but in no way grotesque man – 'comely enough', George Buck wrote, almost 130 years after his death – gradually evolve into Shakespeare's monster.

Nicholas von Poppelau, a nobleman from Silesia – part of modern Poland – definitely met Richard, at court in 1484, and evidently the two men got on well, dining and conversing at length. Nicholas's diary survives only in an eighteenth-century German translation, though it may originally have been written in Latin. He said that the king was 'three fingers taller' than he was himself, although frustratingly there is no portrait of Poppelau to give the measure of this. He was clearly impressed by the king's personality but struck by his physical appearance. There is no withered arm, hunchback or even a raised shoulder in his description. He wrote that Richard was 'a little slimmer and not as bulky as him, also very much more lean; he had very fine-boned arms and legs, also a great heart'.

In the Rous Roll, written during Richard's lifetime and illustrated, like the Salisbury Roll (Plate 20), with charming, though clearly non-portrait, images, John Rous, the clergyman and historian who spent most of his life in or near Warwick and certainly knew the king, describes a good and just ruler. However, his more famous account, his *Historia Regum Angliae*, a history of the kings of England, was written after Richard's death between 1485 and 1491, the year of his own death. It is clearly a propagandist account, written in the wake of regime change, and is probably the origin of all the monstrous later descriptions of Richard. In it, Rous wrote that the king was 'retained within his mother's womb for two years ... emerging with teeth and hair to his shoulders. He was small of stature, with a short face and unequal shoulders, the right higher and the left lower.' The baby born after the long gestation, who came into the world with teeth and long hair, Rous intimates, is not just strange looking but malign, cursed from birth. Later in his history he compares him to the Antichrist. In both accounts, Richard's supposedly abnormal gestation period emphasises his freakish nature in Shakespeare and Rous, even though it is too long in one case and too short in the other.

Later writers, including Polydore Vergil, who never met Richard and whose history of England was commissioned by Henry VII, stress the physical to suggest moral deformity. Rous's 'unequal shoulders' become much more prominent and grotesque. Vergil called him 'lyttle of stature, deformyd of body, thone showlder being higher than thother, a short and sowre cowntenance, which semyd to savor of mischief and utter evydently craft and deceyt'. Sir Thomas More's unfinished *History of Richard III* was written around 1513 and 1518. He also called him 'little of stature' and added that he was 'ill fetured of limmes, croke backed, his left shoulder much higher than his right, hard favoured of visage ... he came into the worlde with the feete forwarde and also not untothed.' More also gave Richard the withered arm. He writes of Richard accusing witchcraft for his condition – and blaming it on his sister-in-law Elizabeth Woodville: 'And therewith he plucked up his doublet sleeve to his elbow upon his left arm, where he showed a werish withered arm and small'. More adds acidly that nobody believed a word of the accusation because they knew he had always had the disability: 'no man was there present but wel knew that his arme was ever such since his birth'. It took 500 years to disprove More: the evidence of the bones was clear: there was no witchcraft and no withered arm either.

The historian George Buck, a descendant of a comrade-in-arms of Richard's, began his history of the king much later, in 1619, but used contemporary oral accounts, including that of John Stow, a sixteenth-century chronicler and historian best known for his 1603 *Survey of London*. He charmingly insisted that Stow 'could not flatter and speak dishonestly ... a man very diligent and much inquisitive to uncover all things concerning the affairs or words or persons of princes'. The supposedly trustworthy Stow, Buck wrote, had 'spoken with some ancient men, who from their owne sight and knowledge affirmed he was of bodily shape comely enough, onely of low stature, which is all the deformity they proportion so monstrously'.

Contemporaries who knew both men must have been struck by the contrast between Richard and his brother Edward IV. Edward stood well over six feet tall. When the antiquaries who found Edward's remains in 1789 in St George's Chapel in Windsor stretched out his bones and measured them, they estimated his height at just over 6 ft 3 in – he would have towered over his brother. Like Henry VIII after him,

Edward was accused by critics of overindulging in all the pleasures of life, and apparently he grew very fat in later years, which some even suggested caused his death. In the companion portraits of Edward and Richard in the Society of Antiquaries collection, though painted after both men were dead, Edward does indeed have a much larger head, and the beginnings of a double chin. Indeed Polydore Vergil claims that Richard persuaded Cambridge-educated cleric Ralph Shaw to give a sermon reinforcing his claim to the throne making use of this striking contrast. Shaw pointed out that while Richard and his father, Richard of York, were small men, both of whom had a short face with compact features, Edward was 'great in stature' with a big head – 'a generous sized face'. For anyone who had missed the suggestions, first made in Edward's lifetime, that he was illegitimate, Shaw nailed the point: 'no man could doubt that Richard was the true son of the Duke'.

Like Stow, many of the early writers comment on how slight Richard was, which some but not all used to suggest moral weakness as well.

Buck cites a speech made before Richard by Archibald Whitelaw, a humanist scholar who had come to his court in 1484 as ambassador from the king of Scotland. Whitelaw, of course, was out to please, so clearly referring to the king's stature to his face was not necessarily an insult. 'Never has so much spirit or greater virtue reigned in such a small body', he told Richard, going on to compare him to a warrior hero Tydeus from the much imitated and reproduced poem *Thebaid* by the Roman author Statius, which would have been known to his educated medieval audience. Tydeus' reputation for valour, though he was as slight as Richard, had endured for 1,400 years, Whitelaw was reminding his listeners.

Richard's face must have struck contemporaries as unusual but not unattractive: all the early writers mention it. Rous says he had 'a short face'. More called him 'hard favoured of visage'. Raphael Holinshed (heavily influenced by Polydore Vergil), in his *Chronicles* (first published in 1577, and a major source for Shakespeare for tales of Richard and many other historical figures), wrote, 'his face was small, but his countenance cruell, and such that at the first aspect a man would judge it to savour and smell of malice, fraud and deceit'. Whitelaw, still working hard to charm, declared, 'Now I look for the first time upon your face, it is the countenance worthy of the highest power and kingliness, illuminated by moral and heroic virtue'.

Many of the portraits of Richard show him twiddling a ring on his finger. In the paintings in the Royal Collection (Plate 21) and National Portrait Gallery he is turning a ring on the little finger of his right hand, in the Society of Antiquaries' portrait (Plate 22), slipping one onto his ring finger. Such gestures were common motifs in medieval and Tudor art, often intended to suggest a betrothal or marriage portrait. However, there are accounts that suggest that Richard was noticeably fidgety and twitchy. Polydore Vergil, as ever, uses this to suggest moral failing, remarking that 'he used constantly to chew his lower lip as if the savage nature in that tiny body was raging against itself'. Holinshed pushed this even further: Richard, he said, 'would bite and chaw busilie his nether lip; as who said that his fierce nature in his cruell bodie alwaies chafed, stirred, and was ever unquiet'.

By late Tudor times, the slight man with the uneven shoulders had become Richard Crookback, crooked in body and mind. The hunchback arrives with Shakespeare in the 1590s. In his *Richard III*, the queen, Elizabeth Woodville, savagely describes Richard as 'that foule hunch-backt toade'. In the earliest text of the play, her insult is 'bunch-backt', but it is 'hunch-backed' in all later versions. Shakespeare's vision of the king, and the word itself, stuck: the *Oxford English Dictionary* cites the play as the earliest use of the term 'hunch back'. However, when the skeleton was found, it graphically demonstrated that Richard suffered from severe scoliosis, a spiral twist in the spine, but there was no trace of kyphosis, where the spine bends forward: ironically, the man for whom the term was coined had no hunch.

Knight and Lund suggest that instead of heaping on fresh insult, Shakespeare may have misunderstood the earlier 'crook back' descriptions – a vivid but accurate description of scoliosis – as implying that he had a hump back. It was Shakespeare's description which stuck.

Portraits of a Long Dead King

Though George Buck was able to write, 'I myself have seen sundry pictures of this king and observed his warlike face', there is no known existing portrait of Richard painted from life. There are sketches in several manuscripts, including the Rous Roll, that were made during his lifetime, but they are clearly not portraits. However, Frederick Hepburn, an expert on Plantagenet and Tudor portraits, has made a particular study of the many paintings of him that survive from the sixteenth and early seventeenth centuries. The majority of such pictures, of which some two dozen are known today, are 'long gallery' portraits painted in the years between about 1590 and 1620. However, it seems that their ultimate source was a portrait in the Royal Collection (Plate 21). This has been dated using dendrochronology, from the tree rings in the oak panel on which it is painted, to between 1504 and 1520. Because of its relatively large size it is likely to date from towards the end of this time frame, but it was first recorded in 1542 in the inventory of the possessions of Henry VIII.

Although the man in the painting looks like a tough customer, he is clearly noble, dignified, and far from Shakespeare's monster. He is portrayed as a pale, strong featured, thin-lipped man, looking towards the right of the painting through narrowed eyes – probably originally towards a lost portrait of his wife. He is sumptuously dressed in a fur-lined black velvet gown, with a jewel in his cap and a jewelled collar. He has several rings on his right hand, including one which he is ostentatiously placing onto his little finger.

In *The English Face*, his classic study of the English portrait tradition, the late David Piper, a former director of the National Portrait Gallery, sees the origin of true portraits of English kings, rather than idealised images of monarchy, in new techniques of humanist realistic portraiture coming into England from the Continent in the late fourteenth and fifteenth centuries, and it is recorded that there were Flemish craftsmen, including weavers, metalworkers, glaziers and painters, working in fifteenth-century Southwark. Hepburn argues that for most people what the king really looked like was unimportant. They needed to know no more than the stylised images of crowned men, barely distinguishable one from another, that are shown on coins from successive reigns. However sometimes a true likeness was essential, as with funeral effigies, and in a few cases these can be compared with paintings to check how realistic they are as portraits.

The bodies of dead monarchs were on view before their funerals and were carried in procession with the face uncovered so that onlookers would know that reports of the death were true. Piper traces the development of realistic effigies displayed instead of the corpse to the period when royal funeral rites became more long drawn out and elaborate, so that displaying the real decaying body was impossible.

The comparison is impossible with Richard, but there are surviving portraits of Henry VII in life and death. A painted portrait made during his life, a gilt bronze effigy from his tomb, and a funeral effigy with a startlingly realistic plaster face which is actually a death mask – now kept in the museum at Westminster Abbey – are among the surviving images. Although the tomb figure is idealised, and the funeral effigy brutally realistic, there is a clear close resemblance between the three-dimensional images and the high-cheek-boned face in the painting.

Are the Later Paintings Based on a Lost Original?

The oldest surviving portraits of Richard were made when he was already lying in his narrow grave. There would have been no effigy made for the hurried burial after his battered body was exposed in Leicester, the face carefully left unmutilated so that he remained recognisable.

It has been suggested above that the Royal Collection portrait (Plate 21) was the crucial source painting on which the later 'long gallery' images were based. This portrait is in itself remarkably authentic in terms of the king's clothing and jewellery, and in the gilt spandrels (the triangles between the arch and the edge of the picture) in the upper corners are tiny profile heads of the Roman emperor Constantine and his mother St Helena – appropriate role models for a would-be crusader king. The chances are that this portrait is essentially a faithful copy of a lost contemporary original. At the same time though there are indications that the portrait was altered soon after it was made, possibly by the same artist. The line of Richard's right shoulder was raised by adding a piece to the magnificent gold collar. The overpainting has now thinned, so that the original line of the shoulder can just be made out. Although it is less clear, Hepburn also believes the lips may have been made thinner and the eyes narrowed, giving him a more grim expression.

Hepburn has suggested, in an essay for the Richard III Society, that these changes were not necessarily an example of Tudor black propaganda. The unknown artist may have painted an accurate copy of the lost original 'and was then asked presumably by someone in authority over him, to make some changes to it'. He believes that the original lost portrait probably flattered the living king by concealing the uneven shoulders.

The portrait owned by the Society of Antiquaries of London (Plate 22), which, based on her DNA work, Turi King believes is probably closest to his appearance in life, may be a little older than the one in the Royal Collection, but was still made at least 25 years after Richard's death. It too shows a long, pale, sharp-featured face, the eyes gazing this time towards our left, where the companion painting of his brother Edward IV would have hung. The narrow hands are twisting a ring on his wedding finger. The eyes are grey-blue, and the hair the light brown to which childhood blonde commonly darkens. The perspective is slightly awkward, but the shoulders do not appear uneven or in any way unusual, though it is hard to tell beneath his red velvet tunic, and cloth-of-gold cape – identical to the one the artist has given his brother – and, again, as in the portrait from the Royal Collection, a magnificent jewelled collar. Hepburn persuasively argues that it, too, was later altered to give Richard a thinner mouth and a more jutting, set jaw – changes reversed in conservation work undertaken in 2007.

When the Society of Antiquaries portrait was shown in an exhibition on Richard at the National Portrait Gallery in 1973, the historians Pamela Tudor-Craig and Claude Blair were struck by the magnificent collar made of openwork gold set with gems and pearls. They found parallels showing that the collar was unquestionably fifteenth century in origin, and too accurately painted to be a mere memory of a type of jewellery in fashion decades earlier: clearly this evidence suggests that the portrait was based on a lost original.

It is probable therefore that the Royal Collection and the Society of Antiquaries portraits reflect two separate lost originals. Both were versions of a single basic image that could be turned to face either left or right and given different costume and jewellery as the occasion required. The image itself would no doubt have resulted from a process of collaboration between Richard and his chosen artist: it would have been important to present the king as he wished to be seen. The Antiquaries portrait, with its later alterations now removed, probably brings us as close as we can get to seeing Richard as he himself wanted to appear.

Richard's Head Reconstructed

None of the later propagandist descriptions of a deformed man matches even the least flattering of the portraits. The bones revealed a slight, delicately built man, with the slender arms and legs, as von Poppelau noted. The twist in his spine was well-balanced, so although it made him shorter than he could have been with a straight back, he would not have appeared deformed. There was no hunch back, and no withered arm.

The Richard III Society commissioned a reconstruction of his face and head (Plate 23), now on display in the new King Richard III Visitor Centre in Leicester, which instantly became one of the most popular and widely reproduced images of the king. Two exact replicas of the battered skull – one now also part of the visitor centre displays – had already been created by Russell Harris of Loughborough University. The replica skulls were made by a technique often used for industrial prototypes, employing a 3D printer to translate a computer model into a robust three-dimensional plastic object, which, unlike the injured and fragile bones, could easily be handled and studied. The computer model which they first built of the skull was based on the sequence of images from CT scans taken of the real skull at Leicester Royal Infirmary (see Chapter 4).

Caroline Wilkinson, Professor of Craniofacial Identification at Dundee University, also used the CT scans, combined with the techniques she has applied in many forensic cases, literally to put flesh on the bones. Building up a computer image, she added the complex layers of flesh and muscle that make up the human face, using accepted data on how muscle depth and facial features relate to the underlying bone structures, weighted for Richard's gender, age and race. She then added the skin, before the head was also translated into a life-size three-dimensional model using a 3D printer. Wilkinson worked blind, without consulting either the portraits or the descriptions. However, when her computer model of the head was complete, she superimposed an image of it, taken at the same angle as the National Portrait Gallery portrait, on a photograph of the painting: the match was startlingly close.

The finished head, given shoulder-length dark brown hair under a jewelled velvet cap, dark eyebrows, dark glass eyes – made before the DNA work was complete, the colouring matched to the then consensus on

Richard's appearance – and hand-tinted skin, appears handsome, smooth skinned, thoughtful and faintly smiling. He looks much younger than the familiar portraits of a man who, aged 32 at the time of his death, would have been judged well into middle age by his contemporaries.

The hair and colouring were added by Janice Aitken, a lecturer at Duncan of Jordanstone College of Art and Design, part of Dundee University, who is also an artist. Aitken could not have done her work blind, so she did consult both the portraits and the contemporary descriptions for clues to his appearance and likely hairstyle and clothing. She also gave him a ruddier complexion – for a man who spent much of his life out of doors and on horseback – than his aristocratic pallor in the paintings.

The result is strikingly lifelike, but though the bone structure and the general shape of the face are unquestionably correct, the accuracy of the outer appearance depends on the trustworthiness of the portraits she used for reference. Hepburn regards the recreated head, founded in science, as a fascinating experiment, but points out that though Wilkinson could recreate the features, she and Aitken could only guess at his habitual facial expression: 'The reconstruction shows a full-faced more approachable Richard, but we need to be wary of taking that as a sign that he was a softer individual than his reputation suggests – to do so would be to make just as much of a moral judgement based on appearance as the medieval writers who linked deformity with bad character.'

So do we now know what Richard really looked like? Perhaps.

Further reading

Hepburn, Frederick (1986) *Portraits of the Later Plantagenets.* Woodbridge, Suffolk: Boydell Press.

Hepburn, Frederick (2014) Earliest portraiture of Richard III. Article for The Richard III Society. Available online at http://www.richardiii. net/2_4_0_riii_appearance.php#portrait (last accessed 20 November 2014).

Piper, David (1957) *The English Face.* London: Thames & Hudson.

Polydore Vergil (1555) *Anglica Historiae.* The Latin text and English translation are available online at http://www.philological.bham.ac.uk/polverg (last accessed 20 November 2014).

Tudor-Craig, P. (1973) *Richard III. National Portrait Gallery, 27 June-7 October 1973* [exhibition catalogue]. London: National Portrait Gallery.

von Poppelau, Nicholas (n.d.) Travel diary.

Nicholas von Poppelau wrote his travel diary, probably sometime between 1484 (when he visited England) and 1494, in likelihood in Latin. The original manuscript seems to be lost. Parts of this were excerpted and translated into German by Samuel Benjamin Klose (1730–98) *Darstellung der inneren Verhältnisse der Stadt Breslau vom Jahre 1458 bis zum Jahre 1526*. The text of this work was edited by Stenzel, G.A. (1847) *Scriptores Rerum Silesiacarum III*, Breslau. The passage quoted in this chapter is Stenzel 1847: 365. The whole manuscript and publication history to 1969 is explained in Armstrong, C.A.J. (1969) *The Usurpation of Richard the Third. Dominicus Mancinus ad Angelum Catonem de occupatione Regni Anglie per Riccardum Tercium libellus*. 2nd edn. Oxford: Clarendon Press, pp. 136–8. The passages quoted here are translated and printed in The Ricardian June 1999, p. 529 by Dr Livia Visser-Fuchs from the most recent edition of the text:Radzikowski, Piotr 1998 *Reisebeschreibung Niclas von Popplau, Ritters, bürtig von Breslau*. Krakow: Trans-Krak.

Walpole, Horace (1768) *Historic Doubts on the Life and Reign of King Richard the Third*. London: J. Dodsley, Pall Mall. Available online at http://books.google.co.uk/books/about/Historic_Doubts_on_the_Life_and_Reign_of.html?id=h0UJAAAAQAAJ&redir_esc=y (last accessed 9 December 2014) and http://www.gutenberg.org/cache/epub/17411/pg17411.html (last accessed 24 November 2014).

Wilkinson, Caroline (2013) Richard III facial reconstruction: Information available at http://www.lifesci.dundee.ac.uk/news/2013/aug/20/cahid-and-djcad-experts-reconstruct-face-richard-iii-528-years-after-his-death (last accessed 9 December 2014) and http://www.le.ac.uk/richardiii/science/facevoice.html (last accessed 9 December 2014).

8

The Big Announcement

The Slow Reveal …

Before dawn on the morning of Monday, 4 February 2013, Richard Buckley was at home wrestling with an unusual dilemma: he knew what he was going to say, but what was he going to wear?

His decades as a professional archaeologist hadn't prepared him for a day like the one he was facing. His usual working kit of battered jumpers and jeans clearly wouldn't do, but should he bring the equally battered hat, the one he had announced to his colleagues he would eat if the excavation uncovered Richard? Would a jacket look too casual? Would a dark suit look too managerial?

Still uncertain, he took out a tweed jacket that he hoped would be sufficiently respectable, but at least look as if he still knew how to operate a trowel …

A Momentous Phone Call (AM, PT, CV, RT)

Late in the afternoon of 5 September 2012, Ather Mirza, the University of Leicester's Director of News, and Peter Thorley, Corporate News Officer, were both still at work when the phone rang. It was Buckley looking for Richard Taylor, who had joined the university a decade earlier as head of marketing, and was now Director of Corporate Affairs and a member of the senior management team. Taylor was at a graduates' reunion in London, so Buckley told Mirza the news: Thorley

The Bones of a King: Richard III Rediscovered, First Edition. The Greyfriars Research Team with Maev Kennedy and Lin Foxhall.
© 2015 University of Leicester. Published 2015 by John Wiley & Sons, Ltd.

looked up in astonishment at the string of unprintable exclamations from his colleague.

Mirza's background was in newspaper journalism; he knew he had just been told a story which would make the front page anywhere in the world. Mathew Morris had gone back with Jo Appleby to excavate the skeleton which he had briefly uncovered 10 days earlier, in the first hours of the dig. They had found a skull with gaping battle wounds – and a torso with a twisted spine.

'It's him!' Mirza said, shocked.

'But we still need to make sure', Buckley said firmly, quite unable to keep the excitement from his own voice.

Mirza recounted the conversation to Thorley very carefully, without mentioning the name Richard. 'It took a minute or two', said Thorley, a graduate of Leicester University's academic companion in the city, De Montfort University, who had worked for the British Psychological Society. 'And then apart from trying to be professional about it, there was a huge human reaction as the penny dropped of the enormity of what had been found.'

'We had joked that if we ever did find him, all hell would break loose', Mirza remembered.

Mirza emailed Taylor in London, asking him to phone urgently. Taylor's phone wasn't working properly, and he wandered around the streets hunting for that rare thing in a twenty-first-century city, a working phone box, eventually finding one that would only take a credit card. He wondered irritably what could be so important, and if the call was going to cost him a fortune.

Mirza broke the news. 'I said oh my goodness me,' Taylor recalled, 'only I probably used slightly more Anglo-Saxon terms. I felt dizzy, actually, literally physically dizzy.'

They all now knew they were sitting on the story of their lives and had very little time to work out how to handle it. They would have to maintain interest in the story for the months it would take the scientists to test the bones, but first they would have to keep secret the news that human remains had been found until the discovery could be assessed and a press conference organised.

Their own families didn't even learn of the discovery, but in London that evening Taylor listened in horror as Vice Chancellor Sir Robert Burgess, chatting with the alumni about all the interesting work the university was engaged in, mentioned in passing that human bones had just been found by the archaeologists. Taylor listened in agony, but Burgess did not refer to the twisted spine, and few in the room registered the significance of the news. Taylor successfully pleaded with one graduate, by now a journalist with 15,000 Twitter followers, not to pass on the news.

The Media over the Car Park

The press office team had known since they sent out their very first press release that the excavation had sparked intense excitement.

On Friday, 24 August, at the height of what journalists call 'the silly season', the time of news famine when most politicians and other news makers are on holidays, the university had invited media to come to the scruffy car park behind the council offices. 'The University of Leicester and Leicester City Council, in association with the Richard III Society, have joined forces to begin a search for the mortal remains of King Richard III', the release had read. 'The project represents the first ever search for the lost grave of an anointed King of England.'

Both Buckley and Morris had been slightly stunned by the result. 'Usually when we do a press day on a dig the *Leicester Mercury* and, if we're really lucky, local radio turn up,' Morris said, 'but that day there were television crews waiting for us when we got to the site.' Half a dozen broadcast crews, scores of UK journalists, and several international news agencies arrived. As the direct descendant of Richard's sister, Michael Ibsen, the Canadian-born cabinetmaker (from whom King took a DNA sample) was present, as was Philippa Langley whose passion for seeking Richard III had launched the project. Their faces went round the world.

The press release, and the members of the team interviewed, had been careful to stress that this was a research excavation. Assuming that after more than a year's careful preparatory work they were actually digging in the right place, they might be lucky enough to uncover 1 per cent of the friary site, and they could not predict what part they might find with any degree of accuracy. Buckley had assured the journalists that 'although in many ways finding the remains of the king is a long shot, it is a challenge we shall undertake enthusiastically.' Privately the archaeologists had given it much longer odds: they had five objectives, beginning with finding the remains of Greyfriars. The fifth was: 'within the choir locate the mortal remains of Richard III'. Buckley and Morris's assessment rated locating the choir as an outside chance, and the final objective 'was not seriously considered possible'.

When the proposal had first crossed Taylor's desk, in an email from Burgess almost two years earlier, he had initially thought it too wild an idea to give serious consideration. However, 'there followed lots of emails from lots of people and gradually the whole thing began to acquire a twang of credibility', he said. 'It was far-fetched and ludicrous, but there was enough in it that was real to make it worth going the journey. But it was essential from the start that there was a genuine research purpose, which we could stand over even if nothing was found except the foundations of a few walls. It was never going to be just a PR stunt.' Buckley had assured Taylor that this could be their last chance of excavating a plot of open land in the city centre and finding the lost Greyfriars church, and if they succeeded it would be a discovery of great local historical and even potentially of national importance. Taylor had been convinced, and he had found £10,000 from the university's marketing budget to put towards the project.

That first press conference had stressed the interest and importance of the excavation for learning more of Leicester's medieval history, and some more nuanced reports had followed. However, the general thrust of the media coverage had been straightforward: the archaeologists were going to dig up the tarmac, and under the large letter R – marking a reserved parking space – they were going to find the last Plantagenet, 'the king under the car park'. The archaeologists, of course, did not look for the grave or place their trenches on the basis of that 'R', and Mirza and Thorley never used that striking phrase, but it became media shorthand for the entire project. In Finland's *Hufvudstadsbladet*, the headline would read 'Rikard III hittad under parkering'. The hunt for Richard had begun.

Mirza and Thorley had started churning out releases, walking a tightrope of both building and managing expectations. Based on daily briefings with the archaeologists, the news they put out lagged a day or two behind events to allow for any unexpected developments. All their early releases stressed the archaeology, because Mirza, with his long experience of news editors, had known that if human remains turned up, with even a remote possibility that Richard had been found, they would never again be able to interest journalists in trenches revealing 'medieval window tracery, glazed floor tile fragments, part of what may be the Greyfriars cloisters walk and a section of wall which they believe could have belonged to the Greyfriars church', as one of the early releases excitedly revealed.

Unknown to the media, and to the archaeologists themselves, within 24 hours of that first press conference, with all the cameras gone except the Darlow Smithson crew following the excavation for what would become an award-winning documentary for Channel 4, and with Carl Vivian filming for the university, Richard would be found.

Vivian, video producer for the University of Leicester and staff member for 14 years, had previously worked for Leicestershire police. It would perhaps have surprised him at that time had he known how useful his experience of both photographing human remains and maintaining absolute discretion about the progress of any investigation would be in his subsequent career. His initial involvement in the project was straightforward, and strictly limited: he was to film a short interview with Buckley about the excavation that was to be sent out with the initial press release. Although he had grown up in Leicestershire, he had no particular interest in history and no experience at all of archaeology. Much to his surprise, after spending two days filming re-enactors clashing about in the mist at the annual commemoration of the Battle at Bosworth and just one day at the car park site he was completely gripped by the story: he decided to give up his annual leave to record every day of the excavation. The images he captured and the films he made went global, viewed online and used in news stories on countless occasions.

By 5 September, with the third trench opened, enough had been discovered to announce the news that 'medieval Greyfriars Church – the burial place of Richard' had been located – information of great interest to archaeologists and medieval historians but not the sensational development the international media were waiting for. Buckley was quoted saying, 'We are extremely excited by the prospect of further discoveries over the next week or so which may take us closer to our goal.' That morning, though, as the press release landed in the media inboxes, Morris and Appleby, with help from King, were already on site, returning to expose and further investigate those two parallel thigh bones, uncovered and buried again in the first hour of the excavation. The long shot was about to become reality.

The Quiet before the Storm

On 5 September, when the Darlow Smithson crew had been working in a different part of the site, Vivian had recorded video footage the media would soon battle to get their hands on. Through the heat of a long afternoon he had remained perched awkwardly on the edge of the trench, looking down as Appleby, hot and uncomfortable in her white boiler suit, delicately exposed the bones one by one. He had been the only other person there when she exposed one verterbra in the thoracic part of the backbone but, baffled, couldn't find the next. She had reached the beginning of the sharp bend in the spine. When, visibly shaken, she had gone to fetch the rest of the team, he had used the time to shoot a sequence which would eventually be endlessly reproduced, a tilting shot along the contorted spine and up towards the battered skull, a moving and startlingly vivid image achieved using available natural light and a delicate touch.

He had gone on to record, in tight close-up, Philippa Langley's shocked reaction when she returned to the site and was told the news. Her jaw literally drops when she is told of the twisted spine, and then she visibly shrugs it off, so convinced that Richard was the victim of Tudor propaganda that the disability meant the skeleton could not be his. Appleby is then heard gently breaking the news that the skull had signs of battle trauma. As Langley comprehends the implications, the colour drains from her face and she has to sit down.

In the week before the find was announced, the team organised the first open day at the site. Leicester locals had been hearing about the excavation on radio and television, hanging around the site every day, peering hopefully through gates and gaps in the fencing, and eagerly asking the archaeologists as they left in the evening if there was any news. 'Some queueing may be needed if large numbers of visitors arrive', the open-day invitation warned. Crowds came from the city and from much further afield, waiting patiently for hours in a queue that stretched around the block.

Press releases followed, detailing the discovery of Richard Herrick's garden path, hailed by Langley as 'an astonishing discovery and a huge step forward', and announcing that the dig was being extended for a third week. And then on 12 September, with the excavation phase complete, the media were invited to pack into the Guildhall and then to view the empty grave. The caution of Mirza and Thorley's early releases was largely abandoned: the skeleton with the twisted spine was described as 'a momentous discovery' with the 'potential to rewrite history'. But it was made absolutely clear that a secure identification of the remains was going to take many months of meticulous research.

Announcing the Bones

Anticipation was high at the press conference, and the team tried to steer a course between undeniable excitement at the possibilities ahead of them and precipitate storylines. Buckley described the archaeology of the site, and Taylor stressed their position: 'We are not saying today that we have found King Richard III. What we are saying is that the search for Richard III has entered a new phase. Our focus is shifting from the archaeological excavation to laboratory analysis. This skeleton certainly has characteristics that warrant extensive further detailed examination.' Appleby described those characteristics, the twisted spine, the slashing skull injury but cautioned against premature excitement: 'We don't know that we've found Richard: he is not the only individual in history to have had scoliosis and not the only medieval man to have received head injuries.' Turi King explained her hope of being able to extract mitochondrial DNA, sequence it and then compare it with a known living relative of Richard's. 'In reality this will be a long process', she warned.

The media reported the health warnings, but only in passing. There was just one story from the day: the Leicester archaeologists had found Richard III. Taylor himself, in an interview with Radio Leicester, abandoned his cautious phrasing at the press conference and described the find as 'mind blowing'.

Waiting for the Results

Although the bones and their condition had been described in some detail at the press conference on 12 September, none of Vivian's vivid images of the skeleton in the grave were released. Instead, the press office team rebuffed a chorus of media pleas for the images of the bones, which Taylor explained had been removed to 'an undisclosed location where further analysis is being undertaken'. In the months that followed there were countless media requests for access to the bones, ranging from civil enquiries to strident demands. In a slightly surreal development, a Bollywood movie was also being made on campus, and the film-makers thought a few scenes with the skeleton would make a striking addition to their work. Their request, like all the others, was politely but unwaveringly rejected. 'Our job was now to gain time for the academic team to withdraw from the public gaze, and get on with their work', Mirza said. So along with all their usual work for the university, a steady flow of news about Richard poured from the press office.

Some stories only received local coverage, but many of the quirkier ones went international. The reconstruction of the Blue Boar Inn, where Richard was believed to have spent his last night in Leicester, was one of those which made news around the world; the model, recreated on a 3D printer from rediscovered measured drawings made by the architect Henry Goddard before the inn was demolished in the nineteenth century, is now on display at the visitor centre. Mirza and Thorley also sent out news of a graphic novel about Richard being created by Emma Vieceli, and of the Victorian builders who had missed the grave by inches. They quoted Foxhall saying – futilely – that the media should not assume that Richard had been found. They passed on the suggestion from the team that the jumble of female bones which had also been excavated could possibly be those of Ellen Luenor, benefactor and founder of the friary, buried around 1350. They reported the excitement of the visit of Archbishop Desmond Tutu to the university and his meeting with key members of the Richard team. They announced that students were mounting a day of Ricardian medieval combat.

At the September press conference the team had said the DNA work could take 'six to eight weeks'. The university had taken over funding the project as a major piece of research, but though work was no longer subject to the ad hoc fundraising of the early stages it was still a slow and tortuous process. The press was expecting an announcement by late October, but in fact, as Taylor recalled, that was wildly over optimistic. The complex and expensive contracts had not even been completed by then, for specialist laboratories where King could carry out the testing in England and France. Instead, on 26 October the press office sent out a release on the first rumble of what would become a storm, reporting that questions had been raised over whether Richard should be reburied in Leicester or whether other locations had a better claim to the honour.

Not a word was released on what the team called 'the wobble'.

Vivian remembers offering Appleby a lift to her home in the countryside after the long session when the bones were put through the scanner at the Leicester Royal Infirmary. It was an almost entirely silent journey. They got on well, and were usually chatty after working together, but that night both were subdued: Vivian was smarting that although he had been present as an observer, he had not been allowed to film. He had noticed how during the long slow process of scanning Appleby had grown increasingly quiet and withdrawn. He sensed she was troubled.

As he learned later, she had been looking at the delicate bones as they went through the scanner, particularly the extraordinarily slender arms and legs, and wondering if they were making a fundamental mistake. Without the definitive evidence of a Y chromosome, sexing skeletal remains is not a straightforward process. There is a continuum, with definitely male and definitely female at opposite ends: she had begun to wonder if they were actually looking at the remains of a woman.

On 24 October, Appleby phoned Foxhall (as head of school), to express her worries that the skeleton might be female. Foxhall, ironically in a meeting in York at the time, told her that she must 'call it as she saw it' – the accuracy and integrity of the academic research was more important than anything else, and if the skeleton was not Richard, then so be it. But, this suggestion struck Foxhall as potentially significant, since she had already looked at John Rous's physical description of Richard as 'slight in body and weak in strength'. The Latin word for 'strength (*vis*) was regarded as a particularly masculine quality, even in Richard's time. To suggest that someone was rather lacking in *vis*, might imply that they looked a bit 'girly'.

Taylor shudders at the memory of the period. 'I think it was the one thing we could not have recovered from. If we'd found nothing except the foundations of the friary: fine. If we'd found a skeleton with a twisted spine and it turned out not to be Richard, fine. But if we'd said we thought we found Richard and it turned out to be a woman, we'd have become an international laughing stock, we'd never have been forgiven.' As the findings of different tests slowly came in, though, crowned by the DNA results, the wobble passed: it was definitely a man, and it was looking increasingly certain that it was the king.

By December, with no date for the promised revelation of the scientific results, sections of the media were growing restless. Mirza and Thorley issued a statement on behalf of the university denying a story, the first of several, that 'additional information' had deliberately been held back at the September press conference. The year ended still without a date for the announcement but with a jolly seasonal release about Richard's Christmas celebrations in 1484, so rollicking that the anonymous author of the Croyland said disapprovingly that he was unable to record them 'because it is shameful to speak of them'.

The Big Day Dawns (AM, PT, RB)

On 4 February, as a chilly damp daylight broke through the clouds, Mirza, Thorley and Taylor were already at the university, excited and acutely nervous, even though the team had done a full dress rehearsal of the press conference the previous day.

The eve of the conference had also seen the release of a truly startling picture, one of the beautiful photographs taken by Vivian that they had been keeping under lock and key. They had chosen the single most striking image, the battered skull glowing like a piece of medieval carved ivory, almost as if in candlelight.

Vivian had filmed the skeleton months earlier, but he had only recently taken these detailed close-up photographs. They were intended as the official excavation record photographs. However, Vivian, who had borrowed a brand new Canon 5D, was apprehensive about using a stills camera after years working on video; he sensed that his photographs would probably also be the images eventually released to the media, and he took as much care over them as if he were shooting a magazine cover. 'It was inconceivable to me that we would ever announce that we had found the remains of Richard without showing people the detail of what we had found', he said. 'They had to be the best record of the bones I could get – but there was no reason why we couldn't try to make them look good too.'

Plate 17 Memorial wall plaque to Anne, Duchess of Exeter, and Sir Thomas St Leger, in the Rutland Chantry Chapel, St George's Chapel, Windsor. Source: Photographed by Angelo Hornak © The Dean and Canons of Windsor.

Plate 18 Michael Ibsen and Wendy Duldig.

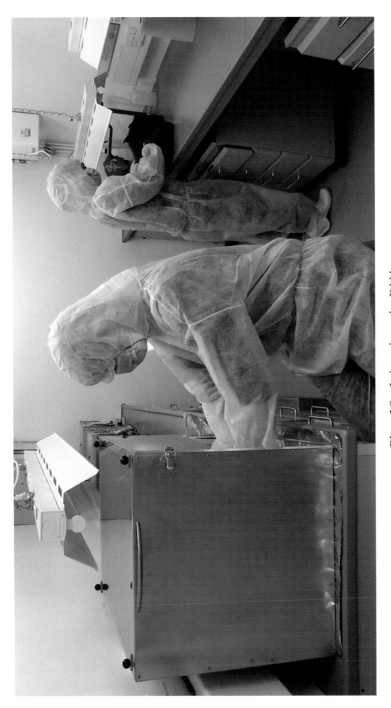

Plate 19 Labwork on the DNA.

Plate 20 Richard III and his wife, Anne, from the Salisbury Roll. *Source*: © 2004 Topfoto.

Plate 21 Richard III, oil on panel, English School, 1520. *Source*: Royal Collection Trust © Her Majesty Queen Elizabeth II, 2014/Bridgeman Images.

Plate 22 Richard III, oil on panel, English School, sixteenth century. *Source*: Society of Antiquaries of London, UK/Bridgeman Images.

Plate 23 A facial reconstruction of King Richard III, unveiled by the Richard III Society on 5 February 2013 in London, England. *Source*: Photograph by Dan Kitwood/Getty Images.

Plate 24   Press conference 4 February 2013, the view from the platform.

He wanted the bones in crisp detail against a dark background. This could have been added digitally, but he wanted the images to be an unmanipulated record of what he had photographed. The day before the skeleton was brought to a laboratory in the School of Archaeology and Ancient History, he had walked down to the Fabric Warehouse in the city centre in his lunch hour and bought all of the best quality black velvet they had in stock.

The bones were set out for him by Appleby, who pointed out the details of the dagger cuts and sword slashes which it was essential he record. Instead of the two powerful lamps he had also brought, which gave too much light and flattened the detail, the bones were lit by small spotlights, turned down low and set around the edge of the velvet cloth. This gave an almost three-dimensional quality to the photographs and brought out the red staining from their centuries lying in the Leicestershire soil. It took a whole day to capture all the images needed, and a second day for the skull alone, which was so fragile it had to be carefully propped and supported when the lower jaw was repositioned.

Once the press office had chosen the image of the battered skull to send out on the eve of the press conference they had carefully captioned it, after much discussion, 'potentially that of King Richard III'. Nevertheless, it was so vivid, and the act of releasing it carried such a weight of certainty, that they answered several phone calls on that Sunday from media asking if they still needed to come to the conference.

By the time the team arrived on Monday, a wall of outside broadcast trucks was already parked outside the building, and journalists were trudging up the hill, weighed down with laptops, cameras and recording equipment. The press conference was due to start at 10.00 a.m., but the doors were opened from 6.30 a.m. The catering staff, who had agreed to come in hours earlier than usual, were explaining to the first hopeful members of the academic staff that the bacon rolls were intended for the ravenous television crews.

They ran through the checklist they had been working on for months. With the lecture theatres unavailable in term time and laboratories, though offering a potentially striking backdrop, being far too cramped a space for the numbers expected, much thought had gone into the venue. The university council chamber was the solution, a large handsome room which had recently been redecorated, and had several adjoining spaces, one with a kitchen.

They had worried about power supplies and measured the distance cables would have to stretch to the outside broadcast vans. For Thorley the logistics meant that he could not be at the actual press conference as it would be his job to load online the prepared press releases and images and distribute them as reams of hard copy. They had ensured there was a live feed to an overflow room; loos and loo paper; coffee, lots of coffee. They had sorted Wi-Fi, after complex discussions with the university's IT staff about how to prevent the entire university network from crashing if every staff member, every student and every journalist logged on simultaneously to follow events. A number of big screens were set up in the Students Union and other parts of the university for staff and students to watch. The green room for the university team to wind down in was ready, but in the end it was barely used as the key members would spend the entire day doing one interview after another. Also, Jon Shears and Michelle Heap, university multimedia experts, had overseen the development of a website which was ready to go live as soon as the announcement was made.

Mathew Morris was already down in the city centre in the car park, waiting to do live breakfast television and radio interviews. He had the awkward assignment of carrying on talking for hours without giving away anything that would be announced later. The previous afternoon, as the academic team had gathered to be told that Turi King and colleagues had managed to extract DNA from the bones, and that this had proved a perfect match to the control region for the mitochondrial DNA sequenced from Michael Ibsen and Wendy Duldig, Morris had to argue his way into the room. Some of his colleagues had felt that if he knew about the DNA he would be unable to keep stalling the media, avid for any clue in advance of the official announcement. He had insisted on hearing the results, and did manage to keep the secret through a string of interviews.

Viewing the Bones

A block away from the council chamber, in a small quiet room off the main floor of the library building, one weary security guard left and another took over, as they had done all through the night, watching in shifts over the bones of a king that lay under a Perspex cover, on Vivian's black-velvet cloth covering four tables pushed together to form an improvised bier. Help with mounting the display had come from an unexpected quarter.

Louise Carr, a student recruitment officer, and by chance a former member of the Richard III Society, worked at a desk strategically placed half way between Taylor's office and the kitchen: every time he had passed, she had pleaded for news of the project. Her interest in Richard had begun when, as a 12-year-old, she had to write a school project on some figure from history. She had written to the Richard III Society, they had sent her a reading list, and the more she had read the more fascinated she had become by the conflicting accounts of this strange king. Now a totally unexpected chapter in his story was unfolding around her. 'I would have been fascinated if they'd found one medieval tile or a bit of broken carved stone. I'd have scrubbed floors or made the tea to be part of the project,' Carr said. Had they found anything, and could she do anything to help, she asked repeatedly, and one day Taylor had paused and replied, 'well ...'

Carr had been given the particularly delicate task of devising a way to let the media see the bones that would keep the remains safe and also treat them with dignity and respect.

Some of the team had feared this might prove such a challenge that the skeleton should not be shown at all, but Mirza, the former news reporter, knew they would never be forgiven if, after waiting for so long, journalists were unable to bear personal witness to the truth of the bones. It was also important to demonstrate that the whole story was not a hoax or a conspiracy, as some of the less credible coverage had suggested. It was going to be tricky enough when he told them that there would be absolutely no photography, or recording of any kind, in the room where the king lay.

With the announcement approaching, the team realised Carr had some very useful skills. As an organiser of open days for prospective students she knew about compiling attendance lists – theirs eventually ran to hundreds of names, arranged in alphabetical order so the *New York Times* was preceded by the *Melton Mowbray Times* – organising seating, desks, lecterns, line-ups of speakers, microphones, timing and all the practicalities of moving large numbers of strangers around the campus.

When she was given the job of organising the viewing of the bones she pored over a map of the campus then headed out on foot, trailed by the head of security and the head of estates, looking for somewhere private, secure, separate from the press conference building. More than that, she wanted to find a room that was also a pleasant, calm space. She found the quiet conference room off the first floor of the main library and then scoured the university again looking for good quality, elegant furniture she could borrow, finally discovering handsome plain oak tables in the law library.

A Perspex cover to protect the bones seemed easy to provide but actually proved the most difficult item on her list to secure. After phoning around university departments, the local museum and libraries in vain, particularly since she was unable to explain exactly what she needed and why, and with only days to spare, she found a firm that could deliver one from stock. She borrowed the specially made mount on which the bones had been photographed and the black velvet cloth to cover it, and then she discovered in a store cupboard some black linen table cloths which had been used for a function.

Carr wanted every detail of her unique challenge, laying out not just human remains but the body of an anointed king, to be perfect. For nights before the big day, she lay sleepless with worry that she had forgotten some small but crucial detail. By late on the Sunday afternoon she had emptied the room and installed the tables. The security was organised, as were the volunteer guides who would lead the journalists to the library and the chaplains who would sit keeping a quiet vigil in the room. Discussions had finalised plans for how to handle anyone who became distressed or even aggressive. Everything on the list was done. She looked again at the black table cloths. And so, as Appleby and Foxhall were about to arrive carrying the bones in three large boxes, to spend much of the evening carefully laying them out, Carr was sprinting across the park in the dusk to her home, to fetch her iron to press the cloths.

When she told this story later during a school visit, a girl the same age as Carr was when she first discovered Richard, came up to ask for the autograph of the woman who became the linen presser to the last Plantagenet.

The Press Conference Begins

By 9.00 a.m. the building was surrounded by broadcast journalists in that familiar anxious state of having to carry live links with absolutely no new information to pass on.

The media pack would have been enraged to know that one journalist already knew the whole story. Peter Warzynski of the *Leicester Mercury*, having signed a confidentiality agreement, actually spent some time embedded in the university press office, brought in to give a working news reporter's view of how the story of the discovery was being released.

He was in the press office when Mirza was trying to think of a phrase conveying that all the different strands of evidence, the dating, the DNA, the injuries, the site, the history, had come together to make it as certain as the team could be that it was Richard. '"Beyond reasonable doubt"?' Warzynski hazarded. His words duly appeared in every report of the press conference.

By 9.30 the room was almost full, and a little group of musicians was playing music from Richard's day – a heavy hint for anyone with an ear for period music.

When the press conference started promptly at 10.00 a.m., opened by Vice Chancellor Professor Sir Robert Burgess and broadcast live by the BBC, the academics at the long desk looked out at a room like nothing they had ever seen before: every seat was full, the walls lined two and three deep with people standing, and at the back of the room on the raised rostrums, a cliff face of camera crews (Plate 24).

The entire event was broadcast live and was followed online by millions. The team went carefully through the evidence point by point: Taylor said what they would announce was 'truly astonishing'.

Buckley gave the dating evidence. Appleby went one by one through the bones and the injuries, and there were audible gasps in the room as Vivian's image of the gaping wound to the base of the skull was flashed up. The bones, she said, presented 'a highly convincing case' that the remains were those of Richard III. Kevin Schürer and Turi King went through their genealogy and DNA work, and then Buckley returned to announce, to whoops and cheers from many in the room, including journalists, that 'beyond reasonable doubt the individual exhumed at Grey Friars on September 12th is indeed Richard III, the last Plantagenet king of England'.

The words of Taylor, and of Sir Peter Soulsby, the mayor of Leicester, announcing that the reinterment would be in Leicester Cathedral, and that a new visitor centre would be built, were almost drowned out in the din of journalists scrambling for their phones and laptops.

Broadcaster and historian Dan Snow was already tweeting: 'David Cameron must sympathise with the mutilated Richard III; both are leaders who have dealt with catastrophic defections.'

Within hours, the story had gone round the world, running at the top of news bulletins and on front pages. The *South China Morning Post* headed it 'Skeleton Under Car Park England's Richard III'. 'Richard III Bones Found at Parking Lot', the *Philippines Daily Inquirer* reported. 'Science Heralds Return of the King' readers learned from the *Geelong Advertiser* in Australia, while in Nepal the *Kathmandu Post* went with 'King Richard III Found after 500 Yrs'. One of the security guards told Carr his family in Guatemala was most excited that he had been involved in protecting the bones; they had read all about it in their local paper.

On Vancouver Island in British Columbia, the *Nanaimo Daily News* rejoiced at discovering a local line: 'Nanoose Family Bloodline Linked to King Richard III'.

The Aftermath

At the end of what for most of the team had been a 14-hour day or longer, most just scattered and went home, too weary for anyone to suggest a group celebration. Both Mirza and Thorley remember feeling a little flat when they finally got home that night: nothing to come in their careers would be as demanding and exciting, they suspected.

There were more results to come in, and academic papers to be published, but they thought they were more or less done with Richard: they were wrong. A year after that press conference, Morris said, 'There's never a week without phone calls about Richard', and for Mirza and Thorley, Taylor, Vivian and the rest of the team, Richard has never gone away. And nearly two years after it, on 2 December 2014, when the results of the DNA analysis were announced to the world, news about Richard III would be trending on news networks once again.

Meanwhile, as well as four awards won by the archaeology team, including an OBE and *Current Archaeology* Archaeologist of the Year for Buckley, the press office team scooped up awards including Outstanding Communications Team from the *Times Higher Education* journal, the Heist award for best PR/Advocacy campaign, gold in the

CASE Circle of Excellence awards, and the science and education title in the European Excellence awards, and they were shortlisted for best communications in the Guardian University Awards.

Mirza and Thorley have been asked to give advice and to speak to other universities and institutions all over the country about how they handled the story. Buckley and Morris have written a book and have speaking engagements to last them throughout another year. Vivian has given talks to many societies, illustrated with his films and photographs. Many others involved in the discovery have given talks to a wide range of conferences, groups and schools throughout the UK and worldwide.

They all expected that, but one of the developments that took them completely by surprise was the challenge from the Plantagenet Alliance, whose members claimed distant relationship with Richard and challenged the terms of the exhumation licence, insisting that there should have been far wider consultation and that Richard should be buried in York. The case lasted longer than anyone expected and delayed the plans for reinterment at Leicester Cathedral by a year.

The team was also ambushed by a backlash that began before the press conference even ended with a tweet from the Cambridge classicist Mary Beard reading, 'Gt fun & a mystery solved that we've found Richard 3. But does it have any HISTORICAL significance? (Uni of Leics overpromoting itself?)'. And Beard's was not the only sceptical voice: to some the very smoothness with which they had handled the operation seemed suspect, making it more show business than archaeology. Even the university logos in the background of the announcement were criticised. Months later Mirza and Thorley were still responding to regular queries about the truth of the discovery of Richard, and the way in which it had been handled. More than a year after the press conference they issued a statement in response to suggestions by Michael Hicks, a professor of history at Winchester University, and archaeologist Martin Biddle that there could be no proof that the skeleton was really Richard. In an interview with *BBC History* magazine, they questioned the accuracy of the DNA and carbon-14 evidence and suggested that the remains could have belonged to anyone who died in the Wars of the Roses.

The statement issued by Mirza and Thorley in March 2014 was almost a re-run of the evidence presented at the press conference, stressing that it was the combination of different strands of research, including the historical evidence for the location of the grave, the nature of the skeleton and the injuries, the dating, the DNA and the isotope evidence, and the genealogical research identifying the closest living relatives, which supported the statement that Richard had been found 'beyond reasonable doubt'.

Both Mirza and Thorley now expect that Richard will never go away, and that they will have to rehearse these arguments many times again in the future. Taylor, now Chief Operating Officer at Loughborough University, remains convinced that throughout they made the best and most honest job of dealing with a discovery with no precedent in the history of the university: 'If we had sat on the results until all the peer reviewed papers were in, it would certainly have leaked, and we would have lost control of the story and how it was told.'

'As it was,' he said, 'the whole story has been a combination of an exciting idea, academic work of the highest quality, good luck, and – without wanting to blow my own trumpet – from a communications perspective I think we handled it really well.' His response to criticism of the presence of university logos is straightforward: 'As for the Leicester University logos – this was a world class piece of research which was going to be reported in every country in the world and seen and read by people who had probably never previously heard of Leicester: why ever would we not have identified the university?' Finally, he comments, 'When Richard is reinterred, I think all the silliness will be forgotten. My hope is that everyone involved will be remembered with credit. I think there's enough credit to go round.'

The Morning after the Night Before and Later

Buckley was sitting at his kitchen table, very tired, all talked out.

The landline rang: it was an Australian radio station, wanting to do an instant interview down the line. Startled, he demanded to know how they had got his private number: well, the researcher explained apologetically, they had looked it up in the telephone directory ...

Foxhall was in her shower at home when her phone rang. Her husband, Hamish Forbes, also an archaeologist, considered telling the caller to go away, then sighed and brought her the phone. She turned off the water and, still dripping, did a live interview with an Australian radio station.

Mirza and Thorley were back in their office, a little later than usual. It was snowing heavily. Another 12-hour day lay ahead: they had three days to get the university's annual report finished. And a press release to send out, based on the work of Dr Philip Shaw of the English department, suggesting that Richard may have spoken with a Brummie accent.

... Late on the afternoon of Tuesday, 2 December 2014, long after the initial furore had died down, King and Schürer made a fresh announcement. Within seconds, media sites were full of the news, this time with the shattering revelation not only that Richard was almost certainly blonde and blue-eyed but also that somewhere in the Beaufort family tree, the paternal line of descent had been broken.

Once again, the team members were the focus of intense media interest.

Further reading

Mirza, Ather (2014) The king under the car park. *Perspectives: Policy and Practice in Higher Education* 18 (4): 1–4.

9

THE AFTERLIFE OF RICHARD III AND THE CITY THAT NEVER FORGOT

Imagine ...

The small boys were restless, the longed-for holidays already dragging. They kicked the cast-iron balustrade of the bridge, with its ornate white and red roses, and threw pebbles into the dark water below. It was flowing too fast to skim the pebbles. It was boring.

'I know!' said one, inspired. 'Let's get our fishing rods and catch that king.'

'What king?'

'You know the king, the rotten king. The one on the sign.'

'What sign?'

'That old stone thing by the bridge, idiot. It says the king was chucked in here, a long time ago, thousands of years ago. Bet he's still here. Bet we can catch him. Let's get the fishing stuff.'

A Hasty Burial in a Modest Church

In 1485 there were far grander churches in Leicester than Greyfriars, including St Mary de Castro, the church within the outer walls of the castle, before Richard's day a Lancastrian stronghold where Henry VI was knighted. Even closer to the castle stood the Newarke, the Church of the Annunciation of Mary, described by Leland soon before it was destroyed in the Reformation as 'not great but exceedingly fair': it now survives only as two arches in a basement of De Montfort University.

The Bones of a King: Richard III Rediscovered, First Edition. The Greyfriars Research Team with Maev Kennedy and Lin Foxhall.
© 2015 University of Leicester. Published 2015 by John Wiley & Sons, Ltd.

Just outside the city walls there was the Augustinians' once grand and wealthy Leicester Abbey – part of its grounds are now the city's Abbey Park – and inside the walls there was also St Martin's, now the cathedral. By comparison, Greyfriars Church, chosen by Henry Tudor, or possibly volunteered by its Franciscan friars, was a modest complex.

Henry may have put Richard's battered body on display, perhaps in the Newarke among the tombs of his Lancastrian cousins, though this is not certain. But, if he hoped to bury Richard's memory along with his corpse, he failed. Even during his lifetime he was compelled by circumstance grudgingly to recognise Richard as a king (see Chapter 2). The site of the grave, and the tomb Henry paid for to mark it, were lost with the church itself. However, Richard was never forgotten, in England or in Leicester.

Many negative memories of Richard were initially preserved in public discourse, perhaps not surprisingly as Henry VII and succeeding Tudor kings established their right to rule. In late November 1530, Cardinal Wolsey, on his way to London to face charges of treason stopped at Leicester. He died and was buried in Leicester Abbey shortly afterwards. On 4 December, the French ambassador to England, Eustace Chapuys, wrote to the King Charles V of France, 'The cardinal of York dies on St Andrews Day, at a place where King Richard was killed. They are both buried in the same church, which the people called the Tyrant's Sepulchre.' Of course, Richard III and Wolsey were not buried in the same church, but it seems likely that in the early sixteenth century many people perceived, or were encouraged to perceive, the two 'tyrants' in the same light.

In 1563, in a poem ('Shores Wife') published in a collection called *Mirror for Magistrates*, Thomas Churchyard (d. 1604) portrays Richard's body as cursed by Edward IV's mistress, herself wronged and already dead:

> I aske of God a vengeance on thy bones,
> Thy stinkinge corps corrupts the ayre I know.

Whether this genuinely reflects a memory of Richard's corpse on display, or one of the other legends which had certainly already sprung up by this time around the fate of Richard's corpse is impossible to be sure.

However, by the seventeenth century, more positive memories of Richard III were already being recorded, notably by the antiquarian George Buck (1560–1622), who held the post of Master of the Revels to James I. Buck's family had owned substantial properties in Yorkshire, which they lost after the Battle of Bosworth, having supported Richard. Buck's major work, only published after his death and dedicated to King James, *The History of the Life and Reigne of Richard the Third*, aimed to resuscitate Richard's character.

Buck claimed to have spoken with John Stow, by that time a very elderly chronicler who had in his own public writings of 1580 remarked on Richard's deformities, following Thomas More's description. However, Buck reports that some said peremptorily that he was not deformed and that John Stow was among them, 'who in all his inquiry could find no such note of deformitie in this king', albeit he had enquired deeply into the subject. And further, he said, Stow declared that he 'had spoken with some ancient men, who from their own sight and knowledge affirmed that he was of bodily shape comely enough, onely of low stature'. Whether or not this reported conversation is accurate, it is interesting to see that already in the seventeenth century more positive depictions, and perhaps memories, of Richard were emerging.

As early as 1768 Horace Walpole, the waspish gossip, art historian and collector, wrote a book called *Historic Doubts on the Life and Reign of Richard the Third*, questioning whether he really had murdered his nephews in the tower.

Historians have kept the story of Richard alive but so have writers and artists, drawn to the story of the most enigmatic of English monarchs, particularly to the murder mystery of the fate of his nephews. In the nineteenth century cheap prints of romantic paintings of the princes in the tower hung in thousands of homes, including *The Children of Edward* by the French artist Paul Delaroche, renowned for his carefully researched English history paintings, which was the crowd pleaser of the Paris Salon of 1831. The picture, showing the boys together on a four poster bed – they have heard a sound and stopped reading, and their dog looks fearfully at a shadow under the door – is now in the Louvre, and a smaller version in the Wallace Collection in London. It has been endlessly reproduced in popular histories, as has Sir John Everett Millais' 1878 painting of the princes as two golden-haired youths clinging fearfully together at the foot of a staircase, now in the collection of Royal Holloway.

In 1924 the Richard III Society was founded as the Fellowship of the White Boar by Saxon Barton, a Liverpool surgeon and amateur historian dedicated to reclaiming the reputation of the king from centuries of Tudor propaganda. By the middle of the century the society was faltering, but then both its membership and popular interest in Richard were revived by Josephine Tey's famous novel about Richard's reputation and the fate of the princes, *The Daughter of Time*, and Sir Laurence Olivier's towering performance in the stage and then film version of the Shakespeare play. The society, which now has an international membership that shot up in the wake of the discovery of the remains, has given many memorials to Leicester, including a dashing statue of Richard with sword in one hand, crown in the other. The sculpture, by James Walter Butler, used to stand in the Castle Gardens but was recently relocated to the newly landscaped cathedral gardens, halfway between the car park site of the king's original grave and his new tomb in St Martin's.

However, long before the Richard III Society was founded, visitors to the city were fascinated by Richard's story. In his evidence to the judicial review of the challenge to the king's reburial in Leicester, Richard Buckley pointed out: 'Richard III has been part of the city's history for over 500 years, and it is documented that people have visited Leicester since at least the early seventeenth century because of this connection.'

A City where Richard Lived on in Legend

The Blue Boar

The streets of the city were threaded with stories of the dead king. According to tradition, Richard spent the night of 20 August 1485 in the Blue Boar Inn, and then rode out to spend the eve of the battle under canvas near the battlefield. The inn, then an imposing modern building, stood on the medieval high street, now Highcross Street. It was a stone's throw from the castle where Richard had stayed on previous visits to the city. There is no proof that he did actually stay in the inn, though the invasion of Henry Tudor and the alarming growth of his army as he marched from Wales to England was an unpredicted disaster, so it is possible that work was being done at the castle and it was not fit for an unscheduled royal visit.

Richard is reputed to have brought his own bed from Nottingham Castle, as according to one account he 'slept ill in strange beds'. This could well have been true: it was common for wealthy medieval travellers to carry their own furnishings and bedding rather than risk the discomfort and probable infestation of lice of a strange bed. It is said that he slept in the best chamber, which was a large room with big windows, and roof timbers painted with tendrils of vine leaves, shown to generations of visitors as the last roof which sheltered the king. The bed, the story continues, was never collected after the battle but remained in the inn for centuries: it is claimed that this is the very grand bed, possibly partly medieval but mostly dating from long after Richard's day, on display at the manor house of Donington-le-Heath in Leicestershire.

The legends of the inn continued with the tale that a seventeenth-century landlady of the Blue Boar, a Mrs Clark, was making the bed one day when a gold coin rolled out onto the floor. She took the bed to pieces, and found a fortune in gold hidden in the base – but the wealth brought her no luck, as she was murdered for it. Her death was a recorded fact, and her killers, Thomas Harrison, who was already on the run with a criminal record, and his accomplice Edward Bradshaw, were tried at the Leicester assizes in 1605. Bradshaw was hanged, and an unfortunate maidservant at the inn, Alice Grimbold, who had apparently been chatted up by Harrison and had told him of her mistress's wealth, was sentenced to be burned at the stake. However, there was no mention at the trial of a hoard of Ricardian treasure, so the story is almost certainly later embroidering of an already sensational yarn.

A further story of the Blue Boar tells that it was originally, like Richard's emblem, the White Boar. In this tale, when the canny landlord hears of the regime change after the devastating defeat of the Plantagenets at Bosworth he acts quickly, and by the time the victors returned to the city with the king's corpse, he has painted the white boar blue – by happy chance the emblem of the earl of Oxford, the commander of the troops at Bosworth for Henry Tudor.

The site of the inn is now marked as a stop on the Richard III historical trail, but the building itself was demolished in 1836, and a starkly modern Travelodge now occupies the site. There are romantic Victorian and early twentieth-century paintings of the inn in its medieval pomp, based on earlier watercolours and engravings. A copy of one painted in 1880 by the local artist John Fulleylove, showing Richard setting out from the inn, was bought at auction in 2013 and presented to the university by local businessman Frank May. It is now on display at the new visitor centre, as is the three-dimensional reconstruction of the Blue Boar Inn (see Chapter 3) given new life by Richard Buckley and Steffan Davies by the creation of a scale model of the building, complete with Richard's bedroom. This was constructed first as a computer model and then on a 3D printer.

Bow Bridge and the horse-trough coffin

The discovery in the car park did nothing to prove or disprove stories about the Blue Boar, but it demolished two of the most famous legends about the king and Leicester.

The original narrow stone Bow Bridge, across which Richard rode towards his fate, was demolished in 1861 and replaced by a much larger bridge with ornate Victorian ironwork incorporating his white roses and boar emblems and his motto, Loyaulte me Lie (Loyalty Binds Me). According to the *Illustrated London News* when the old bridge was demolished a stone recording the Ricardian connection went with it, and so a local builder called Benjamin Broadbent paid for a new one, set into the wall of a factory nearby. The paper described Broadbent as 'a master builder, and one well known for his many acts of munificence'. The report continued, 'This gentleman, unwilling that the remains of a King of England should lie without a stone to mark the place, obtained permission of Mr. A Turner, the owner of the estate, and at his own sole cost inserted a massive stone in the building about to be erected.' Broadbent's plaque, which was moved again when the factory was demolished, reads, 'Near this spot lie the remains of Richard III the last of the Plantagenets 1485', and it compounded the confusion over the fate of the bones.

The *Leicester Chronicle* also reported that while the old bridge was being demolished human bones were found: they were apparently examined by doctors but the science of the day could reveal little about their date. Since the site had originally been part of the Austin Friars' estate, there was nothing surprising about bones turning up, either in the ground or eroded out of a graveyard.

As early as 1611, the historian John Speed recorded that 'as tradition hath delivered', Richard's bones were dug up at the dissolution of the monasteries, and thrown into the river – or in some accounts, buried at the foot of the bridge. Although many historians had argued that this was nonsense, and that there was no evidence for the story, it had been repeated so often that the ULAS application for an exhumation licence for human remains carefully stated that the excavation was intended 'potentially to locate the burial place of Richard III whose remains were interred here in 1485, although these may subsequently have been exhumed and thrown into the nearby River Soar after the Dissolution in 1538.'

The car park proved that the bones remained exactly where they were first buried, as the historian David Baldwin had predicted as far back as 1986. Their discovery also demolished another cherished piece of Leicester folklore: the horse-trough coffin.

John Speed wrote in 1611 of a stone coffin lying outside 'a common inn', and the trough was evidently already a well-known tourist attraction by the time the diarist John Evelyn came in 1684 to 'the old and ragged city of Leicester, large and pleasantly seated but miserably built, the chimney flues like so many smiths' forges'. The city was famous, he wrote, for 'the tomb of the tyrant Richard the Third, which is now converted to a cistern at which (I think) cattle drink'.

Another literary traveller, the remarkable Celia Fiennes, who in the 1690s visited every county in England riding side-saddle, came to Leicester on Holy Thursday, 1698. In her tireless investigation of the library and hospital, the churches and the new guildhall and the old walls by then used 'only to secure gardens that are made of ye ruin'd places that were buildings of strength', she saw Bow Bridge, 'wch is one arch over into ye Priory wch King Richd ye third pass'd over out of ye Priory when he went to fight in Bosworth field wth King Henry the seventh', though she said the stone in the bridge associated with Richard had been removed. She did manage to see the other Ricardian relic that interested her: the horse trough. 'I saw a piece of his tombstone he Lay in, wᶜʰ was Cut out in exact form for his body to Lye in; yᵗ remains to be seen at yᵉ Greyhound in Leaster but is partly broken'. Baldwin has suggested that since there was no Greyhound at that date, Fiennes may have misremembered the name of the The Talbot, a common pub name, often with a sign depicting a talbot, a now extinct hunting dog.

By the eighteenth century, writers including Samuel Carte, a vicar of St Martin's, remembered fragments of stone with a head and shoulder shaped hollow outside the White Horse Tavern. However, in 1758 when Birmingham businessman William Hutton went to Leicester specially to look at 'this trough which had been the repository of one of the most singular bodies that ever existed', nothing remained of it. 'The best intelligence I could obtain', he wrote, 'was that it was destroyed about the latter end of the reign of George the First, and some of the pieces placed as steps in a cellar, at the same inn where it had served as a trough.'

Baldwin suggests it was likely that stone coffins would have been dug up at regular intervals in Leicester as old friary buildings were demolished, and that an enterprising innkeeper could easily have got hold of one as a tourist attraction. The biggest objection to it being Richard's, he says, is that such coffins were used in a much earlier period than the late fifteenth century. In fact the definitive objection, as the excavation proved, was that Richard went into his grave with no coffin of any kind, not even a second-hand early medieval one. Whatever the travellers saw outside the Leicester pubs, it was not the coffin of the last Plantagenet king.

Surprisingly, Robert Woosnam-Savage believes there could well be some garbled truth in one last Ricardian legend about Bow Bridge and the stone which Celia Fiennes sought.

The story goes that as the king rode out on 21 August 1485, the morning sun dazzling on his armour and golden crown – as shown in Fulleylove's painting, though it seems unlikely that Richard would have endured the heat and discomfort of riding in full armour on the eve of a battle – his spur struck a stone of the bridge. An old woman among the crowds watching the spectacle cried out, 'Where your spur should strike on the ride into battle, your head shall be broken on the return' – and this being a fairy tale, of course the prophecy came true. A witch, a curse – Woosnam-Savage assumed that like so much romantic medieval legend, this was a classic piece of confected Victorian gothic. However, he was startled when he traced it back and realised how early the story was. It appears in Richard Baker's 1643 *Chronicle of the Kings of England*, copied almost verbatim from John Speed in 1611, though even then Speed warned that it was hearsay: 'as is the report so let be the credit'.

Woosnam-Savage does not believe in the wise old woman and her chilling prophesy, or that the memory survived of the king's heel or head striking a particular stone – there is no evidence on the skull of such an injury – but he has been brooding about the descriptions of the narrow bridge and the strange cargo carried across it a day later.

The Tudor chronicler Edward Hall was writing decades later but created a particularly vivid picture of the return of the king, based on earlier accounts. Richard was brought back from the battlefield 'naked and despoyled to the skin and nothing left above him, not so much as a clowte to cover his privy members'. The corpse was slung over the back of a horse, trussed 'like a hogge or calfe, the hed and armes hanging on the one side of the horse, and the legges on the other side, and all by spryncled with mire and bloude.' Word would certainly have spread in the town of the strange procession coming their way, and crowds must have gathered to watch a spectacle like nothing any had seen before.

Woosnam-Savage is tempted to wonder if the origin of the story lies in the terrifying and unforgettable sight of the king's dangling body trussed like an animal being taken to market. 'The head was a bloody mess, and would have been visibly so. It was people perhaps seeing this and trying to interpret what they were looking at that may have been the starting point for the tale', he said. Anyone present would certainly have spoken of the extraordinary scene, and as the original eyewitness accounts were passed on and retold, becoming increasingly garbled and embroidered at each telling, the story may eventually have been embellished with the legend of the sinisterly gifted old lady. But this of course, as Woosnam-Savage is only too aware, is speculation.

Rethinking History (NH, PM, ML, BWS)

Horace Walpole worried in the eighteenth century about the reliability of sources for Richard's period:

> The confusions which attended the civil war between the houses of York
> and Lancaster, threw an obscurity over that part of our annals, which it

is almost impossible to dispel. We have scarce any authentic monuments of the reign of Edward the Fourth; and ought to read his history with much distrust, from the boundless partiality of the succeeding writers to the opposite cause. That diffidence should increase as we proceed to the reign of his brother.

The research on the injuries, and the earlier archaeological work on the Bosworth battlefield by Glenn Foard, confirmed the historical accounts of Richard's audacious cavalry charge across the battlefield in an attempt to kill Henry Tudor.

Historian Norman Housley, and biological anthropologist Piers Mitchell – who is also a medical historian – have considered one of the great what ifs of the story of Richard: what if he had killed Henry, turned the tide of the battle, lived and reigned for many more years?

His death, and the propaganda of the victors, fixed his image as a cruel tyrant, and Housley and Mitchell observe that his reputation was so bad by the time of his death that he was increasingly finding it difficult to rally supporters to fight by his side. Most dramatic of all examples was the procrastination of the Stanleys, who held back at the edge of the battle until they were quite sure that they were throwing their forces in on the winning side – Henry's. 'Repeatedly we come back to the shortness of his reign. Experience might have mellowed Richard, allowing his finer qualities to emerge and pushing the ugliness of the usurpation into the background. It is deterministic to claim that Richard could not have created an affinity that would have extended his over-narrow base of support and made more effective use of his strength in the north.' He had qualities, they argue, that could have transformed his reputation if he had lived and reigned for longer. 'Given a good and lasting second marriage, he could have constructed a court life that drew on his lively interest in chivalry and the arts, and with some financial consolidation he might have pursued the aggressive foreign policy that both France and Scotland feared enough to make them give their backing to Tudor. In other words, he might have become a more successful and distinguished king.'

Mark Lansdale, professor of psychology at Leicester, who worked and published on understanding Richard's psychological make up with Julian Boon, has also been reflecting on what the sources say about Richard and what the bones can add to them. He warns of the risk of superimposing twenty-first-century interpretations on the fifteenth century: 'You are trying to establish someone's motivations when they would have had very different attitudes to life and death', he explains. 'For example, they would have had a much greater certainty in the reality of heaven, and lived in much more rigid social structures … Put simply, people lived in a much more brutal environment – twenty-first century scruples don't apply here – this was the Wild West, with an admixture of religion thrown in.' That said, he believes human beings change little in their essential nature. One of Richard's problems, he believes, was Edward – a popular king, a shocking but gossip-worthy womaniser, a war hero, and a giant at well over six feet tall compared to slight Richard.

'His brother would have been a very hard act to follow', says Lansdale. 'Richard's reign puts me in mind of the premierships of Gordon Brown, John Major or Anthony Eden, who all struggled because an immensely powerful leader had disappeared, and everyone was jockeying for power. At the same time the country was riven politically, and under threat from invasion.' And his problems would have been compounded by his personality: 'As king he had to make decisions he had never made before, and had to learn to do this very quickly – it was a huge crisis. He was an immensely competent man – to get a grip on things as well as he did, you would have to be – but there is a difference between being a skilled deputy, and an effective leader. The key forensic work we did was to match Richard to a personality profile that can be described as 'controlling, based upon incipient intolerance to risk'. The problem with controlling personalities is that they can't relax – he wouldn't have given any slack to the nobles and, used to the more relaxed style of Edward IV, they wouldn't have liked that.'

He also thinks that Richard's scoliosis, confirmed by the discovery of the bones, must have had an impact on his character. A pious man could not have been unaware of the common medieval belief that physical deformity reflected moral weakness. 'How well he was able to conceal his scoliosis, and how it affected the way he moved is still being explored, but it is not unreasonable to think that he would have been cautious with strangers, expecting a negative reaction, and that kind of reticence becomes a self-fulfilling prophecy – if you treat other people with suspicion, they are more likely to respond in kind. This is an important part of our picture, because once he was king, he became increasingly socially isolated – most of his male relatives were dead, and he managed to lose the support of several of his most important allies.'

Lansdale sees no evidence that Richard was a psychopath, as some have claimed. While outsiders might expect, given his specialism, that Lansdale would be most interested in the fate of the princes in the tower, which has obsessed generations of historians, in fact he sees nothing particularly unusual, by the standards of the time, in what happened to them: 'It might have raised a few eyebrows that the princes were so young, that they had not reached their age of majority, but otherwise it was not unknown behaviour. Henry VII could be just as opportunistic and cynical with the executions that he ordered throughout his reign, and if you want a real candidate for a psychopath, go to Henry VIII.' Less frequently discussed issues interest him. 'My argument', he says, 'is that this is not a man who is abnormal, but one who is very unlucky. With his personality type, he could have been a good leader under other circumstances, but the pressures of the situation he finds himself in play against the more authoritarian aspects of his character. Under stress, these come out more strongly – and it is understandable: his wife and son were dead, as were most of his male relatives, he was running out of allies and increasingly reliant on the likes of Percy who, when he needed him, turned out to be very poor fare indeed.'

Woosnam-Savage thinks the discovery of Richard will prompt renewed consideration not just of the life of the king himself but of what reliance can be placed on evidence from historical sources. 'The fact that this was a known individual, and not just "anybody" but one of the most famous people in English history, gives a glimpse into the life – as well as the death – of this medieval monarch', he says. 'Although the skeleton itself will never be able to tell us anything about his involvement – or not – with the disappearance of the Princes in the Tower, or anything about certain aspects of his mindset, it aids us in the understanding of how such a person lived, especially when taken in the context of surviving historical documentation. I think that has been one of the most fascinating parts of this journey; the simple fact that a number of points in the historical accounts have apparently been confirmed to lesser and greater degrees by the skeleton.' Revelations throw light on a range of topics: 'Even something like his parasite infestation, or rather lack of other parasites, such as beef and pork tapeworm, tells us something about the cooking of a medieval monarch's food that we may have surmised only from written accounts and medieval kitchen architecture before studying the skeleton'.

As soon as Woosnam-Savage saw the bones in 2012, particularly the battered skull still bearing the vivid signs of sharp force trauma, he was reminded of a line in a Welsh poem written within a few years of Bosworth in praise of Rhys ap Thomas, who fought with Henry Tudor at Bosworth and who has been credited by some with striking the final blow that killed Richard. The line in the poem by Guto'r Glyn, a poet who himself fought in the battle, chillingly, for Woosnam-Savage, described how after 'killing the boar, he shaved his head'. 'A most, simple, apt and evocative description of such wounds,' Woosnam-Savage said. 'Even if Rhys did not kill him, who would have guessed that Glyn's line about how someone "shaved the head of the boar" could perhaps be more than just a metaphor?' However, many scholars would still feel that it would be a mistake to try to read this poetic source too literally.

But if the bones vindicated some historical sources and accounts, they demolished others. 'The finding of Richard even shows up Leicester in a better light: his skeleton wasn't dragged through the city's streets by a jeering mob before being "thrown into the river Soar" after all.' As for the king himself, 'I don't think that the finding of the skeleton necessarily changes the views we generally have of Richard per se but it can help to question and interrogate those views more thoroughly than before', Woosnam-Savage said. 'For instance, we now know that Thomas More was simply wrong about some physical details of Richard: he did not have a withered arm. If More is wrong on this what else is he wrong about? So the discovery has illustrated how we should treat historical evidence with caution. Historians know this already but the public may not be so aware of the processes of historical debate.'

Although Shakespeare took much of his Richard from heavily biased sources like More, he was right concerning many things about the king, including his death in the thick of battle, on foot but fighting to the last.

In the autumn of 2013 the Nottingham Playhouse mounted the first major production of *Richard III* since the announcement that the car park skeleton was indeed Richard. The play, and the fascinating monster

Shakespeare made of Richard, helped keep alive public interest in one of the most enigmatic characters in medieval English history, while great performances in the role have helped make the reputation of great actors. In 1741 David Garrick's Richard electrified London, so realistic and convincing that Samuel Johnson declared, 'If Garrick really believed himself to be that monster, Richard III, he deserved to be hanged every time he performed it.' The artist William Hogarth recorded the performance in a portrait showing Richard rising from his haunted sleep on the eve of Bosworth with a horrified expression and one arm raised to ward off evil: the painting also became a bestselling print.

The critic William Hazlitt wrote that 'the Richard of Shakespeare is towering and lofty; equally impetuous and commanding; haughty, violent and subtle; bold and treacherous; confident in his strength as well as in his cunning; raised high by his birth and higher by his talents and his crimes; a royal usurper, a princely hypocrite, a tyrant and a murderer of the house of Plantagenet.' Hazlitt vividly recorded the early nineteenth-century performance of Edmund Kean in the role: 'Mr Kean's attitude in leaning against the side of the stage before he comes forward to address Lady Anne is one of the most graceful and striking ever witnessed on the stage. It would do for Titian to paint … The concluding scene in which he is killed by Richmond is the most brilliant of the whole. He fights at last like one drunk with wounds; and the attitude in which he stands with his hands stretched out, after his sword is wrested from him, has a preternatural and terrific grandeur, as if his will could not be disarmed, and the very phantoms of his despair had power to kill.'

Laurence Olivier's Richard, regarded as one of the greatest of the twentieth century, was preserved on film. In 1955 *The Guardian* critic called it 'a cinematographic miracle', and described the actor's 'dry humour and a tremendous personality expressed in the varying cadences of a magnificent voice'. Olivier's Richard was also reincarnated in a most unexpected way: John Lydon based his hunched, raging, explosively energetic stage persona Johnny Rotten, with the 1970s' punk band The Sex Pistols, on the filmed performance.

Loveday Ingram, a theatre director renowned for the detailed background research she puts into her plays, was already painfully aware of the weight of theatre history on her shoulders as she prepared to tackle the play for the first time for the 2013 Playhouse production, starring her husband Ian Bartholomew as Richard. She had already started researching and thinking about the play when one morning she turned on Radio 4 and heard the news about the Greyfriars skeleton. 'For days afterwards I couldn't get it out of my mind,' she recalls, 'and every time I turned on the radio or television people seemed to be talking about it. I found it absolutely staggering. I was so excited, to the point of obsession, that I watched and read everything I could find.' Very aware that hers would be the first production of the play since the discovery, she then went to Leicester to meet Buckley, who took the cast on a tour of the Greyfriars site, to discuss exactly how Richard died, blow by blow. 'Shakespeare's Richard is a fascinating character, extremely complex and ambiguous, stunningly villainous but also completely magnetic, witty, charming in a most dangerous way, utterly dominating whenever he is on stage. It was clear to me that what Shakespeare had written was a piece of Tudor propaganda, but I wondered what light from the historical truth I could shine on the play.'

Research rounded out the character for her: 'I don't know whether you could call any medieval king nice, but the more I read about him, the more I could see this was also a chap who did some good things. I firmly believe as a director I have to do the play Shakespeare wrote, but I wondered how to bring some of the real Richard onto the stage.' His physical characteristics were a way in. 'He didn't have a limp, he was light of foot and a good dancer. He didn't have a withered arm. But he was handicapped, he had a disability, he could have been in pain or short of breath sometimes, but there was nothing he could do about that, he had to fight, to lead his army into battle. So he was brave, and he died a terrible death, encircled by his enemies, fighting to the last. He was off his horse, struck down by multiple blows from above, just as Shakespeare said. So I thought we can do that, we can show that.' To suggest the medieval staff weapons – which the budget wouldn't stretch to recreating – she used long poles, painted red in an inspiration the designer took directly from a medieval manuscript illustration.

Ingram believes that all future directors will at least have to consider the truth about Richard revealed in the Leicester car park. Now, though, looking back on her production after almost two years have passed, she wonders if she herself went too far. 'Richard is an irresistibly seductive figure', she reflects. 'In the play he tramples on the audience's sympathies, and then he wins them back again by his sheer charm. I wonder now if he managed to seduce me from over the centuries. I think I got closer to the real Richard – but perhaps further from Shakespeare's play.'

Further reading

Baldwin, D. (1986) *Transactions of the Leicestershire Archaeological and Historical Society* 60:21–24. Available online at http://www.le.ac.uk/lahs/publications/vol51_60.html (last accessed 24 November 2014).

Buck, George (1646) *The History of the Life and Reigne of Richard the Third. Composed in five books.* London: William Wilson. A 1647 edition is available online at http://books.google.co.uk/books?id=ZiFEAAAAcAAJ&printsec=frontcover&dq=George+Buck&hl=en&sa=X&ei=B7WFVMS8HceuU_PcgPgP&ved=0CCIQ6AEwAA#v=onepage&q=George%20Buck&f=false (last accessed 9 December 2014).

Fiennes, Celia (1888) [travels 1698, written 1702] *Through England on a Side Saddle* (1888), edited by Emily Griffiths. London: Field and Tuer, The Leadenhall Press. Available online at http://www.visionofbritain.org.uk/travellers/Fiennes/20 (last accessed 24 November 2014).

Griffiths, R. A. (2014) *Sir Rhys ap Thomas and his Family: A Study in the Wars of the Roses and early Tudor Politics.* Cardiff: University of Wales Press, pp. xv–xvi. The poem by Guto'r Glyn, 'In praise of Sir Rhys ap Tomas of Abermarlais', edited by Dafydd Johnston, is available online at http://www.gutorglyn.net/gutorglyn/poem (last accessed 11 December 2014).

Knight, Sarah and Lund, Mary Ann (2013) Richard Crookback. How the physical remains of Richard III compare with historical and literary accounts of the King. *Times Literary Supplement*, 6 February. http://www.the-tls.co.uk/tls/public/article1208757.ece (last accessed 9 December 2014).

Schwyzer, Philip (2013) *Shakespeare and the Remains of Richard III*. Oxford: Oxford University Press. See pp. 25–8 on the epitaph of Richard III.

Walpole, Horace (1768) *Historic Doubts on the Life and Reign of Richard the Third*. London: J. Dodsley, Pall Mall. Available online at http://books.google.co.uk/books/about/Historic_Doubts_on_the_Life_and_Reign_of.html?id=h0UJAAAAQAAJ&redir_esc=y (last accessed 9 December 2014) and http://www.gutenberg.org/cache/epub/17411/pg17411.html (last accessed 24 November 2014).

10

RICHARD LAID TO REST

The Slow Reveal …

There was a faint scent from the great bunch of white roses brought by an earlier visitor, and the candle flickered in the draught from the door, lighting the copy of a famous portrait and the grey stone slab in the chancel floor of the cathedral. The woman read, puzzled, the carved words: Richard III King of England Killed at Bosworth Field.

'I thought Richard's grave was lost centuries ago,' she said, 'I never knew he was buried here.'

She was right, the guide told her, the grave was lost, probably forever. The slab, beautifully engraved by the calligrapher and stonecutter David Kindersley, was given by the Richard III Society in 1982. It was intended as a memorial because the king would never have a real marked grave; though some had suggested he might lie just 100 yards away, behind the row of Georgian and Victorian redbrick houses on the other side of the road, in sight of the cathedral door.

A local historian, David Baldwin, had even written that Richard's undisturbed grave may still be there to be found – but it was most unlikely that that would ever come about.

The Bones of a King: Richard III Rediscovered, First Edition. The Greyfriars Research Team with Maev Kennedy and Lin Foxhall.
© 2015 University of Leicester. Published 2015 by John Wiley & Sons, Ltd.

Where to Bury Richard?

In the months and years after the discovery of the remains in the Leicester car park, the most minute details of the treatment of the remains were passionately debated and became a subject of public controversy.

The public wrangling over where he should be reburied seemed unstoppable. Rival claims were made for Leicester; Westminster Abbey, where his wife Anne was buried; Middleham, where he lived and his son died; St George's in Windsor Castle with his brother Edward IV; Fotheringhay, where he was born and his parents lie; or York, where he had promised to endow a chantry chapel with 100 priests to pray for the benefit of his soul, though it was never built, and need not be interpreted as indicating Richard's funerary wishes. The debate escalated to questions in Parliament, petitions to 10 Downing Street and a judicial review, which meant work and fundraising for the Leicester Cathedral project had to be put on hold for months.

It had seemed unlikely, when the bones were originally uncovered on Saturday, 25 August 2012 – the first morning of the excavation – that they would prove to be of any significance, and they had been hastily covered up again to protect them from a sudden violent thunderstorm. They were finally excavated on Wednesday, 5 September. Over the weekend Richard Buckley had applied for the exhumation licence. Every line of both the application and the terms of the licence would be analysed in the judicial review in the following year. The intense public concern about every aspect of the treatment of the remains, and their eventual fate, demonstrated not just how important Richard still is to many but also how sensitive many people are about the treatment of human remains.

There would be no confirmation of identity until five months after the press conference announcing the discovery but, despite that, many were in no doubt that Richard had been found: the public debate about how his remains should be treated began immediately. These details really mattered to many people. Long before the first digger blade scraped at the car park tarmac, Philippa Langley, initiator of the Looking for Richard project, had worked with the historical design team of Wendy and David Johnson on a strikingly elaborate proposal for the reburial of the king, detailed down to the dovetail joints of the coffin and the colour of the pall that would cover it as it lay in the cathedral.

Although Langley was convinced her project would lead to Richard being found, few outsiders believed such elaborate advance planning would ever be needed.

Back in 2012, at the cathedral, Pete Hobson, Canon Missioner, then busy on a complex redevelopment of the building next door to the church, and Liz Hudson, Director of Communications, were vaguely aware that Langley had been in touch with the then dean, Vivienne Faull, and that it had something to do with reburying Richard III. It seemed an arcane question, given that so far nobody was digging up any part of Leicester looking for Richard, and therefore most unlikely to impinge in any way on their busy lives. They paid minimal attention. When Richard was indeed found, and came to dominate most of their waking hours, Hobson and Hudson acquired the unique status of project manager and coordinator of the burial of a medieval king. By then their dean had moved on to a new post. Ironically, in view of the controversy that exploded over where Richard should be buried, Faull had become dean of York. Her successor, David Monteith, spoke at the press conference in February 2013, announcing to the world that Richard had been found 'beyond reasonable doubt', and he said that planning had already begun to give the king a new grave within his cathedral.

However, the debate about where the king should be reburied was taken up not just by passionate Ricardians in the United Kingdom and across the world but by local politicians and tourism interests. It became so bitter that when York Minster issued a statement stressing that their church was not a candidate to hold his new tomb, but instead supporting 'the wish of the Chapter of Leicester that Richard should be reinterred in Leicester Cathedral', some of the letters they received were so menacing in tone that they were referred to the minster's security staff.

This level of public interest, and the passionately opposed views, came as something of a shock to both the Leicester Cathedral authorities and the archaeologists.

When Bones are Found (RB, MM LF)

The report on the legal challenge to the exhumation licence for Richard revealed that the Ministry of Justice receives up to 1,200 applications a year for remains buried in the last century, and a further 200 applications to disturb older burials. Archaeologists and builders find human remains every week in Britain, a small and densely populated island. Millennia of burial grounds, from Roman to Victorian, lie packed under its towns and cities, and prehistoric burials regularly turn up in farmland and greenfield development sites and in roadworks – as with the mass grave of decapitated Vikings found in Dorset in 2009.

The ULAS team, including Richard Buckley and Mathew Morris, who led the search for Richard's remains, had previously worked on one of the largest excavations in the city, on the site where the Highcross shopping centre was built. This included the recovery of 1,300 burials from the graveyard of the long lost church of St Peter (see Chapter 3). All were given a Christian reburial by priests from St Martin's.

Although on rare occasions the discovery of human remains becomes a news story, as with the uncovering of a Roman woman in London in 1999 sealed in a lead coffin complete with her funeral garlands, the public rarely learns of the disturbance of so many bones. Scientific study of them, revealing details of diet and disease, life and death, can give fascinating insights into social history, but in almost all cases the individuals will remain completely anonymous. Elaborate memorials were built over the graves of the very rich, but they have often been swept away in later development. Coffin plates only became common from the eighteenth century, and then only for the relatively wealthy. Even where burial ground records survive, in many cases the picture they present will be confused by the fact that, at different periods, graves will have been emptied and the bones gathered up into charnel houses to make space for new burials. The archaeologists in London working on the Bethlem burial ground, opened in 1569 beside the old St Bethlem mental hospital – popularly known as Bedlam – a site which now lies on the line of the Crossrail development, believe that of more than 10,000 people known to have been buried there, few if any will ever be identified.

No artefacts of any kind were found in Richard's grave, nothing which, had his history not been known, could have identified him. The name of the man whose skull was recovered from the River Soar by Bow Bridge in the nineteenth century will never be known. At the time some who believed the story that the king's bones had been dumped in the river thought it was Richard's head.

So if the discovery of some human remains on the Greyfriars site of a medieval burial ground was entirely predictable, the discovery of any named individual from more than 500 years ago was an extraordinarily rare event – so unusual that some archaeologists hoped the bones would be kept above ground and available for permanent study. While the royal connection enthralled the public, for archaeologists it was not the fact that Richard was a king but the fact that his name, age, much of his history and the circumstances of his death were known which made the find so remarkable. However, the law and best professional practice dictate that all human remains of all individuals, however lowly or exalted their original status in life, are treated with great respect.

Detailed advice for the treatment of human remains excavated from Christian burial grounds was published in 2005 by English Heritage and the Church of England: the presumption is against disturbing them, but the document acknowledges that frequently in the modern world this is unavoidable. It also notes that such remains 'are important sources of scientific information'. The guidance takes into account the benefits to research of examining the bones but makes it clear that once studies are complete they should ultimately be reburied in consecrated ground. It draws a clear distinction between human remains from the last century, where it will often be possible to trace relatives, including some who might have personally known the dead individual, and those from an earlier time. When relatives can be found, they should be consulted about reburial, but for remains older than a century such consultation is judged impractical.

The university published the following statement on its website on the practicality of consultation:

> Richard III left no direct descendants. There are a great many distant relatives of Richard III's immediate family alive today, scattered all over the world. Since Richard III lived so long ago, none of these are close relatives. So in the case of Richard III, the only surviving relatives are very distantly related, none will have known him personally, and there are far too many (running into millions) to trace and consult all of them.

This proved far from the last word on the subject. Every line of the original excavation plan, of Richard Buckley's application to exhume the bodies and of the terms of the licence would be analysed in the judicial review in the following year.

When he had applied for the exhumation licence he had known only that the team had found human remains in the area of the Greyfriars site that were of particular interest, and so he applied to lift up to six sets of remains. However, the application specifically provided for the one eventuality which seemed so improbable: 'In the unlikely event that the remains of Richard III are located, the intention is for these to be reinterred at St Martin's Cathedral, Leicester, within four weeks of exhumation.'

Anyone visiting the new King Richard III Visitor Centre can study the terms of the licence duly granted by the Ministry of Justice on 3 September. It deals with both the practical and the ethical concerns, providing that the actual lifting of the bones from the earth must be done 'with care and attention to decency', and screened from the public. The remains must be kept 'safely, privately and decently by the University of Leicester Archaeological Services under the control of a competent member of staff', and should then be deposited at the museum, 'or else be reinterred at St Martin's Cathedral or in a burial ground in which interments may legally take place'. None of the archaeologists foresaw the legal challenge that was to be mounted by the Plantagenet Alliance, a group claiming to be distant relatives of Richard's, who called on the Justice Secretary to revoke the terms of the licence and mount a wide-ranging public consultation on where the king should finally lie. At the time, a spokeswoman for the group, Vanessa Roe, told the media, 'We are the collateral descendants of Richard III, we speak on behalf of him, the only people who can speak on behalf of him.' Their challenge, which raised many general issues of who owns the dead and who should have a say in their disposal, was allowed to be heard on the grounds that the find was 'unprecedented' and so there was 'intense, widespread and legitimate public interest' in the outcome. The legal question was whether the licence had been correctly issued.

The hearings considered statements and detailed arguments from all sides. In his witness statement, Richard Buckley said,

I never considered any other city as a viable contender for the proposed reinterment on the grounds that: Richard III died in Leicester; a king of England (Henry VII) decided in 1485 that Richard III should be buried in Leicester; his remains have lain in Leicester ever since and he otherwise had links to the city during his lifetime. No other documented evidence had come to light to suggest that Richard himself wished to be buried in any of the alternative sites such as at York, Fotheringhay, Middleham or London.

The decision, unequivocally upholding the terms of the exhumation licence, was announced at the High Court in May 2014, and published in a 19,000-word judgement. At St Martin's Cathedral the Bishop of Leicester, Tim Stevens, announced the verdict and said, 'Here in the cathedral, in the diocese, in the city, in the county, we've waited a long time for this.'

However, the dispute has rumbled on, flaring up at every development in the story, including the designs for the tomb, the plans for the reburial service and the opening of the new visitor centre. In the summer months following the announcement of the High Court's decision, a group of those still arguing for a York burial wrote to every member of the houses of Commons and Lords, their argument couched in passionately emotional rather than legal terms:

> This matter for the majority of those who seek answers and receive none from those responsible, is one of simple human dignity about honouring the wishes of a man, as supported by historical contemporary evidence and about paying our respects as a nation with as much love and depth of feeling as we do with the loss of each reigning Monarch and member of the Royal Family.

At the cathedral they hope that Richard's reburial, in a dignified and beautiful space, open freely to all, may eventually help heal some of these scars.

The Cathedral Prepares to Receive Richard

For the cathedral clergy, as for the archaeologists, the discovery of human remains is a common occurrence, and sometimes there are compelling reasons to rebury them. The earliest secure reference to St Martin's Church was in 1220. When any work is being done in a building almost 1,000 years old, or in its environs, human remains are likely to be found, and indeed some were found and excavated during the work at the cathedral landscaping the grounds and preparing the burial site for Richard. Pete Hobson says that he has personally prayed over the reburial of thousands of remains, including those of the Highcross dead – and the three individuals found in the work on the cathedral gardens, part of the Richard project.

He and Liz Hudson had both followed the progress of the excavation, just across St Martin's, the narrow street that separated it from the cathedral. Yet both remember feeling startled at the news that Richard had been found, though they were not immediately aware of how it would change their lives: 'I don't think the full implications for us at the cathedral sank in at all at the beginning', Hobson said. 'There was a feeling that Richard had been found so we would rebury him, and it all seemed relatively straightforward.' That misapprehension rapidly passed.

The cathedral's first design proposal for a ledger, a stone slab set into the cathedral floor, not unlike the 1982 memorial, was received with outrage by some. The cathedral said such a memorial would have 'dignified simplicity', and pointed out that many modern monarchs had been buried under just such grave markers. The Richard III Society, which had already put forward a proposal for an ornate tomb chest, expressed great disappointment and predicted that future visitors would share their disappointment. Some voices put it much more strongly than that.

The eventual design emerged from many meetings and discussions, with ardent debate about the smallest details, including the colour of the stone and the size and style of the lettering.

When Hobson has spoken to people in Leicester about the project, some have expressed concern about the £2,500,000 cost, which included all the work on the building and the re-landscaping of the gardens, which has created a new public space for the city. The cathedral surrounds now include a water feature, which has proved very popular with children and local office workers eating their lunchtime sandwiches. Sometimes they discuss the garden's sculpture, *Towards Stillness*, which was commissioned by Leicestershire County Council from the design firm Dallas Pierce Quintero, a strikingly contemporary intervention in the space. Oriented in the direction of Bosworth, it uses 12 vertical steel plates, with silhouettes of the king on surfaces ranging from brightly polished to rust, set in planting that includes tall grasses and marshy plants to evoke Richard's last battle and the landscape where he met his death.

Hobson has discussed all of this with many people who asked him whether the cathedral should be spending any money at all on Richard, instead of on the poor, and a few who questioned whether the church should be giving a Christian burial to a man with such an infamous reputation. His response is that the money has been raised specifically for the Richard project; it would not have come to the cathedral otherwise and does not in any way affect the work they do every day of every week in the community. 'By an accident of history we are left sitting in the middle of all this,' he said, 'but other people have other interests, the cathedral's bit is God. We do God, they don't.' And as for passing judgement on Richard, that is not something he feels called on to do: 'Richard was indeed a mixed character, but we are all in need of the judgement and mercy of God. The actual Richard is not part of anyone's life today – he is in the hands of God and has been for the last 500 years.'

A Streetscape to Celebrate a King

The work on the spaces immediately around the cathedral mirror the changes in the neighbouring streets following the discovery of Richard's remains in the historic heart of Leicester. Their transformation has been remarkable. In the fifteenth century, Greyfriars lay in the heart of the commercial and religious life of a busy and prosperous town. More than two centuries after Richard's death, the redoubtable traveller Celia Fiennes was quite impressed by Leicester at the very end of the seventeenth century:

> It has 4 gates, the streetes are pretty Large and well pitch'd, there are five parishes; the Market place is a Large space very handsome, with a good Market Cross and town hall … in this Newark wch is a large space of ground are severall good houses some of stone and Brick in which some lawyers live; there is also a new pile of Building all of Brick wch is the Guild Hall where the assizes are kept twice in the yeare and the session quarterly.

Many of the handsome stone, brick and half-timbered medieval buildings Fiennes saw, by then shabby and so old-fashioned they were loved only by antiquarians, were, like the Blue Boar Inn, demolished in the nineteenth century. And, like most English cities, Leicester lost many fine buildings to twentieth-century planners and road building. New roads carved up the densely packed medieval heart of the city, cutting the St Martin's Cathedral quarter off from the castle and riverside, while new commercial and residential developments sprawled out far beyond the line of the old city walls. A mid twentieth-century history of the Alderman Newton's Boys' School remarked gloomily,

> The dirt and grime from the smoky chimneys of a town reputedly renowned for its cleanliness have settled immovably on the building's exterior. In close proximity too, a bus station, a scrap yard, and an undistinguished row of shops and offices scarcely serve as inspirations to the school. The thunder of traffic, north and south bound, produces an atmosphere even less conducive to academic work.

In 2012, when the excavation began, the city also bore many scars of the economic recession. With the exception of the beautiful cathedral and the Guildhall the area around the Greyfriars site was shabby, with the sites of many formerly prosperous businesses marked only by boarded up and decaying buildings. The handsome Victorian gothic buildings of the old school, which had become Leicester Grammar School but was closed in 2008 when the school moved to a new location, lay empty and awaiting redevelopment. Behind the shabby buildings fronting onto the street, the leafy gardens visible in a Victorian photograph taken from the St Martin's spire had all gone, replaced by tatty car parks. Today, the unhappy school historian would be astonished to see the street, with its new paving, lighting and street furniture, and – as throughout what remains of Richard's Leicester – notice boards recounting the unexpected new chapter in its history.

While the 2012 excavation took place behind tall screens, apart from a couple of public open days, there was a viewing platform for the 2013 season when the archaeologists returned to recover more information about the lost friary and the context of Richard's grave. The platform was always crowded, and the archaeologists came to know many of the visitors by name as the same people returned day after day to spend hours standing and watching, undeterred by the fact that the site was never likely to produce any new revelation as exciting as the grave of the last Plantagenet. On the last day, of what, for the foreseeable future, was the last excavation of the site, many said how sad they were that it was all going to be buried and tarred over, and they would never again see what had already become a cherished part of the history of the city, an intense source of local pride. But the site remains in the public gaze: the local authority stepped in and bought the old school and joined it with the scrap of land in the social services car park, just beyond the playground wall, which was the site of the actual grave.

The school buildings have now been transformed into the King Richard III Visitor Centre, which opened in the summer of 2014. The shadowy rooms downstairs take the visitors into the Middle Ages, telling the story of Richard's ancestry, life and death at Bosworth. In striking contrast the twentieth- and twenty-first-century fascination with Richard is recounted in the bright daylight of the rooms upstairs, where the whole story of the excavation is told. The exhibits include not just the 3D printout replica of the skeleton – displayed as if about to be run through the Leicester Infirmary scanner – and the recreation of Richard's head but also Philippa Langley's Union-flag wellies, which she wore on the site, the digger blade that first exposed the bones and the hi-vis jacket Mathew Morris was wearing when he first spotted one leg bone just visible in the red earth.

The final exhibit is the one the visitors find most moving: some spend long periods there in quiet reflection. A pale stone pavilion, with stone benches along the walls that recall the friars' chapter house, whose foundations gave the archaeologists their first clue that their trench had located the lost Greyfriars church, now covers the site of the grave. The rough outlines of the grave itself, the remains of the Victorian wall which came so close to obliterating it, and the traces of the diamond-set medieval tiles which helped confirm to the archaeologists that they had really found the choir of the church, can be seen through the thick glass slabs in the floor. The trench where Jo Appleby spent perhaps the most extraordinary day of her career carefully exposing the bones, one by one, lies empty apart from a light projection of the outline of the skeleton as she uncovered it and the two yellow plastic pegs that were placed by the archaeologists to mark the head and foot of the body.

Cut into the stonework wall over the grave are the words of a prayer which during his lifetime was written into Richard's own Book of Hours, now in the library of Lambeth Palace in London. It reads:

> Lord Jesus Christ, deign to free me, your servant King Richard, from every tribulation, sorrow and trouble in which I am placed … Hear me in the name of all your goodness, for which I give thanks, and for all the gifts granted to me, because you made me from nothing and redeemed me out of your bounteous Love and pity from eternal damnation to promising eternal life.

Although such prayers were common in many surviving examples of beautiful and costly books once owned by monarchs, it is impossible not to read them as a poignant echo of Richard's short and difficult life and terrible death. The words are also a reminder of why the ceremonies across the road in the cathedral, though grand and solemn, were not a funeral.

It must surely have been true that the defeated king was buried on the orders of the victor, as the historian Polydore Vergil wrote, 'sine ullo funere honore', without the appropriate funeral honours for an anointed king. However, to have been buried in the consecrated ground within the church, as the archaeology showed he was, he must have had at least a minimal funeral service. It was not true, as a Yorkshire schoolteacher called William Burton claimed, that Richard was 'an ypocryte, a croche bake, and berried in a dike like a dogge'. His words, in 1491, just six years after the king's death, were preserved in York's civic records, and probably reflected what many believed had happened to the stripped and humiliated corpse.

Francis Bacon, in his 1622 *Historie of the Raigne of King Henry the Seventh*, clearly felt that all had not been done well. He wrote that Richard was 'obscurely buried', but he was anxious to absolve the victor of Bosworth from any blame. Instead, he blamed the friars, claiming they shared the popular hatred of the dead man as a tyrant: 'For though the King of his noblenesse gave charge unto the Friers of Leicester to see an honourable interrment to be given to it, yet the Religious People themselves (being not free from the humours of the Vulgar) neglected it; wherein neverthelesse they did not then incurre any mans blame or censure.'

That seems inconceivable.

The evidence of the grave was clear. Richard certainly did not have the honours he would have received if he had won at Bosworth, reigned for many more years and perhaps had a great state funeral at Westminster Abbey. The grave was quickly and roughly dug, smashing through some of the floor tiles, which shattered into the pit, and it was slightly too short even for someone of Richard's height. He went into it, too, without a coffin or apparently even a shroud, but it was in a position of respect within the church, a space close to the high altar reserved for only the burials of the elite and the esteemed. Whether the friars were asked to undertake the burial, or volunteered, they must have wanted to make short work of interring a body which had been lying in the open for several days in August. However, they were Franciscan friars; they saw burying the dead, and ensuring that their souls were committed to the mercy and keeping of God, as part of their pastoral role in medieval society. They would certainly have laid him into the ground with prayers for his soul. Richard had had a Christian funeral in 1485 in which his soul was consigned to God; the reinterment of his bones did not call for a repeat of the rites.

Although, Hobson said, the cathedral community was determined to avoid any fake medieval pageantry, and instead wanted to create a twenty-first-century memorial and ceremony for a fifteenth-century king, they also wanted to follow good historical practice. There was no exact precedent for the ceremony they were charged with organising, but they did extensive research with advice from the historian Julian Litten, author of *The English Way of Death*, a landmark study of the traditions of death and burial of both the great and humble.

The cathedral authorities considered the occasions when royal figures were moved from one grave to another, something which has happened surprisingly frequently. Alfred the Great was exhumed and reburied at least twice in Winchester; Richard III moved Henry VI from Chertsey to Windsor; James VI reburied his mother, Mary Queen of Scots, executed on Elizabeth's orders, in a magnificent tomb in Westminster Abbey. Richard himself played a leading role in the spectacular ceremony organised by Edward IV, when his brother reburied the bodies of their father and brother Edmund at Fotheringhay. There must have been another ceremony when their remains were moved and reburied yet again on the orders of Elizabeth I when their end of the church had become derelict. The cathedral chapter described the reburial of Richard as 'an event of national and international importance' – but at the heart of it, the dean said, was a church which had prepared with great care 'to offer him lasting sanctuary and peace'.

Although there was so much discussion before most if not all the Ricardians were finally agreed on the design of the stone tomb, there was universal welcome for the poetic idea of commissioning a coffin from Michael Ibsen, the cabinetmaker who was also Richard's sixteen times great-nephew. Ibsen, who had never even considered making a coffin before, was startled but touched by the invitation, and he kept a copy of *The English Way of Death* by his bench in his workshop. 'It was an extraordinary thing to be asked to contribute', Ibsen said. 'This wasn't just a piece of furniture, it was something intensely personal. I had been asked to make something that was layered with meaning for many people. I saw my coffin as a way of adding another element that would have significance, something that would tell a little more of the story.'

The original suggestion was for the remains to be contained in an ossuary, a small box especially designed for this purpose, but some felt this was an undignified way to treat the bones, which had been lying as they were buried for so long. The final decision was to rebury them in as close as possible to the original position in which they had lain in the ground. Litten advised that in the fifteenth century royal remains were more likely to have been placed in a body-shaped lead casket than in a wooden coffin, and the casket would then be laid directly into the vault. The burial excavated in the car park by the archaeologists in 2013, only a few metres from Richard's grave, was sealed in lead inside a stone sarcophagus. Richard's bones, together with any remaining fragments of the samples taken for DNA testing and isotope analysis, have therefore been sealed into a lead lining inside Ibsen's wooden casket.

Ibsen constructed a frame inside his coffin to hold the lead casket in place, choosing, for its symbolism, yew: the wood of the longbows of the English archers who had played a crucial role in so many battles. Then, when it came to sourcing the timber for the casket itself, he had an inspiration. He remembered that Willy Bullough, owner of the sawmill in Whitney-on-Wye where he buys most of his timber, had once mentioned that some of his supplies come from the Duchy of Cornwall, the estate of the Prince of Wales. Word came back to Ibsen that the Duchy was delighted by the idea of timber coming from the forests of the present Prince of Wales to make a coffin for Richard, whose own son Edward held the title for less than a year of his short life.

The coffin is far plainer than most familiar modern coffins, without handles or ornament apart from the beautiful English oak: Ibsen said modestly that he can neither draw nor carve, but in any case felt that the coffin should be simple, elegant and evocative. 'It was certainly never just another job to me', Ibsen said. 'It was the last service I could do for Richard. He was a king, but he was also part of my family.'

A King Reburied

A review of the plans for 26 March 2015 uncovers the intricacy and care which so many people bestowed on ensuring a fitting, stately burial for Richard III with beautiful music, flowers, candlelight and Christian prayers, in a cathedral prepared for the presence of national and international figures, including the leaders of the Anglican, Roman Catholic and many other faiths in England, and representatives of the city which sheltered the remains of a king for more than 500 years. Last time, his body came back from Bosworth field humiliatingly slung naked over the back of a horse to be hastily buried in a makeshift grave. The twenty-first-century planning extended the ceremonies to a week.

It was felt appropriate that his body should be brought with dignity along the route from the field of battle, his coffined remains beginning their formal progress from Fenn Lane Farm. The fields on both sides of a narrow road there were only identified in 2010 as the true site of Bosworth field and the place where, in a two-hour battle, the final scenes of the Wars of the Roses were played out: the ground where he lost his final desperate fight to keep his crown and his life. From there, the route of the cortege was carefully planned to incorporate visits to the villages and towns associated with Richard's last days and death, including Market Bosworth; Dadlington, where some of the battle dead were buried in the parish churchyard; and Sutton Cheney, where it is believed Richard heard his final Mass at St James's Church on the eve of the battle.

It was agreed that, nearing the culmination of the route, when Richard's remains reached Leicester crossing Bow Bridge as in 1485, they should be met by the mayor and other civic dignitaries before being carried on a horse-drawn hearse to be received into the cathedral. St Martin's was a parish church when Richard was buried in the friary across the road, but it has been the principle church of the Leicester Diocese since 1927, and since the decision was made to reinter Richard within its precincts, work on the building and its surroundings have created a new space suitable to hold the bones of a king in honour.

Every detail of events was subject to minute discussion, out of which emerged plans for the termination of one of the most extraordinary periods in the history of the University of Leicester to coincide with the final moments of Richard's last journey. It was decided that Richard Buckley would hand over the exhumation licence under which the king's bones were excavated at the point at which his cortege reached the church door – the act demonstrating the formal transfer of care of the remains which he and his colleagues had looked after since September 2012, from the university to the cathedral.

The first time, Richard's battered body was exposed, in a nearby church or possibly in Greyfriars, just a few metres away, to prove to the gleeful, fearful or merely curious that a king was dead and another head wore the crown. The second time, it was agreed, the body should lie for three days on a bier covered by a magnificent, specially embroidered pall, allowing everyone to visit and share a moment of contemplation of the fate of kings and all mortal men, before its burial in an English oak coffin made by a craftsman whose DNA proved he was of Richard's family.

The old slab in the cathedral floor given by the Richard III society, cut with the words 'Richard III King of England Killed at Bosworth Field 22nd August 1485', looked so like a tombstone that it convinced many casual visitors to the church. By coincidence, the day when the works programme reached the point when the slab had to be lifted to make way for the new tomb was 22 August 2014, the anniversary of the battle. The new tomb, a brick-lined vault beneath the crossing, was designed by the architects van Heyningen and Haward, who have also created the new spaces in the cathedral. It is sealed with a great slab of fossil-rich Swaledale limestone quarried in Yorkshire, tilted towards the east and the rising sun, polished till it gleams and so deeply incised with a cross that light spills through the cut, a symbol of the resurrection. Richard's name, dates, motto and emblems are carved into the dark Kilkenny-marble plinth.

No one can foretell the future: the Franciscans who buried Richard in 1485 surely thought their church would stand for centuries if not forever, when in fact it barely lasted another 50 years, destroyed in the dissolution of the monasteries in 1538. This time, some, including some archaeologists and historians, wondered if the new tomb could be designed so that it could easily be reopened, allowing access to the remains if science moves on so that new tests and new revelations become possible. However, David Monteith, Dean of Leicester, has insisted that what the cathedral could offer Richard was undisturbed sanctuary. His tomb would be sealed. Even the remaining fragments of the samples taken for testing have been carefully interred with the bones, and the scientists have retained nothing: the evidence gained from the years of research remains, but the mortal remains of a king have been returned to the earth forever.

Further reading

English Heritage and the Church of England (2005) *Guidance for Best Practice for Treatment of Human Remains Excavated from Christian Burial Grounds in England*. Swindon: English Heritage. Available at: https://www.english-heritage.org.uk/publications/human-remains-excavated-from-christian-burial-grounds-in-england (last accessed 9 December 2014).

Litten, Julian (1991) The English Way of Death: *The Common Funeral Since 1450*. London: Robert Hale Ltd.

Appendix 1

Close Maternal-line Relatives of Richard III

Historical accounts record Richard III as having one shoulder higher than the other; sustaining battle injuries and being killed at the Battle of Bosworth; and as being brought back to Leicester and subsequently buried in the choir of the church of the Greyfriars. However, albeit there is no record of even one of these features also being true of any of Richard's relatives, could there be the slightest chance that the burial is actually that of a female-line relative of Richard III of the right age, who also suffered a spinal abnormality, who died at the Battle of Bosworth, and who would therefore also show evidence of battle injuries, who was brought back to Leicester and buried in the choir of the church of the Greyfriars in Leicester and carry the same mtDNA type?

In order to attempt to answer this question, the inheritance of Richard's mtDNA was traced for seven generations, from his maternal great-great-grandmother down and out through his network of cousins, identifying any males who would have been alive at the time of Bosworth and who might be candidates for the skeleton in the site of the Greyfriars. It is not possible to trace the line further back than this as the identity of his maternal great-great-great-grandmother is unknown. A summary of this genealogy is given here. In order to simplify the genealogical information, every individual in the overall tree has been assigned a unique number. Additionally, the overall tree has been broken down into a series of component family sub-trees. Females carrying the mtDNA who married and passed this on to

The Bones of a King: Richard III Rediscovered, First Edition. The Greyfriars Research Team with Maev Kennedy and Lin Foxhall.
© 2015 University of Leicester. Published 2015 by John Wiley & Sons, Ltd.

children of their own will appear in two family sub-trees, as daughter in the first, then as mother in the second. The descent from sons is not included since they cannot pass on the mtDNA. Spouses marrying into the network are included where appropriate, but since these do not carry the mtDNA their identification number is ~~struck through~~. Males carrying the same mtDNA type as Richard, but NOT at risk of being confused with the skeleton in the Greyfriars friary (as either already dead, known to have survived beyond Bosworth or alive at the time of Bosworth but clearly too old or too young) have their identification number in **bold type**.

This lineage was reconstructed using a wide variety of documentary sources.

Tree 1

The name of Richard III's great-great-grandmother [1] is uncertain. She was the wife of Sir Payne Roët of Guienne (or Paon de Roët) [2]. They had three daughters:

[3]   Isabel (Isabelle), became a nun (Canoness of the Convent of St Waudru, Mons) and died childless.

[4]   Phillippa (*c*.1346–*c*.1387), married the poet Geoffrey Chaucer [6] when aged about 10. Details of offspring [7–10] are shown below, *Tree 2*.

[5]   Katherine (*c*.1350–1403), Richard's great-grandmother, who married first Sir Hugh Swynford (*c*.1366–) [~~11~~], and second, as third wife, John of Gaunt, Duke of Lancaster (–1399) [~~12~~], son of Edward III and father of Henry IV (from his first wife Blanche). Details of offspring [13–19] are shown below, *Tree 3*.

Tree 2

Phillippa de Roët [4] is recorded as having up to four children, although some suggest only three. It is also possible that some (or all) of these children were actually fathered by John of Gaunt [~~12~~] rather than her husband, Geoffrey [6][24–26]. All four children are believed to have died childless, the Chaucer family having died out by the fifteenth century.

[7] Elizabeth (*c*.1364–), a nun in Barking Abbey.
[8] Thomas (*c*.1367–).
[9] Agnes, a lady in waiting at Henry IV's coronation in 1399.
[10] Lewis (*c*.1381–). (Possibly not their child.)

Tree 3

Katherine de Roët [5] had seven children from her two husbands, three with Hugh Swynford [11] and four with John of Gaunt [12] (all born out of wedlock but subsequently legitimated by charter under Richard II, 1397):

[13] Blanche (1367–9).
[14] Thomas (1368–1432).
[15] Margaret (*c*.1369–), became a nun and died childless.
[16] John Beaufort (1373–1410), first Earl of Somerset, Marquis of Dorset and Lord High Admiral of England.
[17] Henry Beaufort (*c*.1374–1447), Bishop of Winchester and Cardinal, Lord Chancellor.
[18] Thomas Beaufort (*c*.1377–1426), first Duke of Exeter.
[19] Joan Beaufort (*c*.1379–1440), who married, first, Sir Robert Ferrers [20], fifth Baron Botcher of Wem in 1391 and, second, Ralph Neville, first Earl of Westmorland [21]. Details of offspring [22–37] are shown below, *Tree 4*.

Tree 4

Joan Beaufort [19], Richard's grandmother, had sixteen children, two daughters by her first husband, Robert Ferrers [20], and five daughters and nine sons by her second husband, Ralph Neville [21], as follows:

[22] Elizabeth Ferrers (1393–1434), who married John de Greystoke [38], fourth Baron Greystoke (1389–1436), in 1407. Details of offspring [39–50] are shown below, *Tree 5*.
[23] Margaret Ferrers (1394–1458), who married Ralph Neville [51] (–1458) in *c*.1413. The marriage is recorded as resulting in only one son, John Neville [52] of Oversley (*c*.1416–82), Sheriff for Lincolnshire.

[24] Katherine Neville (*c.*1400–*c.*1484), married four times: to John de Mowbray, second Duke of Norfolk [53]; Thomas Strangeways [54], John, Viscount Beaumont; and John Woodville. Details of offspring [55–57] are shown below, *Tree 6.*

[25] Eleanor Neville (–1472), who married, first, Richard le Despenser [58], fourth Baron Burghersh, and had no issue, and, second, Henry Percy [59], second Earl of Northumberland. Details of offspring [60–69] are shown below, *Tree 7.*

[26] Richard Neville (1400–60), fifth Earl of Salisbury.

[27] Robert Neville (–1457).

[28] William Neville (–1463), first Earl of Kent.

[29] Anne Neville, who married Humphrey Stafford [70], sixth Earl of Stafford and first Duke of Buckingham (1402–60), who died at the Battle of Northampton. Details of offspring [71–80] are shown below, *Tree 8.*

[30] Edward Neville (–1476).

[31] Cecily Neville (1415–95), mother of Edward IV [86] and Richard III [93], married Richard Plantagenet [81] (–1460), third Duke of York, Protector of England, died at the Battle of Wakefield. Details of offspring [82–94] are shown below, *Tree 9.*

[32] George Neville (–1469).

[33] Joan Neville, died childless.

[34] John Neville, died young.

[35] Cuthbert Neville, died young.

[36] Thomas Neville, died young.

[37] Henry Neville, died young.

Tree 5

Elizabeth Ferrers [22] had six sons and six daughters from her marriage with John de Greystoke[38], fourth Baron Greystoke (*c.*1389–1436), as follows:

[39] Richard, died without issue before his father.

[40] Henry, died without issue before his father.

[41] William, died without issue before his father.

[42] Ralph (–1487), Baron Greystoke, buried in Kirkham Monastery.

[43] Joan (1408–56), married, first, John Darcy [95] seventh Baron Darcy of Knaith (succeeding his brother Philip), and, second, William Stoke [96]. Details of offspring [97–104] are shown below *Tree 10.*

[44] Anne (–1477), married in 1432 to Ralph Bigod [~~106~~] of Settrington, who died at the Battle of Towton. Details of offspring [107–112] are shown below, *Tree 11*.

[45] Thomas, died unmarried before 1487 (as brother Ralph succeeded by granddaughter).

[46] Eleanor, married Ralph Eure [~~115~~]. Details of offspring [116–127] are shown below, *Tree 12*.

[47] John, died unmarried before 1487 (as brother Ralph succeeded by granddaughter).

[48] Catherine, became a nun and died unmarried.

[49] Matilda, died unmarried.

[50] Elizabeth (1428–), married Roger Thornton [~~128~~] in 1440. Details of offspring [129–130] are shown below, *Tree 13*.

Tree 6

Katherine Neville [24] had one son from her first marriage to John de Mowbray [~~53~~] and two daughters from her marriage to Thomas Strangeways [~~54~~], as follows:

[55] John de Mowbray (–1461), third Duke of Norfolk.

[56] Joan Strangeways, who married William Willoughby [~~131~~], with whom she had a daughter, Cecily [132], who married Edward Sutton [~~158~~], second Baron Dudley, but had no children born prior to Bosworth.

[57] Catherine Strangeways, who married Henry Grey [~~133~~], fourth Baron of Codnor, yet remained childless.

Tree 7

Eleanor Neville [25] married, first, Richard le Despenser [~~58~~], fourth Baron Burghersh (1396–1414), yet this young marriage was childless. Her second marriage to Henry Percy [~~59~~], second Earl of Northumberland (1393–1455), produced seven sons and three daughters, as follows:

[60] John (1418–), died before his father (pre-Bosworth).

[61] Henry (1421–61), third Earl of Northumberland, died at the Battle of Towton. His son, Henry, fourth Earl of Northumberland (who would not have shared mtDNA with Richard III), led

troops at Bosworth in the Yorkist cause but failed to engage. After Bosworth he was imprisoned by Henry VII but was subsequently released and allowed to retain his titles and land.

[62] Thomas (1433–60), first Baron Egremont, died at the Battle of Northampton.

[63] Katherine (1423–75), married Edmund Grey [~~134~~], first Earl of Kent (1416–90). Details of offspring [135–138] are shown below, *Tree 13*.

[64] George (1424–74).

[65] Ralph (1425–64), died at the Battle of Hedgeley Moor.

[66] Richard (1427–61), died at the Battle of Towton.

[67] William (1428–62).

[68] Anne, died unmarried.

[69] Joan, died unmarried.

Tree 8

Anne Neville [29] had six sons, two of whom were twins, and four daughters through her marriage with Humphrey Stafford [~~70~~], sixth Earl of Stafford and first Duke of Buckingham, as follows:

[71] Humphrey (1425–58), seventh Earl of Stafford. Married Margaret Beaufort (daughter of the second duke of Somerset) and fathered Henry, second Duke of Buckingham, who was instrumental in persuading Parliament to declare Edward V illegitimate and subsequently offer the throne to Richard III. He later switched his allegiance and rebelled against Richard in favour of Henry Tudor, but the rebellion failed and Buckingham was beheaded for treason in 1483. His widow, Catherine, subsequently married Jasper Tudor.

[72] Henry (*c*.1425–71), married Margaret Beaufort (daughter of the first duke of Somerset), as her third husband. She had previously married John de la Pole [~~149~~] (subsequently the second duke of Suffolk) at a very early age, yet the marriage was dissolved before she reached the age of 12. Her second marriage was to Edmund Tudor, first Earl of Richmond, with whom she had Henry Tudor (later Henry VII). Her fourth marriage, following Henry Stafford's death, was with Thomas Stanley, first Earl of Derby.

[73] John (1427–73), first Earl of Wiltshire.

[74] Edward, died young.

[75] Margaret (1435–75), married Sir Robert Dunham [~~139~~] (1430–) with whom she had a son, Sir John Dunham [140] (1450–1524), who was knighted by Henry VII at the Battle of Blackheath in 1497.

[76] Catherine (1437–76), married John Talbot [~~141~~], third Earl of Shrewsbury, third Earl of Waterford, twelfth Baron Strange of Blackmore (1448–73). Details of offspring [142–144] are shown below, *Tree 15*.

[77] George (1439–), twin of below, died young.

[78] William (1439–), twin of above, died young.

[79] Joan (1442–84), not known to have married.

[80] Anne (1446–72), not known to have married.

Tree 9

Cecily Neville [31] married Richard Plantagenet [~~81~~], third Duke of York and had thirteen children as follows:

[82] Henry (1438–*c*.1440).

[83] Anne of York (1439–76), married, first, Henry Holland [~~145~~], third Duke of Exeter, by whom she had a single daughter, Anne [147], who died without issue. Secondly, she married Sir Thomas St Leger [~~146~~], by whom she has a single daughter, Anne St Leger [148], Baroness de Rous, all of whose male children with George Manners were born after the Battle of Bosworth. Anne St Leger's daughter Katherine is the common maternal ancestor of the two living individuals (Michael Ibsen and Wendy Duldig) from whom DNA samples were taken.

[84] Henry (1441–), died in infancy.

[85] Edward (1442–83), Duke of York, later Edward IV.

[86] Edmund (1443–60), Earl of Rutland, died at the Battle of Wakefield.

[87] Elizabeth (1444–1503), married John de la Pole [~~149~~], second Duke of Suffolk. Details of offspring [150–160] are shown below, *Tree 16*.

[88] Margaret (1446–1503), married Charles I [~~161~~], Duke of Burgundy (the Bold) and died childless.

[89] William (1447–), died young.
[90] John (1448–), died young.
[91] George (1449–78), first Duke of Clarence.
[92] Thomas (1451–), died young.
[93] Richard (1452–85), Duke of Gloucester, later Richard III.
[94] Ursula (1455–), died young.

Tree 10

Joan Greystoke [43] is believed to have had five sons and three daughters with her first husband John Darcy [95], seventh Baron Darcy of Knaith, of Temple Hurst, Yorkshire, as follows. She married, secondly, William Stoke [96] in 1458, yet had no further children. The children of her first marriage were as follows:

[97] Richard (1424–58), married Eleanor Scrope.
[98] John (*c*.1426–61).
[99] George, died young, unmarried.
[100] Elizabeth, died young, unmarried.
[101] Thomas, died young, unmarried.
[102] Philip, died young, unmarried.
[103] Jane, married John Beaumont [105]. Details relating to this marriage, shown below, are unclear, see *Tree 17.*
[104] Eleanor, died young, unmarried.

Tree 11

Anne Greystoke [44] married Ralph Bigod [106] of Settrington in 1432 and had six children, two sons and four daughters, as are shown below:

[107] John (of Settrington), died at the Battle of Towton, 1461.
[108] Thomas (*c*.1435–). Death unknown, but too old to be a skeleton at The Greyfriars friary.
[109] Anne, believed to have died young.
[110] Catherine (*c*.1439–). Death unknown, believed to have been unmarried.
[111] Matilda (*c*.1440–). Death unknown, believed to have been unmarried.

[112]   Agnes, who married Thomas Stillington [~~113~~], by whom she had a daughter, Catherine [114], whose own sons all died after Bosworth.

However, note that some web-based genealogies record Anne and Ralph as having fifteen children. Yet the Visitation of Yorkshire 1584/85 attributes Ralph Bigod (of Scagglethorphe, next to Settrington) as having nine children through a marriage to Margaret Plumpton (daughter of Sir Robert Plumpton) through whom the line descended. This is presumably either a second marriage or a different Ralph Bigod. None of the children from the second family would have carried the same mtDNA as Richard III.

Tree 12

Eleanor (Ellinor) Greystoke [46], married Ralph Eure [~~115~~] in 1440 and had seven sons and five daughters, as follows. (Some accounts suggest six of each; the confusion arises because it is not entirely clear if they had two sons called John (*Johanni*) or two daughters called Joan (*Johanna*)). Ralph Eure was killed at the Battle of Towton in 1461:

[116]   Joan (*c.*1438–), died unmarried.
[117]   William (*c.*1440–84), heir to Ralph. Married Margaret, daughter of Sir Robert Constable of Hainborough.
[118]   Ralph (*c.*1442–*c.*1484). Will proved at York, 19 June 1484.
[119]   Elizabeth (*c.*1444–81), died before 1484. Married three times. Details of offspring [164–167] are shown below, *Tree 18.*
[120]   Henry (*c.*1446–), twin of below, died in childhood.
[121]   John (*c.*1446–), twin of below, died in childhood.
[122]   Margaret/Margery (*c.*1448–), unmarried, a nun at Watton.
[123]   Robert (*c.*1450–) was a Knight of the Order of St John of Jerusalem, details of death unknown.
[124]   John (*c.*1452–*c.*1493). Will proved at York, 11 June 1493, buried at Hutton Bushell.
[125]   Anne (*c.*1454–), recorded as marrying Thomas Rokeby (who fought at the Battle of Bramham Moor), details of any children are unclear, but they would be too young to be confused with Skeleton 1.

[**126**]   Hugh (*c*.1456–*c*.1523), rector of Huggate, and later Brompton in Pickering Lythe. Will proved at York, 16 April, 1523.

[127]   Mary (*c*.1458–), recorded as marrying Hilton (name uncertain) in 1483, details of any children unclear but would be too young to be confused with Skeleton 1.

Tree 13

Elizabeth Greystoke [50] married Roger Thornton [~~128~~] in 1440 and had two daughters, as follows:

[129]   Elizabeth (*c*.1450–), married George[~~168~~] Lord Lumley (*c*.1444–1507). Details of offspring [169–171] are shown below, *Tree 19*.

[130]   Joan, is given as unmarried in some sources, but it is also possible that she could have married Richard Ogle. Any resulting children would be too young to be confused with Skeleton 1.

Tree 14

Katherine Percy [63] married Edmund Grey [~~134~~], first Earl of Kent and had two sons and two daughters as follows:

[**135**]   Anthony, married Eleanor, sister of Elizabeth Woodville, wife of Edward IV, and died childless in 1480.

[**136**]   George (1454–1505), second Earl of Kent.

[**137**]   Elizabeth (–1472), married Sir Robert de Greystock [~~172~~] (*c*.1443–83) and died without having any sons.

[**138**]   Anne, married John Grey [~~173~~], eighth Baron Grey of Wilton (*c*.1443–99). Details of offspring [174–183] are shown below, *Tree 20*.

Tree 15

Catherine Stafford [76] married John Talbot [~~141~~], third Earl of Shrewsbury, third Earl of Waterford, twelfth Baron Strange of Blackmore (1448–73) and had two sons and a daughter:

[142] George (1468–1528), fourth Earl of Shrewsbury, fourth Earl of Waterford, tenth Baron Talbot, ninth Baron Furnivall (1468–1528). Fought with Henry at Bosworth, as did his uncle and guardian, Sir Gilbert Talbot.

[143] Thomas (1470–), believed to have died young, but too young to be Skeleton 1.

[144] Anne (1472–), married Thomas Butler. Any children would have been born after Bosworth.

Tree 16

Elizabeth of York [87] married John de la Pole [~~149~~], second Duke of Suffolk and had seven sons and four daughters:

[150] John de la Pole (*c*.1462–87), first Earl of Lincoln. Married Lady Margaret FitzAlan, with whom he had a son (Edward) who died young. He was the *de facto* heir to Richard III (his maternal uncle) following Bosworth, yet initially sided with Henry VII. Subsequently he led a short-lived Yorkist rebellion and was defeated and killed at the Battle of Stoke.

[151] Geoffrey (1464–), died young.

[152] Edward (1466–85), Archdeacon of Richmond.

[153] Elizabeth (*c*.1468–89), married Henry Lovel, eighth Baron Morley yet had no children.

[154] Edmund (1471–1513), third Duke of Suffolk, beheaded by Henry VIII as a Yorkist pretender.

[155] Dorothy (1472–), died young.

[156] Humphrey (1474–1513), a cleric.

[157] Anne (1476–95), died unmarried, a nun.

[158] Catherine (*c*.1477–1513), married William Stourton, fifth Baron Stourton yet had no children.

[159] William (1478–1539), of Wingfield Castle, yet often kept in the Tower of London. Married Katherine Stourton but had no children.

[160] Richard (1480–1525), lived in exile as a Yorkist pretender following death of his brothers, allying himself with Louis XII of France. Two planned invasions, however, never took place and

he died fighting alongside Francis I at the Battle of Pavia. He was known as the 'White Rose'.

Tree 17

Jane Darcy [103] married John Beaumont [~~105~~]. Details relating to this marriage are unclear, yet Foster *County Families* gives a John Beaumont of Newsome as marrying Jane, who could be Jane Darcy. This marriage resulted in two sons, Adam and Henry, both of whom were living during the reign of Henry VII. Some sources suggest that Jane's marriage was dissolved.

Tree 18

Elizabeth Eure [119] married three times, the first time to Sir William Bulmer [~~161~~], the second to Sir James Strangeways [~~162~~] and the third to John Ellerker [~~163~~]. The first marriage resulted in a daughter, the second marriage a daughter and two sons, the third marriage was childless:

[164] Anne, no details are known, but if she had had a son he would certainly have been too young to have fought at Bosworth.
[165] Felicia (1467–), married William Aske (1465–1512) in 1482. Their daughter, Alice, was born after Bosworth.
[166] Ralph, born after 1469 and therefore too young to be Skeleton 1.
[167] Edward, born after 1469 and therefore too young to be Skeleton 1.

Tree 19

Elizabeth Thornton [129], married George[~~168~~] Lord Lumley and had three sons:

[169] Thomas (1460–87, buried in Lumley, Durham), who married Elizabeth Plantagenet, illegitimate daughter of Edward IV and Elizabeth Waite. Their son, Richard, became third Baron Lumley.
[170] Roger (1475–1530).

[**171**]   Ralph, death date is unknown but he would have been aged less than 10 at the time of Bosworth.

Tree 20

Anne Grey [138], married John Grey [~~173~~], eighth Baron Grey of Wilton (*c*.1443–99). Richardson, *Royal Ancestry* records them as having seven sons [174–179] and three daughters [180–183]. However, other sources record John Grey marrying as his second wife Elizabeth Vaughan, daughter of Sir Thomas Vaughan and widow of Sir Thomas Cokesey, with the first marriage resulting in only one child, Edmund:

[**174**]   Reginald, died before his father in 1499.

[**175**]   Edmund (*c*.1469–1511), became ninth Baron.

[**176**]   Richard, details uncertain but he would have been aged 14 or younger at the time of Bosworth.

[**177**]   Peter, details uncertain but he would have been aged 14 or younger at the time of Bosworth.

[**178**]   Edward, details uncertain but he would have been aged 14 or younger at the time of Bosworth.

[**179**]   George, details uncertain but he would have been aged 14 or younger at the time of Bosworth.

[**180**]   Thomas, details uncertain but he would have been aged 14 or younger at the time of Bosworth.

[**181**]   Jane (1473–), married Sir Watkin Vaughan. Any children would have been born after Bosworth.

[**182**]   Katherine (1475–), married Sir Thomas Rotherham. Any children would have been born after Bosworth.

[**183**]   Tacy (*c*.1484–), married John Gyse. Any children would have been born after Bosworth.

What does the information from this web of relatives descended from Sir Payne Roët and his wife tell us?

It traces seven generations of descendants and has identified 144 individuals who would have shared the same mtDNA as Richard III, of whom 82 were male, excluding Richard himself. Of these males, 81 could not be Skeleton 1 as they are known to have died either before or after Bosworth or were clearly too old or too young at the time of

Bosworth (1485). This leaves just one candidate male: Robert Eure, born around 1450, whose death is unknown (Richard was born in 1452). However, there is no record of the family having fought at Bosworth and, being a Knight of the Order of St John of Jerusalem (Knights Hospitaller), he is likely to have spent time in the Mediterranean, especially Rhodes, and could even have died there. In addition, there are four females who *could* in theory have passed on the mtDNA to a future generation but for whom no clear details are known. However, importantly, no record of any marriage for any of these women is recorded, so it is reasonable to assume that they did not have children.

Descendants of Sir Payne Roët of Guienne

1-Sir Payne Roët of Guienne
 +?
 ├ 2-Isabel de Roet
 ├ 2-Phillippa de Roet b. 1346, d. 1387
 │ +Geoffrey Chaucer
 │ ├ 3-Elizabeth Chaucer b. 1364
 │ ├ 3-Thomas Chaucer b. 1367
 │ ├ 3-Agnes Chaucer
 │ └ 3-Lewis Chaucer b. 1381, possibly not their child
 └ 2-Katherine de Roet b. 1350, d. 1403
    +Unknown
    ├ 3-Blanche b. 1367, d. 1369
    ├ 3-Thomas b. 1368, d. 1369
    ├ 3-Margaret b. 1369
    ├ 3-John Beaufort first Earl of Somerset b. 1373, d. 1440
    ├ 3-Henry Beaufort b. 1374, d. 1447
    ├ 3-Thomas Beaufort b. 1377, d. 1426
    └ 3-Joan Beaufort b. 1379, d. 1440
       +(1st husband) Robert Ferrers
       ├ 4-Elizabeth Ferrers b. 1393
          +John de Greystoke b. 1389, d. 1436
          ├ 5-Richard de Greystoke
          ├ 5-Henry de Greystoke
          ├ 5-William de Greystoke
          ├ 5-Joan de Greystoke b. 1408, d. 1456
          │ +(1st husband) John Darcy
          │ ├ 6-Richard Darcy b. 1424, d. 1458
          │ ├ 6-John Darcy b. 1426, d. 1461
          │ ├ 6-George Darcy
          │ ├ 6-Elizabeth Darcy
          │ ├ 6-Thomas Darcy
          │ ├ 6-Philip Darcy
          │ ├ 6-Jane Darcy
          │ │ +John Beaumont
          │ │ ├ 7-Adam Beaumont
          │ │ └ 7-Henry Beaumont
          │ └ 6-Eleanor Darcy
          │ +(2nd husband) William Stoke
          ├ 5-Elizabeth de Greystoke b. 1428
          │ +Roger Thornton
          │ ├ 6-Elizabeth Thornton b. c.1450
          │ │ +George Lord Lumley
          │ │ ├ 7-Thomas Lumley b. 1460, d. 1487, (Lumley, Durham)
          │ │ ├ 7-Roger Lumley b. 1475, d. 1530
          │ │ └ 7-Ralph Lumley
          │ └ 6-Joan Thornton
          ├ 5-Anne de Greystoke b. 1477
          │ +Ralph Bigod
          │ ├ 6-John Bigod d. 1461, Battle of Towton
          │ ├ 6-Thomas Bigod b. c.1435

Descendants of Sir Payne Roët of Guienne (*continued*).

```
        ├ 6-Anne Bigod
        ├ 6-Catherine Bigod b. c.1439
        ├ 6-Matilda Bigod b. c.1439
        └ 6-Agnes Bigod
      ├ 5-Ralph de Greystoke b. 1487
      ├ 5-Thomas de Greystoke d. 1487
      ├ 5-Eleanor de Greystoke
          +Ralph Eure d. 1461, Battle of Towton
          ├ 6-Joan Eure b. c.1438
          ├ 6-William Eure b. 1440, d. 1484
          ├ 6-Ralph Eure b. 1442, d. 1484
          ├ 6-Elizabeth Eure b. 1444, d. 1481
              +(1st husband) Sir William Bulmer
              └ 7-Anne Bulmer
              +(2nd husband) Sir James Strangeways
              ├ 7-Felicia Strangeways b. 1467
              ├ 7-Ralph Strangeways b. 1469
              └ 7-Edward Strangeways b. c.1469
              +(3rd husband) John Ellerker
          ├ 6-Henry (twin of John) Eure b. c.1446
          ├ 6-John (twin of Henry) Eure b. c.1446
          ├ 6-Margaret/Margery Eure b. c.1448
          ├ 6-Robert Eure b. c.1450
          ├ 6-John Eure b. 1452, d. c.1493, (Huttun Bushell)
          ├ 6-Anne Eure b. c.1454
          ├ 6-Hugh Eure b. c.1456, d. c.1523
          └ 6-Mary Eure b. c.1458
      ├ 5-John de Greystoke d. c.1487
      ├ 5-Catherine de Greystoke
      └ 5-Matilda de Greystoke
   └ 4-Margaret Ferrers b. 1394, d. 1458
      +Ralph Neville b. 1394, d. 1458
      └ 5-John Neville b. 1416, d. 1482
   +Ralph Neville  (see Joan Beaufort above)
   ├ 4-Katherine Neville b. 1400, d. 1484
      +John de Mowbray
      └ 5-John de Mowbray
      +Thomas Strangeways
      ├ 5-Joan Strangeways
      └ 5-Catherine Strangeways
   ├ 4-Richard Neville b. 1400, d. 1460
   ├ 4-Cecily Neville b. 1415, d. 1495
      +Richard Plantagenet
      ├ 5-Henry Plantagenet b. 1438, d. c.1440
      ├ 5-Anne of York Plantagenet b. 1439, d. 1476
      ├ 5-Henry Plantagenet b. 1441
      ├ 5-Edward Plantagenet b. 1442, d. 1483
      ├ 5-Edmund Plantagenet b. 1443, d. 1460, Battle of Wakefiled
      ├ 5-Elizabeth Plantagenet of York b. 1444, d. 1503
          +John de la Pole
```

Descendants of Sir Payne Roët of Guienne (*continued*).

```
        ├ 6-John de la Pole b. c.1462, d. 1487
        ├ 6-Geoffrey de la Pole b. 1464
        ├ 6-Elizabeth de la Pole b. c.1468, d. 1489
        ├ 6-Edmund de la Pole b. 1471, d. 1543
        ├ 6-Dorothy de la Pole b. 1472
        ├ 6-Humphrey de la Pole b. 1474, d. 1513
        ├ 6-Anne de la Pole b. 1476, d. 1495
        ├ 6-Catherine de la Pole b. c.1477, d. 1513
        ├ 6-William de la Pole b. 1478, d. 1539
        └ 6-Richard de la Pole b. 1480, d. 1525
      ├ 5-Margaret Plantagenet b. 1446, d. 1503
      ├ 5-William Plantagenet b. 1447
      ├ 5-John Plantagenet b. 1448
      ├ 5-George Plantagenet b. 1449, d. 1478
      ├ 5-Thomas Plantagenet b. 1451
      ├ 5-Richard Plantagenet b. 1452, d. 1485
      └ 5-Ursula Plantagenet b. 1455
  ├ 4-Robert Neville b. 1457
  ├ 4-William Neville b. 1463
  ├ 4-Eleonor Neville b. 1472
    +(1st husband) Richard le Despenser
    +Henry Percy b. 1393, d. 1455
    ├ 5-John Percy b. 1418
    ├ 5-Henry Percy b. 1421, d. 1461
    ├ 5-Katherine Percy b. 1423, d. 1475
      +Edmund Grey
      ├ 6-Anthony Grey
      ├ 6-Anne Grey b. c.1443, d. 1499
        +John Grey
        ├ 7-Reginald Grey
        ├ 7-Edmund Grey b. c.1469, d. c.1511
        ├ 7-Richard Grey
        ├ 7-Peter Grey
        ├ 7-Edward Grey
        ├ 7-George Grey
        ├ 7-Thomas Grey
        ├ 7-Jane Grey b. 1473
        ├ 7-Katherine Grey b. 1475
        └ 7-Tacy Grey b. c.1484
      ├ 6-George Grey b. 1454, d. 1505
      └ 6-Elizabeth Grey d. c.1472
    ├ 5-George Percy b. 1424, d. 1474
    ├ 5-Ralph Percy b. 1427, d. 1464
    ├ 5-William Percy b. 1428, d. 1462
    ├ 5-Thomas Percy b. 1433, d. 1460
    ├ 5-Anne Percy
    └ 5-Joan Percy
  ├ 4-Anne Neville
    +Humphrey Stafford
    ├ 5-Humphrey Stafford b. 1425, d. 1458
```

Descendants of Sir Payne Roët of Guienne (*continued*).

```
        ⌐ 5-Henry Stafford b. c.1425, d. 1471
        ⌐ 5-John Stafford b. 1427, d. 1473
        ⌐ 5-Edward Stafford
        ⌐ 5-Margaret Stafford b. 1435, d. 1475
        ⌐ 5-Catherine Stafford b. 1437, d. 1475
          ⌐ +John Talbot
          ⌐ 6-George Talbot b. 1468, d. 1528
          ⌐ 6-Thomas Talbot b. 1470
          └ 6-Anne Talbot b. 1472
        ⌐ 5-George (twin of William) Stafford b. 1439
        ⌐ 5-William (twin of George) Stafford b. 1439
        ⌐ 5-Joan Stafford b. 1442, d. 1484
        └ 5-Anne Stafford b. 1446, d. 1472
     ⌐ 4-Edward Neville b. 1476
     ⌐ 4-George Neville
     ⌐ 4-Joan Neville
     ⌐ 4-Cuthbert Neville
     ⌐ 4-Thomas Neville
     └ 4-Henry Neville
```

APPENDIX 2

The Male Line

The Bones of a King: Richard III Rediscovered, First Edition. The Greyfriars Research Team with Maev Kennedy and Lin Foxhall.
© 2015 University of Leicester. Published 2015 by John Wiley & Sons, Ltd.

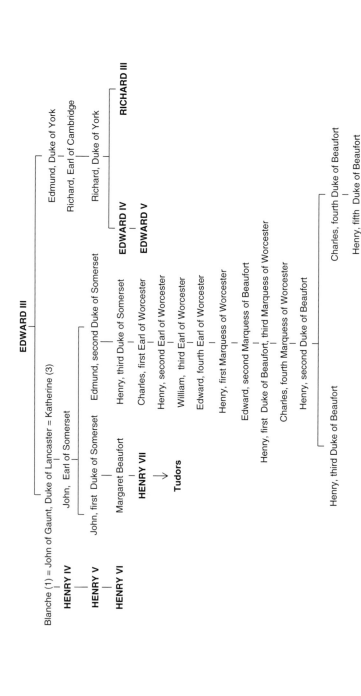

EDWARD III

Blanche (1) = John of Gaunt, Duke of Lancaster = Katherine (3)

John, Earl of Somerset

HENRY IV

HENRY V

HENRY VI

John, first Duke of Somerset

Edmund, second Duke of Somerset

Margaret Beaufort

HENRY VII

→ **Tudors**

Henry, third Duke of Somerset

Charles, first Earl of Worcester

Henry, second Earl of Worcester

William, third Earl of Worcester

Edward, fourth Earl of Worcester

Henry, first Marquess of Worcester

Edward, second Marquess of Beaufort

Henry, first Duke of Beaufort, third Marquess of Worcester

Charles, fourth Marquess of Worcester

Henry, second Duke of Beaufort

Henry, third Duke of Beaufort

Charles, fourth Duke of Beaufort

Henry, fifth Duke of Beaufort

Edmund, Duke of York

Richard, Earl of Cambridge

Richard, Duke of York

EDWARD IV

EDWARD V

RICHARD III

Index

Page numbers in *italics* refer to illustrations. Photographic plates are referred to with the abbreviation *pl.*

The Bones of a King: Richard III Rediscovered, First Edition. The Greyfriars Research Team with Maev Kennedy and Lin Foxhall.
© 2015 University of Leicester. Published 2015 by John Wiley & Sons, Ltd.